GLIMPSES IN THE TWILIGHT

"Of an ancient fresco on the wall of the Refectory—comprising lifelike representations of members of the community, long dead and buried—the Old Prior remarked with deep feeling, 'These pictures seemed to me the only certain realities: we ourselves are but as shadows, never continuing in one stay; and only catching faint Glimpses in the Twilight of friends long lost, who we trust now walk in white in a kindlier and better land.'" —*John of Pavia: A Tale of Truth and Trust.*

"The Body is the prison of the Soul for ordinary mortals. We can see merely what comes before its windows; we can take cognisance only of what is brought within its bars. But the adept has found the key of his prison, and can emerge from it at pleasure. It is no longer a prison for him—merely a dwelling. In other words, the adept can project his soul out of the body to any place he pleases with the rapidity of thought."—SINNETT'S *Occult World.*

"Until the day break, and the shadows flee away."—*Song of Solomon.*

GLIMPSES
N THE TWILIGHT

BEING

VARIOUS NOTES, RECORDS, AND EXAMPLES

OF

THE SUPERNATURAL

BY THE

REV. FREDERICK GEORGE LEE, D.D.

Fide et constantiâ

WILLIAM BLACKWOOD AND SONS
EDINBURGH AND LONDON
MDCCCLXXXV

"How near
We tread the confines of the spirit-world!
How thin the veil that hides it! Who but feels
Some time, in Night's dim silence and dead noon
Conscious that those we deem so far are near,
The lost are present? Who that has not heard
Of strange mysterious warnings, or perchance
The work of Guardian Angel, or belike
Of friend who, having loved us, loves us still,
And who, now free, would guard us, captives yet?
Who has not felt, in hour of need or woe,
Illapses more than earthly? This be sure:
That when we solve—God grant we solve it well!—
That last and greatest riddle, when our eyes
Begin to open on the spirit-land,
Then we shall learn how mixed and intertwined
Through all our course has been that land with this."

—*The Seven Churches of Asia*, by the
Rev. Dr John Mason Neale.

THIS VOLUME

IS INSCRIBED TO

AUBREY DE VERE

WITH RESPECT AND ADMIRATION.

CONTENTS.

"Twilight above a rough and rugged road,
Where rocks on either side their shadows cast;
Devious our way, and darkened hollows lie
Where shades are deepest. On the hill-crests near
Move forms that beckon upwards, pointing out
Glimpses of shadowed light, and gleams of Heaven,
To cheer the wanderer on his path below,
And link those resting here with those who strive."

—*The Sorrows of Sewallis.*

INTRODUCTION

GLIMPSES IN THE TWILIGHT.

INTRODUCTION.

Of late years it cannot but have been noted by the thoughtful and observant, that the Christian Religion has been too commonly and too generally disregarded. The nation as a nation, it is to be feared, is losing its hold upon religion. Comparing the Present with the Past, à great and dangerous silent revolution is being quietly wrought out. Whatever changes may have been hitherto effected for the worse, a belief in Almighty God and His revealed religion has in the main dominated and advantaged our fellow-countrymen. The Supernatural, interwoven by religious rites and observances into public and private life, has invariably exercised a vast and beneficial influence on both. The unction and crowning of the sovereign; the implied admission of the coronation rite, that all power comes from God; the invocation of His sacred Name before the daily labours of each House of Parliament; the importance and sanctity of an oath; the proclamation against vice and immorality solemnly made in the Law Courts of the realm;[1] the admission that our ships of commerce and war go forth under the protection of the Almighty; that death is "the visitation of God,"—all tell of the Supernatural and of Religion. And at no time as yet have our rulers been called upon to undertake the difficult and dangerous task of governing a people devoid of any belief in God, a future state, the existence of bright and glorious angels on the one hand, of dark and fallen spirits on the other, and of a just and

[1] In the 'Bucks Advertiser' for July 5, 1884, under the heading, "Summer Assizes," Sir Watkin Williams being the judge on circuit, I read, with great regret, the following: "The customary attendance at church was dispensed with, and at noon his lordship opened the Commission and at once proceeded to business. The time-honoured 'Proclamation against Vice and Immorality' was not read; and it is understood to be one of the features of the new system that it should be discontinued." It is a remarkable fact that this judge died of heart disease at Nottingham on the 17th of July, during the circuit of the judges referred to.

righteous system of future rewards and punishments.

Yet now a small, but able and resolute minority—a minority which knows its own mind, and is determinedly bent on accomplishing its purpose—has been for some time labouring to abolish God from His own universe. In education, politics, law-making, and the administration of the laws, the Almighty is as a consequence either scarcely recognised or contemptuously set aside. In effecting this revolution, the aggressors are few, but have proved themselves strong; the defenders are in a large majority, but are aimless, wayward, and have shown themselves impotent.[1]

So that, amongst that large body of per-

[1] "In spite of many efforts to deride, to explain, or to improve upon the Christian system; in spite of the extent to which all faith in Christianity may here and there have died out, no rival system has been able, since the cessation of Mohammedan invasion, to obtain a firm foothold in any Christian land. The 'Religion of Humanity' may boast of a few eccentric enthusiasts amongst the cultured, as 'Spiritualism' may count its thousands amongst the less informed; but neither possesses the qualities necessary to rival the Christian system as satisfying the intellect, filling the heart, and dominating the will. The future life set forth by 'Spiritualism' may indeed be called a state of 'other-worldliness.' That system is emphatically an unspiritual religion."—Professor St George Mivart, 'Dublin Review,' p. 65, July 1884.

sons who prefer shifting sentiment, nebulous notions, and hazy convictions, to the old dogmatic system of ancient Christendom, the Supernatural and the Miraculous, together with all that is involved in the use of those terms, are quietly put away.

Since the Tudor changes—certain of which were fundamental and radical—the descent from faith to want of faith has been exceedingly facile. First came misbelief, the Ancient Faith misrepresented and perverted, an acceptance of the repulsive system of Calvin, held earnestly, but proving ruinous to any sound belief and moral integrity. It is to this system that some of the modern atheistic writers so constantly refer, when they still further misrepresent and caricature Christianity. It is to the disagreeable morality of Calvinism that they so frequently direct their keen criticism and fierce satire. Then, subsequently to the Tudor alterations, came by degrees a loss of this or that detail of the faith, more especially of everything that seemed to imply that the Christian Church was as much a living, energising, acting power now, as it had been in the earlier or subsequent centuries of its existence; and that the Miraculous and Supernatural—both on their dark and bright sides, witchcraft, possession, and necromancy on the one hand, as well as the guardianship of angels, the power of the saints, and the influence of things sacramental on the other—were still active and potent. Eventually Unbelief walked in and scattered its interminable disputations and doubts.

Thus remarks a thoughtful and able writer, Mr Newton Crossland, on a repudiation of the Supernatural by non-dogmatic Christians: "It has been frequently asserted that when Christ had established His worship, He withdrew from the world His displays of miraculous power: but there is no warrant to be found in Scripture for this opinion; and if the maintenance of His divine Religion requires His miraculous intervention, there never was a time when this intervention was more needed than at the present day, when Pagan reasoning and scoffing infidelity are taking possession of the minds of our 'leading philosophers' and 'scientific guides.' There never has been an age in which these miraculous gifts have not been manifested; but philosophers and sceptics have called the miracles 'tricks' or 'delusions.' Whenever your Rationalist meets with a circumstance which he cannot explain, he immediately and coolly denounces it as 'imaginary.'"

Hence it has been discovered that a Christianity which does not permanently rest on the Supernatural is no Christianity at all. When, in my hearing, the late Dean Stanley, in reply to a criticism on the Westminster Abbey communion of a Unitarian, asked triumphantly, "Might it not be argued that Unitarianism is Christianity robbed of its absurdities?" it became perfectly evident to myself to what an extent, and how rapidly, English religion was moving away from "the old paths" down to the mud-bank of misbelief.

The same, to a great extent, is the case abroad. The irreligious divisions of bygone centuries are cursing the descendants of those who first helped to originate and seal them. The country of Calvin is a spiritual desert. In the land of Luther, Force rather than God has come to be regarded as of the greater interest and moment. France, since 1792, let it be noted, has had no fewer than twenty-one new and different Constitutions, while religion there has been, during the last ninety years, rather tolerated than upheld.

Hence the disorder, unquiet, and social dangers which afflict the nations, now apparently being left to themselves to work out the awful problems of life without God or religion, and of man without an immortal soul.

What said M. Andrieux, the noted atheistic revolutionist, at the so-called "Council of Naples"? Here are his exact and clearly expressed sentiments:—

"Seeing that the idea of God is the source and mainstay of all despotism and of all iniquity, and that the Christian Religion is the most perfect and terrible personification of that idea; and that the totality of its doctrines is the very negation of Modern Thought,—the Free Thinkers resolve to work for the abolition of Christianity root and branch, and for its total destruction, by every means in their power, even, if necessary, by revolutionary violence and force."

As yet the English political allies of this advanced Liberal, and his fellow-workers, have not become quite as outspoken or plain-spoken. They veil their plans at present, and are certainly discreet in so doing; for John Bull believes himself to own the purest form of religion, and the wisest and most workable systems of Government, that were ever invented. With reasonable wisdom, the allies in question are bound, therefore, to be reticent and obscure in their public pronouncements. Travelling too fast, they might court disaster. But their policy, as regards that of their foreign allies, is fundamentally one and the same. To abolish Religion in law-making, to undermine it also in the administration of the law, to corrupt the lower classes by an artfully designed system of atheistic national education (which in England is doing its deadly work, slowly, it may be, but most efficaciously), is, in the long-run, the surest method of enabling those active revolutionary destructives eventually to place M. Andrieux's programme of naked atheism for acceptance before the British public.

With thousands, therefore, anything that indicates a belief in the Supernatural is frowned upon, derided, and condemned. Anonymous public writers — themselves many of them

Freemasons,[1] and some members of anti-Christian Secret Societies,[2] whose masked rulers govern them with a rod of iron from abroad —use the sledge-hammer of criticism,[3] and warn off those inquirers concerning the Supernatural who pine for something more acceptable than the cold cynicism of an ever-sneering Indifference, or the dry husks and worthless mumblings of an effeminate Agnosticism.

On the other hand, numerous societies, both in London and elsewhere, exist for the sys-

[1] No fewer than fifty "members of the gallery"—reporters of the Parliamentary debates—are Freemasons, and some are members of Secret Societies. Their lodge is styled "The Gallery Lodge of Freemasons," and much efficient work is expected from them.

[2] "There can be no doubt that the practice of these occult arts is in the present day alarmingly on the increase; and that they are frequently employed by the Secret Societies to injure persons who are obnoxious to them, as well as by fanatics and others for various delusive, immoral, or revengeful purposes."—Letter of "Anti-Mesmer" in the 'Tablet' of 21st September 1878.

"In view of the increasing power of the Secret Societies in this and in other countries, he believes that the subject referred to [Mesmerism] deserves the most serious consideration of all who have at heart the eradication of vice and error, and the protection and wellbeing of Christian society."—'The Secret of the Sects: a Caution for the Times,' p. 7. (Privately printed.)

[3] "There is not a single influential newspaper in England—I mean, of course, leading journals, those which are supposed to mould public opinion—upon which some "Secret Society man," in one capacity or another, is not to be found, pledged to keep their unknown rulers well informed concerning all that they desire to know."—*Letter to the Author.* I may add, that I myself have abundantly verified the perfect accuracy of this curious statement, and am acquainted with the names and labours of several of such agents.

tematic investigation of supernatural occurrences,[1] and for testing the reality of ancient[2] witchcraft, mesmerism,[3] magic, and modern

[1] The following are the objects of the new "Society for Psychical Research," the offices of which are in Dean's Yard, Westminster :—

1. "An examination of the nature and extent of any influence which may be exerted by one mind upon another, apart from any generally recognised mode of perception.

2. "The study of hypnotism, and the forms of the so-called 'mesmeric trance,' with its alleged insensibility to pain; clairvoyant, and other allied *phenomena*.

3. "A critical revision of Reichenbach's researches with certain organisations called 'sensitive,' and an inquiry whether such organisations possess any power of perception beyond a highly exalted sensibility of the recognised sensory organs.

4. "A careful investigation of any reports, resting on strong testimony, regarding apparitions at the moment of death, or otherwise, regarding disturbances in houses reputed to be haunted.

5. "An inquiry into the various physical *phenomena* commonly called 'spiritualistic,' with an attempt to discover their causes and general laws.

6. "The collection and collation of existing materials bearing on the history of these subjects."

The objects of the "Theosophical Society" are as follows: 1. "To form a universal fraternity of Humanity, without distinction of faith, colour, or race; 2. To encourage the study of the literature of religions and the science of the East, and to point out their importance; 3. To investigate the unknown laws of Nature and physical powers which lie latent in man." Its founders "appeal for support to all who love Humanity, and desire the abolition of those detestable barriers erected by race, by intolerant faiths, and by social castes, which have so long and so grievously arrested Human Progress."

[2] "Nor do I see, ... in face of the penalties denounced against the crime both in the Old and New Testament, and the history of Saul, how we are justified in denying that witchcraft, like demoniacal possession, was once at least, if it be not still, a hideous reality."—'Christians and the Old Testament,' p. 9. By Rev. H. N. Oxenham, M.A. London: 1884.

[3] "The science of Animal Magnetism, set on foot by Mesmer,

spiritualism—quite a work of supererogation, in my judgment, for there can be no reasonable doubt of their only too true reality, power, and activity. Independent of these societies, thousands of persons by private *séances* have become followers of the spiritualists, and many have ended their inquiries in a state of temporary or permanent lunacy. The frightful and almost unbearable unrest of unbelief,[1] followed sometimes by earnest and prolonged inquiries into the ways and works of the modern spiritualists, and occasionally ending with a state of "possession" by torturing spirits, which not unfrequently ensues, have in several recent cases—round which a dark shadow of mystery distinctly hung—as I myself well enough know, subsequently resulted in the suicide of the experimentalists.[2]

was a formal attempt to revive a well-known and ancient branch of the magic art. . . . On the strength of this identity, Ennemoser, a professor of magic, and author of an interesting history of the art, incorporates the mesmeric system into the science of magic, as an integral and indeed principal part of it."—'Origines Protestanticæ,' p. 327. London (without a date).

[1] "Destruction and unhappiness is in their ways, and the way of peace have they not known: there is no fear of God before their eyes."—Psalm xiv. 7.

[2] Mrs Eliza Ravenshaw of Malvern Link thus wrote to me in 1878, in reference to one of my volumes on the Supernatural: "I was so much interested in the part called 'Modern Necromancy.' I

Here in England, with many, I repeat, a belief in religion, and a conviction of the reality and truth of the Supernatural, have been of late years roughly pushed aside. What previous generations have accepted,[1] the present sceptical generation rejects. In the place of a belief in the Supernatural, we have what some American pointedly termed "a firm faith in the almighty dollar." Added to this, we find an absorbing love of gain, the most luxurious habits, with too many a perfect indifference to the general good of the community and country, and a towering self-

am so glad you have written so strongly against it. I heard only a few weeks ago that a certain Spiritualist, before coming to stay with her sister-in-law (an acquaintance of mine), wrote to beg her brother and sister would sleep with their bedroom doors open during her visit, as she was so terrified at night by fears of devils coming to seize her. She had, as she averred, lately had a message from a deceased brother *begging her to destroy herself, as he wanted her in the Spirit-World.*"

[1] "I never fear to avow my belief that warnings from the other world are sometimes communicated to us in this ; and that, absurd as the stories of apparitions generally are, they are not always false, but that the spirits of the dead have been sometimes permitted to appear. I believe this, because I cannot refuse my assent to the evidence which exists of such things, and to the universal comment of all men who have not learnt to think otherwise. Perhaps you will not despise this as a mere superstition, when I say that Kant, the profoundest thinker of modern ages, came by the severest reckoning to the same conclusion. But if these things are, then there is a state after death ; and if there be a state after death, it is reasonable to suppose that such things should be."—Robert Southey.

ishness. At the same time, in London alone, from forty to fifty thousand children are being annually sent forth from the atheistic Board Schools and others, often without the smallest fear of God or the slightest regard for man—the direct outcome of education without religion. Under Darwin's tuition for the more educated classes—alike in kind to that referred to—even the natural virtues are being disregarded,—prudence, which perfects the intellect; justice, which perfects the will; temperance, which teaches men to master themselves in the solicitations of Pleasure; and fortitude, which makes them brave under disaster and suffering, and strong and enduring under pain. So that the problems of governing huge masses of people without any aid from the beneficent influences of Religion, whether Natural or Revealed, and of maintaining a successful struggle with the advancing and energetic Demon of Revolution, are problems which may well puzzle the adroit statesman, and occasionally awe the most self-confident optimist.

Should any one wish to learn the true nature of Darwin's tuition, here are his exact words:—

"Science and Christ have nothing to do with each other, except in as far as the habit of scientific investigation makes a man cautious about accepting any proofs. *As far as I am concerned, I do not believe that any revelation has ever been made.* With regard to a future life, every one must draw his own conclusions from vague and contradictory probabilities."[1]

A plainer denial of all revelation could not have been made. But this is not the only outcome of the painful and elaborate cogitations of the new "gospellers of the gutter." Here is another, standing even on a lower plane:—

"I may, without violation of any confidence, mention that, both *vivâ voce* and in writing, Mr Darwin was much less reticent to myself than in his letter to Jena. For, in answer to the direct question, I felt myself justified, some years since, in addressing that immortal expert in biology as to the bearing of his researches on the existence of an *anima* or soul in man. *He distinctly stated that, in his opinion, a vital or 'spiritual' principle, apart from inherent*

[1] Letter dated from Down, Beckenham, Kent, June 5. 1879, signed "Charles Darwin," addressed to a student at Jena.

somatic energy, had no more locus standi *in the human than in any other races of the animal kingdom—a conclusion that seems a mere corollary of, and indeed a position tantamount with, his essential doctrine of human and bestial identity of nature and genesis.*"[1]

Of course, if this be the case, there is no place for God, the human soul, conscience, free-will, moral responsibility, a future state, or any hope of another life in any shape or form. The present life is the be-all and end-all of existence. We are but developed apes of polished instincts, but with no souls. The Incarnation is but a dream; the Supernatural a delusion. Our only duties are to feed and breed. "Let us eat and drink, for to-morrow we die."[2]

Yet, what said the most popular preacher of the Establishment in 1882, at St Paul's Cathedral, concerning Darwin's degrading theories?

"These reflections may naturally lead us to think of the eminent man [Charles Darwin] whose death during the past week is an event

[1] Dr Robert Lewins in the 'Journal of Science.'

[2] 1 Cor. xv. 32.

of European importance; since he has been the author of nothing less than a revolution in the modern way of treating a large district of thought, while his works have shed high distinction upon English science."[1]

[1] 'The Recovery of St Thomas,' &c., a Sermon, with a Prefatory Note on the late Mr Darwin. By H. P. Liddon, D.D. Second Edition. London: 1882. The "Prefatory Note," covering thirteen pages, embodies a somewhat laboured attempt to defend Mr Darwin and his "revolution" in question, while the body of the Sermon (pp. 25, 26) contains—what many will regret to read—a denial of the Catholic doctrine of the Holy Eucharist. The Canon waxes eloquent in admiration of Darwin's treatise on the loves and habits of earthworms; a curious, and, I presume, to some minds, an exceedingly elevating dissertation.

On the general question of Darwinism an ex-Canon of Inverness writes to me thus forcibly and practically as follows: "We have great reason to be thankful that the Darwinian hypothesis has not so established itself amongst us, as to make the Prefatory Note attached to Canon Liddon's Sermon necessary; for by no method of interpretation can the language of Holy Scripture be made wide enough to re-echo the orang-outang theory of man's natural history. Even the ancient philosophers agreed that the human race approached nearer to perfection when it came from the hands of its Maker, and, in common with other things, had been subject ever since to *progressive deterioration*. To Darwinism, however, it has been reserved to reverse the Revelation of God with respect to the creation of man, body, soul, mental powers, moral sense, and the origin of his religion—ascribing the whole *to structure*, derived from old and new world monkeys,—matter producing life, structure, function, progressive development from the irrational to the rational, without the help of anything *but time and the exigencies and efforts of individuals, who are the alone creators*, in the great onward movement of self-transmutation and development. Now this is a theory which, in its religious aspects, subverts the whole scheme of Christianity. It destroys our moral nature in its relation to that scheme. It materialises our minds. It reduces us from men who have souls to mere structural machines. It annihilates our faith by mere self brute force, and it implies utter blasphemy

This, of course, is most remarkable and startling testimony from a dignitary of the Established Church preached in the pulpit of its chief sanctuary in London. The revolution referred to *is* a revolution indeed. Others—bishops, deans, and several inferior clergymen—joined in the sustained chorus of laudation. Well-selected and grand adjectives abounded. The British Public thoroughly approved of their use. And Darwin's body was buried, with psalms and Christian prayers, in the once-glorious abbey of Westminster.

On the whole, however, I myself am free to confess that the following sentiments of a distinguished Cambridge graduate, embodied in such plain-spoken terms, are somewhat more to the point—more in accordance with the due propriety of things, though perhaps not quite so popular:—

"Those who fondly cling to the silly delusion that England is a Christian country should take to heart the fact, which has lately taken place, of the high national honour paid to the notorious atheist, Darwin, by burial in West-

against the divine and human character of our Incarnate Lord, now in heaven, making intercession for us—blasphemy which I feel to be so dreadful that I shrink with horror from the very thought of it."

minster Abbey. It is in vain that the apologists of this impiety would hide themselves under the pretence that the honours which England thus gives are accorded to him not as an atheist, but as 'a great naturalist.' This is false, even according to the very professions of those who pleaded for the desecration. They urged his claim to Abbey honours on the very ground of his having been the chief promoter of the atheistic mock-doctrine of evolution of species and ape-descent of man. It is, therefore, as the high priest of dirt-worship that the English nation has assigned to him the privilege of being interred in a temple dedicated to the worship of the Creator."[1]

The position, as regards the subject of this volume, has been thus ably and accurately stated in a long and appreciative review of my book, 'The Other World,' in which the critic surveys the position from a lofty standing-point, and describes it with a master's hand :—

"The sceptical leaders have had matters very much their own way. Their exuberant laudation of themselves and their colleagues, and the altitude of contemptuous superiority

[1] Rev. F. H. Laing, D.D., of the University of Cambridge.

which they are wont to assume, have successfully imposed upon many, to the destruction of their faith. Their undaunted confidence, —'We are they that ought to speak; we are the People, and wisdom will die with us,'—and the more than Bolingbrokian flippancy which claims to have confuted everything at which it sneers, have told with woful effect upon the many whom any novelty will attract; upon the shallow and the half educated, upon the conceited and those whose ambition it is to make themselves notorious; and upon the yet more numerous class who would be glad to break away from all religious obligation."[1]

On the other hand, certain critics are prolific of critical politeness, and positively redundant in their condemnatory and crushing adjectives.

Thus one writes, concerning a treatise of my own, as follows:—

"The whole work displays an absence of capacity to appreciate the value of evidence, or to distinguish between fact and fiction, which itself is more astounding than any of the marvels which are related, although it is thrown into the shade by the still more re-

[1] 'The Church Quarterly Review,' p. 193. London: April 1877.

markable absence of any perception of the ludicrous. After all, the covers of the volumes are more worthy of notice than the pages which these covers contain."[1]

Another, dealing with dreams, visions, and apparitions, thus settles all the questions involved, by a few strokes of his pen :—

"Of course all such visions are subjective merely. It is the living in whose 'mind's eye' only the ghost is seen; because the history of the place suggests the image of the dead." ["Not at all," I remark; "for in many cases two or more persons have at the same time seen, and have described apparitions, in almost identical terms."] "Real ghosts and apparitions, in short, if such things were, would not correspond always and exclusively to the ideas, and beliefs, and expectations of the living." ["How," let me ask, "can the writer possibly know this? For disembodied spirits which could not be identified, would have no object in appearing."] "That such a correspondence may invariably be traced is the best possible reason for concluding that the ghosts and apparitions have no objective truth."[2]

[1] 'Times,' April 19, 1876.

[2] 'Standard,' October 5, 1880.

A third critic is now quoted—a critic of one of my books on the supernatural—remarkable alike for his moderation and good taste :—

"If we did not think the book in style, as in all other respects, so weak as to move no sentiment higher than of amusement, we should regard it as dangerous. As it is, we caution against it those whom its title may attract, and we warn every father of a family against admitting it into his circle without reading it, not only to see what indescribable rubbish the author has gathered together, but what views lurk behind its foolish phraseology. For our own part, we have never been called on to review a book from which we recoil with equal dislike and regret."[1]

Others follow from various serials, showing how a mere plain and modest statement of facts regarding the Supernatural affects and afflicts writers who obviously reject it and laugh it to scorn :—

"Dr Lee is evidently sincere in what he writes," as the 'Dublin University Magazine' allows ; "but sincerity, no matter how sincere, is no excuse for folly—no excuse for the evil

[1] 'Sunday Times,' May 2, 1877.

which may be wrought by presenting a grovelling creed of superstition and credulity." [1]

To believe too much is thus seen to be "a sin against public opinion and taste" never to be forgiven; to believe too little, or nothing at all, is, from the Materialist's point of view, the "one thing needful," and to deserve the highest commendation.

Another savage writer, apparently an angry Agnostic — maintains that my right, even to considerate treatment, has been altogether forfeited :—

"We would not have ventured to disturb the medieval serenity of a strange but guileless antiquarian relic; but the truculence of his tone deprives Dr Lee of any right to considerate treatment. It shows all the irritability as well as the weakness of anility. The bitterness with which any scepticism about his pet prodigies is met, is proportioned to the strain put upon our faith in our own senses, to find that any grown man could swallow, without an attempt at discrimination, such a mass of heterogeneous absurdity." [2]

[1] 'Dublin University Magazine,' p. 128, July 1875.
[2] 'Pall Mall Gazette,' June 5, 1875.

And yet another—most probably, from internal evidence, a disciple of Bain—accuses me of cruelty, and of a desire to shed innocent blood :—

"Such a book . . . comes to prove that Superstition is still alive, still cruel; that the eyes of her votaries are blinded as of yore, and that their feet would fain be swift to shed innocent blood. It would be easy and true to say that Mr Lee's book is a mere farrago of unauthenticated marvels, piled together to form a buttress to the author's creed."[1]

The 'Spectator,' a little less anti-supernatural than the bitter and savage materialistic critics already quoted, remarked that "There must always exist for believers in the immortality of the soul a certain *prima facie* probability that the dead should revisit the living,"—a position which, to my own mind, is incompatible with firm faith. The article concludes thus: "Regarding the remainder of Dr Lee's volumes, which are filled with the wildest histories of magic and witchcraft, we can really make no remark beyond asking the question—Is the respected

[1] 'Academy,' July 10, 1875.

vicar himself an instance of the return of departed spirits? Surely the man who penned many of these pages must have been born at the very latest in the seventeenth century."[1]

Of course the literary disciples of those who deny that man has a soul, or that there is any Creator of heaven and earth, or any disembodied spirit, will, as we have seen, laugh to scorn every notion relating to the Supernatural, whether on its dark or light side. Both as regards its broad principle and its various details, such persons will reject the notion altogether, and style those who adopt it "fools," "cruel," and all the other choice terms which in my case the critics in question have been so kind as, metaphorically, to have thrown at my head. If there be no God, there can, of course, be no sin against God; and if there be no such thing as sin in general, there can be no such sin as necromancy and witchcraft, nor as intercourse and dealing with evil spirits in particular. Once concede as true the degraded position taken up by Darwin, that man owns no soul—a position more degraded than that occupied by the lowest un-

[1] 'Spectator,' August 23, 1875.

civilised nations of the earth—and all religion is utterly brought to nought. In truth, the frequent conceit and impiety of many phases of what are termed "Modern Thought" and "Free Thought"—whose scribes are becoming numerous and bolder—are only equalled by their rank blasphemy and intellectual absurdity.

The lamps of these modern lights, in fact, are obviously without oil. Their owners, after much deep thinking, have only carefully "bottled the fog," [1] and are sagely proceeding "to analyse it." The late Mr Stuart Mill—a personage of huge self-consciousness, and always so well pleased with himself—maintained that "this World was a bungled business, in which no clear-sighted man could see any signs either of wisdom or of God." Another, the son of a much-overrated schoolmaster, has declared that "the existence of God is an unverifiable hypothesis;" a third, Mr R. Congreve of Wadham College, in setting forth what he holds to be the plain duty of man, suggests that "the professed servants of Humanity must lead in the struggle to elimi-

[1] Such useful and elevating work has been actually attempted by a band of scientific experimentalists—with what success, however, I am unable to declare.

nate God; and that this is the essential element in the whole existing perplexity, is forcing itself upon all." To take another example, Mr Herbert Spencer, who rejects the idea of a personal God, believes that we are "ever in presence of an Infinite and Eternal Energy, from which all things proceed;" but at the same time maintains that we do not know, and never can know, anything more, or in fact anything at all, about this said Infinite and Eternal Energy. Such fog though it may be successfully bottled, surely cannot be analysed. Mr Frederick Harrison again —an accomplished gentleman, who apparently worships himself (not by any means a peculiar *cultus*)—tells us that "Humanity is the grandest object of reverence within the region of the Real and the Known—Humanity, with the world on which it rests as its base and environment." Now Humanity is nothing less than the sum total of the whole human race, including the dead, the living, and those yet to be born; so that Mr Harrison's Object of adoration is by no means as yet complete. As a religious maxim, "Meditate on the Human race" is about as sensible as "Meditate on the Unknowable." On this lucid and refreshing exposition by Mr Harrison, a third personage, Sir James Stephen, has written a convincing criticism, maintaining that Mr Harrison's dissertations about effort, energy, and force,—both infinite and eternal,—are simply a batch of empty words, mere prosaic jargon, without either meaning or sense. To talk about the worship of mankind, he practically affirms, is to be simply idiotic. "Mankind is the object of our worship—mankind, a stupid, ignorant, half-beast of a creature, the most distinguished specimens of which have passed their lives in chasing chimeras, and believing and forcing others to believe in fairy tales about them—a creature made up mostly of units, of which a majority cannot even read, whilst only a small minority have the time, or the means, or the ability to devote any considerable part of their thoughts to anything but daily labour. For my part," he continues, "I would as soon worship the ugliest idol in India, before which a majority of the Queen's subjects chop off the heads of poor little goats."[1]

[1] The 'Nineteenth Century' for June 1884

Thus an English judge of the nineteenth century only borrows from a Jewish monarch, who lived nearly three thousand years ago, that sage and reasonable conclusion—"The fool hath said in his heart, There is no God."[1] The race so righteously disparaged by King David is certainly not extinct. It is still breeding; and just as some persons prefer darkness to light, so others apparently prefer foolishness to wisdom. Where people, proclaiming themselves wise, jabber foolishness, of course fools congregate.

Such modern dreamers—physiologists, materialists indebted to Lucretius for notions and ideas, dogmatists, and "philosophers," as they term themselves—have maintained, as the outcome of their dreams and researches, that "there is no matter without force and no force without matter;" in other words, that there is neither God nor spirit, whether embodied or disembodied; neither Creator nor soul. Thus they have directly invaded the domain of Faith, and, being bold, and acting on the timid and weak, may work untold mischief.

For it is by faith, and not by science, that

[1] Psalm xiv. 1.

men learn that life here is worth living; for only in the life to come will all difficulties and inequalities be smoothed. The rough places will be then made plain, and the crooked ways straight. Faith is the rod and staff that supports man in the trials, disappointments, and sorrows of his pilgrimage below; and it is the light of Faith which directly illumines his path, and shall lighten the darkness of the valley of the shadow of death, where demons gather, but angels glide, in his last earthly extremity.

ALL SAINTS' VICARAGE, LAMBETH,
September 8, 1884.

APPARITIONS AND HAUNTED LOCALITIES

APPARITIONS AND HAUNTED LOCALITIES

CHAPTER I.

APPARITIONS AND HAUNTED LOCALITIES.

In the present age of unbelief and scepticism, when universal traditions regarding things spiritual are being flung aside as useless, and when so many persons profess to reject the doctrine of the immortality of the soul as well as that of the resurrection of the body, it may not be out of place to gather together and set forth various records of remarkable facts and well-authenticated traditions in support of the Supernatural. These examples, gathered from various sources, of varying interest and of different kinds, are—the large majority of them, at all events—now published for the first time, and have been intrusted to the author for publication with the direct and excellent intention of duly preserving such instances of supernatural intervention, and in the reasonable hope that, when the reader perceives that such examples, as a whole, are not only in perfect harmony with the universal traditions of mankind — with pagan history and traditions, as well as with the recorded history of God's chosen people—but also with the Christian revelation and sacred tradition, he will be induced to take, "with many grains of salt," the dogmatic utterances and often rash conclusions of persons who loftily claim for themselves—and whose friends and literary trumpeters claim for them—the designations of "leaders of thought," "advanced philosophers," "great thinkers," and "intellectual benefactors of mankind."

This compilation has been duly and directly made from the standing-point of one who believes heartily and firmly in all the great doctrines of Christianity; who holds that God Almighty has not left man to grope in the dark, but, on the contrary, has condescendingly vouchsafed to reveal Himself by seers and prophets, by apostles and evangelists; and Whose merciful and blessed revelation in our Divine Lord—of Whom there shall be a living witness in the world until the end of time—is the greatest source of comfort and consolation to thousands.

The subjects of prophecy, miracles, angelic aid and intervention, intimations and warnings by dreams, the reality of witchcraft and demonology, the efficacy of prayer, the gift of spiritual vision, the power of "discerning of spirits,"[1] the dangers of practising the black art, and of seeking intercourse with, or aid from, fallen spirits, will each and all be illustrated and exemplified in the following pages; and where a few explanatory notes and elementary comments seem to be required, they will from time to time be provided.

No abstract theory will be advanced, however much needed or desirable, with the intention of bringing into intellectual harmony all the varied examples of the Supernatural here recorded. But it will be abundantly shown that the student of Holy Scripture may in numerous cases readily find therein many remarkable and impressive parallels; while the ordinary traditions of Christians, from the day of Pentecost to the present time, will supply many more.

[1] 1 Cor. xii. 10.

It will, no doubt, have been observed that, as a rule, the general body of newspaper conductors and editors appear to be in direct opposition to any belief in the Supernatural of any sort or kind. When not directly condemnatory of all such belief, they are too often cynical and almost invariably destructive in their critical method.[1] Many of these writers not only scornfully reject the Christian Religion, but deny alike the doctrines of the immortality of the soul and the resurrection of the body. One such writer has maintained that, because direct instances of the reality of spiritual manifestations have from time to time been remarked and recognised in all ages, "therefore" —note the illogical consequence—"humanity has been attacked by a series of mental epidemics and crazy delusions." The doctrine of the immortality of the soul in the eyes of such appears to be of less importance than the great question of how to dispose of the sewage of London; while the reality and eternity of the

[1] "Of course all such visions are subjective. *It is the living in whose 'mind's eye' only the ghost is seen*; because the history of the place suggests the image of the dead. Real ghosts and apparitions, in short, *if such things were*, would not correspond always and exclusively to the ideas and beliefs and expectations of the living."—'Standard,' October 5, 1880.

future life are of no moment whatsoever in comparison with the pressing need of vaccination, or a knowledge by telephone or electricity of the exact state of the Funds. In fact, the supremely confident and over-dogmatic "great thinkers," maintaining that scepticism is a duty,[1] are succeeding in completely demolishing some of our most sacred ideas, and in reducing the ordinary British mind to the dry and dead level of a rationalistic and utilitarian philosophy.

Yet, as John Wesley so acutely and reasonably remarked, "If but one account of the intercourse of men with separate spirits be admitted, the whole castle-in-the-air (Deism, Atheism, and Materialism) falls to the ground."

Let the following records therefore be carefully studied. The sneers of the cynical, be it remembered, and the scoffs of the unbelieving, most certainly cannot alter facts.

[1] "Scepticism is the highest of duties; blind faith the one unpardonable sin."—'Lay Sermons,' by T. H. Huxley, p. 21. London.

"Five-sixths of the public are taught Adamitic monogenism—*i.e.*, of Adam and Eve being the parents of all mankind—as if it were an established truth, and believe it. I do not, and I am not acquainted with any man of science or duly instructed person who does."—T. H. Huxley in the 'Fortnightly Review,' "On the Methods and Results of Ethnology."

THE GHOST OF THE NUT-WALK.[1]

There is an old farmhouse, anciently a gentleman's mansion, situated at no great distance from Wendover in Buckinghamshire, which I have recently learnt had had the reputation of being haunted for a considerable period. Many years ago it was tenanted by its owners, a family of the name of Theed,[2] and several later members of this race were not only confident of the fact of its being haunted, but were sometimes inconvenienced by the night noises, sighs, and sounds, which were occasionally heard in its northern wing. Here were the kitchen and scullery, over them being two attic bedrooms. But both of these latter rooms were disused—the windows in one being boarded up, and the other being only used as a store-place for seeds and apples.[3]

[1] I am indebted for this account to a Buckinghamshire friend—from the exact words of whose several letters on the subject the narrative above has been carefully framed.

[2] This family, now extinct thereabouts, were succeeded by strangers of the name of Pargiter, who came out of Warwickshire in 1818. These, again, have died out (1856). Another race are now the tenants.

[3] An old shepherd named Baldwin Thorne—long since dead—used to aver that whenever he went into a storehouse for wool, adjacent to the old house, he heard the Squire's pitiful voice crying out, "Mercy, mercy! God a' mercy!" but never saw anything. Other workmen and farm-labourers had often seen the apparition in the nut-walk, but had never spoken to it.

I went to stay at the house in the year 1854, in order to be near some friends who rented a considerable tract in the county for partridge-shooting in the autumn. At the time I knew nothing of the reported ghostly visitant, and very little of the locality, except that a baronet (Sir F. Bernard-Morland) who lived near was a friend of mine—our friendship having been first formed at school—and I had no other friends thereabouts. I am quite certain, however, that he had never mentioned anything about the ghost, or anything likely to arouse curiosity with regard to the house. On returning thither late at night from a hard day's shooting, in the month of November, a friend who had driven me in his gig, and was driving to his own home, put me down—not at the chief gate of the place, which lay in another direction, but at a spot from which, as he directed me, if I walked through a narrow fir-plantation, and then over a stile into another banked-up walk, hedged in on both sides with filbert-trees, I should reach the kitchen and fruit-garden of the house by a near cut, and save myself and him a considerable *détour*.

It was a fine night. The moon was up;

but there were some heavy clouds in the sky towards the eastern horizon. On reaching the stile I vaulted over it, holding my gun in my left hand. No sooner had I reached the nut-walk, the trees of which had been arched together and made to grow so as to form a kind of continuous bower, than I distinctly saw what I thought was an old man, with his back towards me, stooping in his gait, about eight or ten feet before me. He did not seem to walk, but to glide, with a curious smooth motion, and to be about a foot off the ground. I called out "Holloa! who's there?" but he took no notice, and glided on. I myself promptly followed. In an instant I seemed to realise the undoubted fact that the form was shadowy, strange, and supernatural. I then stopped for a few moments. The weird form, which emitted a curious kind of light, as I then noticed, stopped too. I went on: it went on. Then it sighed several times, with a deep, long-drawn, unearthly sigh, which terrified me considerably; and at once turning round—its features being vague and indistinct—it gave a piercing shriek, and suddenly vanished close before my eyes. At that moment a sound as of mocking, jeering voices, with laughter, rose on every side. This seemed to come from a large multitude of invisible persons quite near. The laughter was then repeated, as by voices up in the air, but fainter and fainter; and I must say I was exceedingly terrified. I listened for some minutes, expecting to see the form again, or to hear the voices and laughter; but all was at once still. Perfect silence reigned; not a sound was heard. Even the wind seemed to have sunk; and there was no repetition of this remarkable occurrence.

I reached the old house shortly; and after having refreshed myself with a plain but substantial meal, and being resolved to say nothing about what I had seen and heard to the tenants of the house, went to bed.

Afterwards I found, on inquiry, that "old Squire Theed used to be seen o' nights in the nut-walks;"[1] but not by every one, only by some. It was a part of the grounds of the house always avoided by servants. Two females, coming home from Wen-

[1] "It may be that part of the temporal sufferings of those who have to pay the penalty of their transgressions *somewhere*, is to be confined after death to that locality on earth where such transgressions of the divine law were actually perpetrated."—'The Future Life.' Repentance is possible even *inter pontem et fontem*.

dover Fair, as I was told, had recently seen the old Squire, "wafting himself along"—as the phrase used had it—and heard the ghostly mockings, though they themselves crossed towards the house by a pathway through Cow-leas Mead. The account of the apparition, and of the weird laughter, given by other independent persons, who either alone or together had witnessed the same, tallied almost exactly with that here recorded.

The current tradition, explanatory of all this, was that a young woman and her infant child had been murdered in the house and buried in the walk by the Squire, who subsequently made away with himself, being haunted by his victim. This tradition certainly has truth for its foundation, and is generally accepted.

The following example deserves to be preserved here, because of certain of its remarkable characteristics:—

A HAUNTED HOUSE IN BRUSSELS.

Haunted houses are not of frequent occurrence in Belgium. Even in the old Flemish towns, where solemn nooks, grim shadows, and lugubrious legends abound, a haunted house is a rarity. Modernised Brussels, however, possesses one. It stands in that part of the upper town called the Quartier Léopold, and is not noticeable externally, or suggestive of weird associations, having been cast by its architect in the same monotonous mould as its congeners. It was the property of a learned Professor, who occupied it himself, with the exception of a set of rooms, which a bill in the fanlight over the street door announced were "to be let furnished." I am an ocular witness that for five-and-twenty years the bill was never taken down. Lodgers there were a-many, the situation being attractive, but never one that remained over the second day; for no sooner was the lodger installed than he began to feel an uncontrollable desire to cancel his agreement, and be quit of the house. The more plucky and pertinacious held out a trifle longer than the rest, but the result was invariable in all cases. One would have said an invisible tenant was already in possession, who resented the intrusion of strangers, and expelled them by an occult effort of will. The ghostliness went no further than this, and was unaccompanied, as far as I know, by any alarming sights or sounds.

Some declared the Professor himself to be at the root of the mystery. I knew him well by sight. His appearance was certainly against him. He was a living skeleton, yellow, haggard, hatchet-faced, mere cuticle and cartilage. He had a wife and daughter, but they were a forlorn pair. After a sickly season the wife died. Somewhat later I saw a narrow coffin carried in at the door—it was the daughter's; and finally the Professor died also, and went to his grave, the malicious insinuated, without a mourner. Since his decease the cobwebs have covered his window-panes, and the grass has overgrown his threshold; but still in the fanlight may be seen the immemorial yellow *affiche*, "Appartement garni à louer présentement."

I once went to look at this apartment myself, though not on my own behalf. The Professor received me, and after showing the rooms, which had a depressing appearance, he proceeded, in a peculiar, far-away voice, that seemed on the outside of him, to lay down certain conditions and restrictions of an unusual character. While combating these, I became conscious of a rising desire to curtail the interview, and escape from the room and the Professor's presence. Was this the current rumour influencing my imagination, or was the unseen tenant of the apartment already at work on me, with his peremptory notice to quit? Whatever the cause, my stay was of the briefest, and my impatience to be gone had probably betrayed itself, for, as I went down the stair, I heard a husky, rattlesnake sort of sibilation from the upper landing.

I may add that, coming home one night by a side street, which commands a view of the back of the Professor's premises, I observed an upper window illuminated. As he and his were all dead and gone at that time, and the house shut up, it struck me as singular. The light, too, was singular in itself, being dull, uniform, and without radiation—not such as would proceed from lamp or candle. A policeman in the street attributed it to a reflection from some neighbouring window; but as the hour was late, and no other light visible in any direction, the solution failed to satisfy me. I should not, however, have given the circumstance further thought, had it not brought to my mind an incident, analogous in character, connected with a so-called haunted house in England — in the county of Somerset—that I had heard of long ago.

The following is the same writer's record of it :—

A LUMINOUS CHAMBER.

In the year 1840 I was detained for several months in the sleepy old town of Taunton. My chief associate during that time was a fox-hunting squire—a bluff, hearty, genial type of his order, with just sufficient intellectuality to temper his animal exuberance. Many were our merry rides among the thorpes and hamlets of pleasant Somersetshire; and it was in one of these excursions, while the evening sky was like molten copper, and a fiery March wind coursed, like a race-horse, over the open downs, that he related to me the story of what he called his "luminous chamber."

Coming back from the hunt after dark, he said he had frequently observed a central window, in an old hall not far from the roadside, illuminated. All the other windows were dark, but from this one a wan, dreary light was visible; and as the owners had deserted the place, and he knew it had no occupant, the lighted window became a puzzle to him.

On one occasion, having a brother squire with him, and both carrying good store of port wine under their girdles, they declared they would solve the mystery of the luminous chamber then and there. The lodge was still tenanted by an aged porter; him they roused up, and after some delay, having obtained a lantern and the keys of the hall, they proceeded to make their entry. Before opening the great door, however, my squire averred he had made careful inspection of the front of the house from the lawn. Sure enough, the central window *was* illuminated: an eerie, forlorn-looking light made it stand out in contrast to the rest—a dismal light, that seemed to have nothing in common with the world, or the life that is. The two squires visited all the other rooms, leaving the luminous one till the last. There was nothing noticeable in any of them; they were totally obscure. But on entering the luminous room, a marked change was perceptible. The light in it was not full, but sufficiently so beneath them to distinguish its various articles of furniture, which were common and scanty enough. What struck them most was the uniform diffusion of the light: it was as strong *under* the table as *on* the table, so that no single object projected any shadow on the floor, nor did they themselves project any shadow. Looking into a great mirror over the mantelpiece, nothing could be weirder, the squire declared, than the reflection in it of the dim, wan-lighted chamber, and of the two awe-stricken faces that glared on them from the midst—his own and his companion's. He told me, too, that he had not been many seconds in the room before a sick faintness stole over him; a feeling—such was his expression, I remember—as if his life *were being sucked out of him.* His friend owned afterwards to a similar sensation. The upshot of it was, that both squires decamped, crestfallen, and made no further attempt at solving the mystery.

It had always been the same, the old porter grumbled: the family had never occupied the room; but there were no ghosts—*the room had a light of its own.*

A less sceptical spirit might have opined that the room was *full* of ghosts,—an awful conclave, viewless, inscrutable, but from whom emanated that deathly and deadly luminousness.

My squires must have gone the way of all squires ere this. "After life's fitful fever," do they "sleep well"? Or have they both been "sucked" into the luminous medium, as a penalty for the intrusion?

The following relates to a well-known case, and is from the pen of a late Bishop of the Established Church in Wales:—

Ghosts remind me that I never told you a story Mrs —— related to us when she was here last, about the haunted house in Berkeley Square: S—— pointed it out to me last spring. One side of it looks towards the street, which, crossing Mount Street, runs into the square opposite Lansdowne House, and the other side into the square itself. The dilapidated, forsaken, dusty look of this house, quite suits a reputation for ghosts. By the way, I am not sure whether it is the corner house, or next door to the corner house, but

Lady M—— declares that the real site is at the end of Charles Street, where the street opens into Berkeley Square. This house, she says, is watched strictly by police. None of its inhabitants ever cross its doorstep, and false coining is supposed to be carried on there, but has never been detected. Miss H—— (who repeated the tale to Mrs P——) was told by some Roman Catholic friends of hers, that a family they knew hired the haunted house—wherever it is—in Berkeley Square for a London season, as there were daughters to be brought out, one of whom was already engaged. They spent a short time in the house without finding anything amiss; then they invited the young lady's lover to join them, and the next bedroom, which they had not occupied, was made ready for him, and the housemaid was either sleeping there, or else still busy with the preparations at twelve o'clock the night before his arrival. The hour had no sooner struck than piercing shrieks were heard, loud enough to rouse the whole household. They rushed up-stairs, flung open the door of the haunted room, and found the unfortunate housemaid lying at the foot of the bed in strong convulsions. Her eyes were fixed, with a stare of expressive terror, upon a remote corner of the chamber, and an agony of fear seemed to possess her, yet the bystanders saw nothing. They took her to St George's Hospital, where she died in the morning, refusing to the last to give any account of what she had seen: she could not speak of it, she said—it was far too horrible. The expected guest arrived that day. He was told the story, and that it was arranged that he should not occupy the haunted room. He voted it all nonsense, and insisted upon sleeping there. He, however, agreed to sit up until past twelve, and to ring if anything unusual occurred. "But," he added, "on no account come to me when I ring first, because I may be unnecessarily alarmed, and seize the bell on the impulse of the moment: wait until you hear a second ring." His betrothed expostulated in vain. He did not believe in apparitions, and he would solve the mystery. She listened, in a misery of suspense, when the time of trial drew nigh. At last the bell rang once, but faintly. Then there was an interval of a few dreadful minutes, and a tremendous peal sounded through the house. Every one hurried breathless to the haunted room. They found the guest exactly in the same place where the dead housemaid had lain, convulsed as she was, his eyes fixed in horror upon the same spot where hers had been fixed the night before; and, like her, he never revealed his experiences. They were too awful, he said, even to mention. The family left the house at once.

The two following accounts, quite independent of that above, and of each other, are set forth here as having been supplied by persons who profess to be acquainted with the circumstances of the house in question :—

No. 1.—The chronicle will tell you that the house is still under the influence of the magic spell thrown around it by its late occupant, who practised for years her magic tricks in the rooms on the first floor. This tenant was a lady of high family, who had lived in solitude and celibacy, spending her whole life in the pursuit of forbidden knowledge. She is described at great length in the memoirs of a French adept, who came over to England to assist in the work on which she was engaged —that of extracting from a deceased minister the secret motive which had actuated him in a certain parliamentary measure, by which the career of a member of her own family had been ruined. "Milédi," says the adept, "was a little woman, verging on old age, but full of life and vigour. Her eyes were black, and sparkling with fire. When conversing rapidly, they seemed to throw out sparks from beneath her broad, black, bushy eyebrows, over which fell in disorder thick masses of hair, white as the driven snow." After a visit of some days with the lady, and many *séances*, to one of which Sir Edward Bulwer[1] was invited, the object was accomplished, but imperfectly,— "and," says the adept, "the bitter exclamation which fell from her lips on becoming convinced of her failing power touched me to the heart's core. 'Too old, too old!' she cried, as the instrument she had been using in her vocation dropped from her hand, and she sank against the wall."

[1] His impressions of the house in Berkeley Square supplied Bulwer with materials for his story, "The Haunted and the Haunters," in 'Blackwood's Magazine,' August 1859.

No. 2.—Of all the haunted houses that I have heard of, the corner house in B—— S—— is the most terrible. It is stated that, owing to previous experience of the house, the late proprietor was loath to let it; but he was persuaded by a gentleman who was about to be married to let him the house. The house was furnished for the newly married couple, who were to occupy it on their return from abroad. When they were expected back, the mother-in-law went to put the house in order for them. The first night she slept in the house her maid heard a scream, and going into her mistress's bedroom, found her quite dead. In consequence of this calamity, the house was not occupied by the family. Soon after this a man expressed his determination to sleep in the haunted house with his dog. On arriving at the house the dog refused to enter, and was carried in against his will. The man slept in the house with the dog in his room, and he and the dog were found dead; the dog appeared as if he had been strangled. On another occasion, a gentleman occupied the room where these tragedies had occurred, his man-servant sleeping on the landing outside the door. In the night the gentleman was aroused by a noise outside the door, and found his servant dead. Since these events have happened, the house has remained vacant.

Here is a remarkable and well-attested case of the apparition of a living person, himself unconscious of his appearance, to a man wide awake :—

APPARITION OF A LIVING MAN.[1]

My late father, after his appointment to the Deanery of Cashel in 1829, discovered, in the Registry office there, an old tally of twelve acres of glebe, in Coleman parish, part of the Union of the Deanery—no glebe being then known. Further search revealed that his predecessor in the dignity, the Very Rev. Joseph Palmer, M.A., had employed Mr Jerry Ives, a solicitor in Waterford, to serve an ejectment on the owner of the town land, in which the glebe was said to be; but for some unexplained cause the case had not been proceeded with. My father, however, took the necessary steps and recovered the glebe, after

[1] Communicated by the Rev. B. W. Adams, D.D., Rector of Santry.

a trial in the superior courts. About three weeks before the trial, my father was lying awake one night, in Londonderry Hotel, Dublin, when an apparition of a middle-sized, stout gentleman, in grey shooting-coat, red vest, drab breeches, top-boots, hunting-cap, and riding-whip in hand, entered the room. On my father asking, "Who are you?" he replied, "I am Jerry Ives of Waterford," and immediately sinking down on the floor in a black heap, disappeared. My father lighted a candle, found the door locked, as he had left it, but no Mr Ives anywhere in the room. He had never even seen Mr Ives (who had retired from professional duties), nor did he know anything of his appearance. Accordingly he resolved to inquire next morning of his own solicitor, Mr Robert Montgomery, something concerning Mr Ives's personal appearance, and, if it coincided with that of the man in the vision (so unlike a professional man), to have a special commissioner sent down from the Court to take his evidence, as it was important for the success of the case. Mr Montgomery exactly described the figure of the vision, adding that he had received a letter that morning from Mr Ives accepting his invitation to dine with him when he came up to the trial. My father, however, insisted on a special commissioner going down, which he did by that night's mail. Next morning he took Mr Ives's evidence, to his great surprise, as he maintained that he had never felt better in his life. After the commissioner left, Mr Ives went about his place until dinner-time; and having eaten a hearty dinner, settled himself in his easy-chair to read the newspaper, when in a few minutes he expired.

The following—communicated likewise by Dr Adams—is another of the numerous examples of apparitions of persons at the time of death,—so numerous that there is scarcely a family or locality in which such have not been known:—

APPARITION AT THE TIME OF DEATH.

In December 1825, my youngest sisters, when on a visit to my grandfather, about fourteen miles distant from my father's house, occupied a double-bedded room. A few days after Christmas, on retiring to their room at night, the youngest, aged eleven, saw my father's old steward, James M'Keown, standing inside the door. She was not frightened, as she supposed that he had come with some message. Before she had time to address him, he walked in between the beds, and disappeared. On returning home, a few days afterwards, she heard that M'Keown had died in his own house after a short illness, and about the same time as the vision had appeared.

APPARITION AFTER DEATH.[1]

A member of this congregation (Santry, in Ireland), about five years ago, lost his eldest daughter, aged seventeen, in consumption, which loss the bereaved mother took very much to heart; until she heard that a friend of her sister, living in Liverpool, who had never seen the girl, but who had invited her over for change of air, had written to her aunt in Dublin asking her description, saying that a young lady had appeared to her by night and charged her to tell her parents in Ireland not to fret, as she was happy. Her description

[1] The above example, and the two others which immediately follow, are from the pen of Dr Adams, Rector of Santry—to whom, for his obliging courtesy, I here tender my best thanks.

exactly resembled the person seen in the vision.

APPARITION OF A LIVING MAN.

On December 21, 1861, my eldest brother, living about forty-nine miles from Dublin, where I then resided, awoke about midnight, when he at once perceived that a dim supernatural light was shining in the room, by which he beheld me sitting on the floor, with my back to him, apparently reading by the light in front of me. He remarked that my hair was shorter than I usually wore it. Knowing it to be a vision, he was not alarmed, and said to himself that I was most likely at that time engaged reading with one of our nieces, then dying at Sandymount, near Dublin, and who died that night. Though I was not then with her, I had been there during the day. My brother turned on his other side in bed, and endeavoured to go to sleep, but was unable, until near morning, for whenever he looked he still perceived the vision, until it vanished in the morning light. On coming up to the funeral, he was surprised to see that I had had my hair cut short, exactly as represented in the vision, a few days before it had appeared to me.

VISION OF AN ANGEL.

My eldest son, aged eleven years and a half, after a few days' illness, died 10th March 1869, of diphtheria. A few nights after, my widowed mother, then living at Malasside, about four miles distant from my house, saw a supernatural light in her room, about midnight, and as it were a ladder extending from the ceiling to the floor, down which descended an angel in white, with my little son in his arms, who had his arm around the angel's neck. My mother, who was wide awake, said, "Oh come, Arthur, back again!" at which the angel replied that he could not; and, gradually ascending the ladder, disappeared through an apparent trap-door, from which the light appeared to shine,—a vision having evidently been graciously sent to comfort us in our sad bereavement.

THE SINGING-GALLERY GHOST.

An archæologist, with two of his young sons, who were visiting the place in question for the first time, and had just arrived, was examining the chancel of an old church in Oxfordshire, in a town where he and his family had come to sojourn for six weeks, in a house near the church. The eldest son asked his father's leave to go out of the church, which he was proceeding to do by the western door, when all at once the boy, looking up some stairs which led to a singing and organ gallery at the west end of the church, saw at the top the figure of a woman in a shroud standing erect with the hands crossed. Very much alarmed, he ran home to his mother, and gave her a minute description of the apparition, describing the ancient shroud, tied at the head and the feet, with great correctness. He was distinct and precise in his account of it; and in answer to the question, how he knew it *was* an apparition, explained that the form was transparent, and that he could see through it. Neither argument nor remark could shake his conviction, or lead him to alter the narrative he gave.

On a subsequent day the archæologist in question entering into conversation with the sexton's wife, asked her if on any occasion she had ever seen anything ghostly or supernatural in or about the church. Affirming that she utterly disbelieved in ghosts, she remarked in reply that she had been at all hours of the day and night both in church and churchyard, but had never seen anything of the sort. She had sometimes heard old and decayed coffins give way and fall in the vaults of the church, causing an "unkid noise, but nothing more."

She wound up, however, thus: "There are lots of people in the town who say they have seen what is called 'the Singing-Gallery Ghost.' But I never have. It is a tall woman in a shroud, with her hands crossed and tied at the wrists. Sometimes she stands at the top of the stairs, and sometimes she is seen standing in the recess of the buttress outside. But I have never seen her."

THE RESTLESS SUICIDE.[1]

I had been invited to go to a clerical conference in the south of England, where, as I was given to understand, a few leading

[1] The above is from the pen of a clergyman in the diocese of Rochester—himself the person mentioned in the narrative as having seen this apparition.

clergy were to assemble to discuss several very practical questions relating to their work and office. The conference was to last three days, but unanticipated circumstances prevented my going until the second day. The clergyman at whose house the conference was to be held was a stranger to me, though some correspondence had passed between us. On arriving at the cathedral town, I found that I had a drive of five miles before me. This was at once taken, and on reaching my destination, I received a very cordial welcome from my host. His wife directed that I should be shown to my bedroom, and apologised for its size, its northern aspect, and the scantiness of its furniture, remarking that it was only used when the house was quite full.

I was just in time to attend the latter part of the second day's conference, after which we dined, and in due course I went to bed. In the middle of the night I awoke much oppressed with the feeling that something like a large animal appeared to be lying on my chest, and that I had a difficulty in breathing.

Arousing myself at once, I sat up in the bed, recovering my breath immediately; when, in the dimness of the gloom, I thought I beheld the bent figure of a person, clothed in a long dressing-gown or similar flowing garment, slowly gliding backwards and forwards around the room.

Upon this I struck a light and lit the candle by my bedside. Even in the glare of the candle I still continued to see the gliding shadowy form moving as before, though it was obscure in outline and dim in colour. It soon began to fade away, though its motion was continued. My curiosity being greatly excited, I kept the light burning for at least half an hour; but the figure did not reappear. I lay awake a little unnerved until the morning began to dawn; and then, being weary, fell asleep.

When I went down to breakfast, somewhat late, the lady of the house, noticing that I looked pale and fatigued—as indeed was the case—inquired, with some obvious nervousness, if I had slept comfortably. I hesitatingly replied in the negative; but without giving the why and the wherefore, or appearing to be at all disconcerted. Later in the day, when the subject was again mentioned by her, I learnt that a tradition existed that the man-servant of a previous rector had committed suicide in that room,—which, as a rule, was never used; and that many persons had seen the indistinct form of the restless apparition incessantly gliding backwards and forwards round the large bedstead. At other times a constant tramping across the floor of the room was heard; and reports existed that piercing shrieks sometimes came therefrom in the stillness of night.

THE HAUNTED HOUSE OF HOTWELLS.

My father[1] purchased the freehold of a small and comfortable house, called "Hotwells," with two acres of land, near Bristol, about the year 1829. It stood quite alone—away from the village, but not far from the village church; and there he intended to settle, having quitted his old house in London, and given up his profession (the legal). He bought the place quite a bargain. It had

[1] I am indebted for the above to the courtesy of Mr James W. Wayland, sometime of Bath.

been dilapidated, but the owner had covenanted to put it into repair, on condition of recovering a fair amount for the absolute freehold. This was paid, and everything settled, in the spring of 1831.

My father, with my youngest sister, a man-servant, and two maid-servants, went to reside there in April; when, within a fortnight, both the female servants gave notice to leave. The house, they maintained, was haunted by two animals—a large ape and a huge black dog. One or the other of those creatures appeared in several of the rooms, and was constantly passing them in the passages and on the stairs; while the strange noises—which were heard elsewhere—alarmed them greatly. In an empty attic the most frightful sounds were heard, as of people being strangled; and sometimes noises and shouts, as of twenty or thirty persons being beaten severely, came from the courtyard. When they went to investigate the cause of such noises, nothing was seen, nothing heard. The yard was then as still and silent as the grave, and no explanation of the mystery was forthcoming. On several nights some of the villagers were induced to keep watch; but they would do so only with lights and lanterns, and in a considerable company. On these occasions the noises then were only heard in the attics; but, about midnight, the apparitions of the ape and black dog appeared in the courtyard, and were seen by five persons at once. They seemed to come up through a closed grating from a large cellar underneath an outhouse, and to rush out into the darkness beyond the gates of the enclosure. At least a dozen times these apparitions were seen by the tenants and the villagers, though my father and the man-servant (who had both heard strange enough noises) had never seen anything. Early in November 1831, however, when he had changed servants two or three times, he was awaked in the middle of the night by a frightful scream, which came, or seemed to come, from the roof of the house; and noises simultaneously reached him which seemed as if twenty or thirty chattering workmen were removing the tiles, and flinging them down as fast as possible into the garden below. He hastily got up, assumed part of his clothes and dressing-gown, and, summoning the man-servant, went down with him to the front-door, armed with a brace of loaded pistols and a blunderbuss. They expected to find thieves, or a body of lunatics, or Chartist rioters on an errand of destruction. But on opening the door and making examination, not a soul was to be seen—not a sound heard. None of the tiles had been removed; while the garden was perfectly still and deserted.

Similar occurrences, differing somewhat in detail, took place again and again. My father, who was a most unimaginative and prosaic man, came to the distinct conclusion that the house was haunted—as certainly seems to have been the case—and got rid of it to a retired Bristol tradesman in 1832.

He in turn, I am told, found his life unbearable there, was unable to dispose of it, and so turned it into three cottages. But even the cottagers—having similar experiences—refused to live there: the spot got a bad reputation; the windows of the untenanted place were broken; the premises in due course went to ruin, and in a few years were pulled down.

Two details of interest should be added: first, that common Report had long and deliberately maintained that a series of murders had been committed in the house in the early part of the present century, about 1807, and that a noted "gentleman highwayman" who, with certain accomplices, had plied his trade on the old Bath and Exeter road, was supposed to have been the murderer;[1] and secondly, that so recently as the year 1869, "a huge black dog, with a monster riding on its back," was seen from time to time by several persons in the field on which the old mansion-house of Hotwells once stood, as reported in the Bristol newspapers of the time.[2]

THE GHOST OF MANNINGTON HALL.

The Rev. Augustus Jessopp, D.D., who took his degree at St John's College, Cambridge, in 1848, sometime Head-master of Helston Grammar-School, subsequently Head-master of King Edward VI.'s School, Norwich,

[1] He was known as "Gentleman Jack," and believed to have been a member of a noble family in Cornwall. He died in bed, but in despair, without the consolations of religion, and eventually a dangerous maniac.

[2] Amongst these cited before Squire Harford, were John W. Jackson, Charles Higham, Robert Brownson, Henry Gill, Richard Fox, William Colehurst, James Hampton, Harry Hampton, and Benjamin Byles, whose affidavit to that effect I have seen.

and now Rector of Scarning, near East Durham, sent to the 'Athenæum' the following curious narrative, written, as he declares, when all the circumstances were fresh in his recollection.

On October 10, 1879, he spent the night at Mannington Hall, the seat of Lord Orford. He was in perfect health and spirits, and, though a little anxious about various things, conscious of nothing approaching weariness. He passed a pleasant evening, without any reference in conversation to the Supernatural. The story, as recorded, proceeds thus:—

"The main object of my going over to Mannington was to examine and take notes upon some very rare book in Lord Orford's library, which I had been anxiously wishing to get a sight of for some years, but had never been fortunate enough to meet with up to this time. I asked leave to sit up for some hours, and make transcripts. His lordship at first wished me to let his valet remain in attendance to see all lights put out; but as this would have embarrassed me and compelled me to go to bed earlier than I wished, and as it seemed likely that I should be occupied till two or three in the morning, it was agreed that I should be left to my own devices, and the servants should be allowed to retire. By eleven o'clock I was the only person downstairs, and I was very soon busily at work, and absorbed in my occupation.

"The room in which I was writing is a large one, with a huge fireplace and a grand old chimney, and it is needless to say that it is furnished with every comfort and luxury. The library opens into this room, and I had to pass out from where I was sitting into this library and get upon a chair to reach the volumes I wanted to examine. There were six small volumes in all. I took them down and placed them at my right hand in a little pile, and set to work—sometimes reading, sometimes writing. As I finished with a book, I placed it in front of me. There were four silver candlesticks upon the table, the candles all burning; and as I am a chilly person, I sat myself at one corner of the table, with the fire at my left, and at intervals, as I had finished with a book, I rose, knocked the fire together, and stood up to warm my feet. I continued in this way at my task till nearly one o'clock. I had got on better than I expected, and I had only one more book to occupy me. I rose, wound up my watch, and opened a bottle of seltzer water, and I remember thinking to myself that I should get to bed by two after all. I set to work at the last little book. I had been engaged upon it about half an hour, and was just beginning to think that my work was drawing to a close, when, *as I was actually writing*, I saw a large white hand within a foot of my elbow. Turning my head, there sat a figure of a somewhat large man, with his back to the fire, bending slightly over the table, and apparently examining the pile of books that I had been at work upon. The man's face was turned away from me, but I saw his closely cut reddish-brown hair, his ear and shaved cheek, the eyebrow, the corner of the right eye, the side of the forehead, and the large high cheekbone. He was dressed in what I can only describe as a kind of ecclesiastical habit of thick corded silk or some such material, close up to the throat, and a narrow rim or edging, of about an inch broad, of satin or velvet, serving as a stand-up collar, and fitting close to the chin. The right hand, which had first attracted my attention, was clasping, without any great pressure, the left hand; both hands were in perfect repose, and the large blue veins of the right hand was like the hand of Velasquez's magnificent Dead Knight in the National Gallery. I looked at my visitor for some seconds, and was perfectly sure that he was not a reality. A thousand thoughts came crowding upon me, but not the least feeling of alarm, or even uneasiness; curiosity and a strong interest were uppermost. For an instant I felt eager to make a sketch of my friend, and I looked at a tray on my right for a pencil; then I thought, 'Up-stairs I have a sketch-book—shall I fetch it?' There he sat, and I was fascinated—afraid not of his staying, but lest he should go. Stopping in my writing, I lifted my left hand from the paper, stretched it out to the pile of books, and moved the top one. I cannot explain why I did this. My arm passed in front of the figure, and it vanished. I was simply disappointed, and nothing more. I went on with my writing as if nothing had happened, perhaps for another five minutes, and I had actually got to the last few words of what I had determined to extract, when the figure appeared again, exactly in the same place and attitude as before. I saw the hands close to my own; I turned my head again to examine him more closely, and I was framing a sentence to address to him, when I discovered that I did not dare to speak. *I was afraid of the sound of my own voice.* There he sat, and there sat I. I turned my head again to my work, and finished writing the two or three words I still had to write. The paper and my notes are at this moment before me, and exhibit not the slightest tremor or nervousness. I could point out the words I was writing when the phantom came and when he disappeared. Having finished my task, I shut the book and threw it on the table: it made a slight noise as it fell—the figure vanished.

"Throwing myself back in my chair, I sat for some seconds looking at the fire with a curious mixture of feeling, and I remember wondering whether my friend would come again, and if he did, whether he would hide the fire from me. Then first there stole upon me a dread and a suspicion that I was beginning to lose my nerve. I remember yawning; then I rose, lit my bedroom candle, took my books into the inner library, mounted the chair as before, and replaced five of the volumes; the sixth I brought back and laid upon the table where I had been writing when the phantom did me the honour to appear to me. By this time I had lost all sense of uneasiness. I blew out the four candles and marched off to bed, where I slept the sleep of the just or the guilty—I know not which, but I slept very soundly."

The following account of a headless apparition in a Berkshire village may here reasonably follow :—

A HAUNTED HOUSE AT BRACKNELL.

"About fifteen or eighteen years ago," writes "A Believer in the Supernatural," "I had driven a young lady-friend from the village of Sandhurst, in Berkshire, to Windsor, where we spent the day. On our return at night, the moon being full, it was shining brilliantly. On turning out of the Bracknell road into the village, we had to pass a house which in former years had the reputation of being haunted; but, on the occasion to which I am referring, such a subject as ghosts was very far from my thoughts. I was chatting with my companion till we came to the meadow at the back of the so-called 'Haunted House,' when we both saw standing in the middle of the meadow a figure of a most brilliant white. It seemed to me to look like a man without a head, and with a remarkably white frock on the rest of his body. I stopped the horse I was driving, and giving the reins to my friend, was about to descend and go into the field to see what the object was, when, before I had time to alight, the figure began to approach us, and came within a few feet of the hedge, when it so suddenly disappeared as to cause us both to be much more alarmed than at the sight of the spectre.

"On arriving at the house where my lady-friend lived, we acquainted her family with what we had seen. Her father, a very old gentleman, expressed no surprise, but told me that he had often had persons come screaming into his house, stating what they had seen in the road and about the grounds adjoining this haunted house. Occasionally it was a man in white, then a lady with her head cut off, and other dreadful things which they said they had seen.

"During my stay in the village of Sandhurst, I conversed with a man who had lived in the house some time for the purpose of minding it. He told me that he and his wife could rarely get any sleep, owing to the continual nocturnal noises heard, such as chains being drawn up and down stairs, the rustling of silk dresses, the opening and shutting of doors, &c.

"After all this lapse of years, I can give no explanation of what I saw except as I have now described it."

The following singular narrative is full of interest, supported as it is by the testimony of that which follows :—

THE SHUDDER.[1]

In a lonely neighbourhood on the verge of Enfield Chace stands an old house, much beaten by wind and weather. It was inhabited, when I knew it, by two elderly people, maiden sisters, with whom I had some acquaintance, and who once invited me to dine with them, and meet a circle of local guests. I well remember my walk thither.

[1] 'Notes and Queries,' 5th April 1873, signed "J. Westwood."

It led me up a steep ascent of oak avenue, opening out at the top on what was called the "ridge-road" of the Chace. It was the close of a splendid autumn afternoon: through the mossy boles of the great oaks I saw—

> ". . . the golden Autumn woodland reel
> Athwart the smoke of burning flowers."

The Year was dying with more than its wonted pomp, "wrapping itself in its gorgeous robes, like a grander Cæsar."

On reaching my destination, the sun had already dipped below the horizon, and the eastern front of the house projected a black shadow at its foot. What was there in the aspect of the pile that reminded me of the corpse described by the poet—the corpse that—

> "Was calm and cold, as it did hold
> Some secret, glorying"?

I crossed the threshold with repugnance.

Having some changes to make in my attire, a servant led the way to an upper chamber, and left me. No sooner was he gone than I became conscious of a peculiar sound in the room—a sort of shuddering sound, as of suppressed dread. It seemed close to me. I gave little heed to it at first, setting it down for the wind in the chimney, or a draught from the half-open door; but, moving about the room, I perceived that the sound moved with me. Whichever way I turned it followed me. I went to the furthest extremity of the chamber—it was there also. Beginning to feel uneasy, and being quite unable to account for the singularity, I completed my toilet in haste, and ascended to the drawing-room, hoping I should thus leave the uncomfortable sound behind me—but not so. It was on the landing on the stair; it went down with me—always the same sound of shuddering horror, faint, but audible, and always close at hand. Even at the dinner-table, when the conversation flagged, I heard it unmistakably several times, and so near, that if there were an entity connected with it, *we were two on one chair.* It seemed to be noticed by nobody else, but it ended by harassing and distressing me, and I was relieved to think I had not to sleep in the house that night.

At an early hour, several of the guests having far to go, the party broke up, and it was a satisfaction to me to breathe the fresh, wholesome air of the night, and feel rid at last of my shuddering incubus.

When I met my hosts again, it was under another and unhaunted roof. On my telling them what had occurred to me, they smiled, and said it was perfectly true; but added, they were so used to the sound that it had ceased to perturb them. Sometimes, they said, it would be quiet for weeks; at others it followed them from room to room, from floor to floor, pertinaciously, as it had followed me. They could give me no explanation of the phenomenon. It was a sound, no more, and quite harmless.

Perhaps so; but of what strange horror, not ended with life, but perpetuated in the limbo of invisible things, was that sound the exponent?

THE PROMISE FULFILLED.

It is on record that the Rev. Theodore Alois Buckley,[1] one of the chaplains of Christ

[1] Theodore Alois William Buckley, born 27th July 1825; graduated B.A. at Christ Church, Oxon.; was the author of several useful books, and died 30th January 1856. He was buried at Woking Cemetery, with the following inscription on his tomb:—

"The love of learning made thee early known,
But Death as early struck the flower half-blown."

See also the 'Gentleman's Magazine' for March 1856.

Church, Oxford, at the close of a conversation upon the subject of apparitions with his friend Mr Kenneth R. H. Mackenzie, and in consequence of it, entered into a compact that, if after his death it were permitted by the Almighty for his spirit to return to his friend to indicate the certainty and reality of the life beyond the grave, such a return should take place. A corresponding understanding was at the same time made by Mr Mackenzie. Here is the remarkable sequel :—

Mr Buckley, a learned and well-read man, whose life, however, had been partially unhappy and unfortunate, died on the 30th of January 1856.

Three days afterwards, half an hour after midnight, Mr Kenneth Mackenzie, lying on one side in bed awake, watching the candle expiring, and without thinking of his friend, nor being at all aware of his death, suddenly felt from behind him a cold clammy hand very gently placed upon his forehead. On starting up and looking round, he saw the spirit of Buckley, in his usual dress, standing at his bedside with a portfolio under his arm, exactly as he had so often seen him in life.

Immediately the figure was recognised by the astonished Mackenzie, it retreated towards the window; but after remaining there most distinctly visible both in form and feature for more than two minutes, it slowly faded away. Twice afterwards it appeared.

WARNINGS OF DANGER OR DEATH, BY DREAM OR OTHERWISE

CHAPTER II.

WARNINGS OF DANGER OR DEATH, BY DREAM OR OTHERWISE.

THE various cases of warnings of approaching death, or of preservation from danger, by dream, intuitive prevision, or unseen angelic messenger, now to be set forth, will be read with interest by all who believe in the reality of those most sacred written records and ancient traditional convictions, both of Jews and Christians, preserved in Holy Scripture—convictions directly and distinctly shared by most of the Pagan nations of old, and found to have an actual existence even amongst many of the savage peoples of the earth at the present day. To the atheist and agnostic,[1] or to their literary

[1] "No man has an intellectual right to say that there is no God, till he has explored the secrets of the universe, and mastered all the subtle problems connected with organised life and the government of

scavengers, such will be pushed aside with profound contempt. So be it. The germs of old truths apparently, however, cannot be altogether destroyed. Though knowledge may everywhere increase, a certain number of men shall still testify to the value and excellence of the things of old. A witness for God, whether men hear or whether they forbear, shall still remain upon earth and declare His will. "Lo, I am with you alway, even unto the end of the world."

the world. Hence it is simply astounding that men can avow themselves to be atheists; and it is a striking proof of the power that lies have not merely to corrupt the heart, but to deprave the intellect. The man that avows himself to be an atheist, proclaims himself to be a god upon earth. The man that says there is no God, asserts that there is no being in the universe superior to himself, and the arrogance of the assertion is only rivalled by its blasphemy. . . . Denying the existence of God, the atheist, as a matter of course, denies the possibility of revelation,—denies, too, the existence of a divine law. With him, then, truth and falsehood, right and wrong, virtue and vice, honesty and dishonesty, morality and immorality, are names rather than principles—words of little or no meaning. How can it be otherwise when he believes in no future state, and acknowledges responsibility to no divine tribunal? True, the atheist may talk of the harshness of human law, and the rights of human brotherhood; but we have already seen what value is attached to those claims when they come into collision with the claims of supposed self-interest."—'The Modern Atheist,' by C. B. Brigstocke, M.A., pp. 11, 12. London: 1881.

WARNINGS OF DEATH.

Spirit-rappings at Bampton, Oxfordshire, two hundred years ago.

A strange relation touching the family of one Captain Wood of Bampton, near Brizenorton, in Oxfordshire, captain in the late Wars for the King, what strange knockings used to be heard a little before the death of those of that family. The first knocking that was heard, or at least observed, was about a year after the restoration of the King, in the afternoon, a little before night, as it was apprehended by Mrs Elenor Wood, mother to Captain Basil Wood, who only heard it, none being then by or about the house but herself, at which she was very much disturbed, thinking it boded some ill to her or hers; and within fourteen nights after, she had news of the death of her son-in-law, Mr George Smith, who died in London. About three years after that, there were three great knocks given very audibly to all that were then in the house—viz., to the foresaid Mrs Elenor Wood, Mr Basil Wood, and his wife Mrs Hester, and some servants. Which knocks were so remarkable that one of the maids came from the well, which was about twenty yards from the place, to see what was the matter. And Mrs Elenor Wood, and another maid that was in the house, saw three great pans of lard shake and totter so upon a shelf in the milk-house, that they were like to fall down. Upon this violent knocking Mr Basil Wood and his wife, being then in the hall, came presently into the milk-house to their mother, where finding her somewhat disturbed, and inquiring the reason, she replied, "God Almighty only knew the matter—she could tell nothing; but she heard the knocking:" which being within doors, Mr Basil Wood concluded must be for some of the family at home, that upon the door being for a friend abroad. Which according fell out, three of the family, according to the number of knocks, dying within little more than half a year after—viz., Mrs Hester Wood, wife to Mr Basil Wood, a child of Mr Wood's sister, and Mrs Elenor Wood, his mother. About August 1674, Mr Basil Wood, junior, son of Basil aforesaid, living at Exeter, in Devonshire, heard the same kind of knocking; at which being disturbed, he wrote word of it to his father here at Bampton,—viz., that on Sunday he and his wife, and her sister, and his brother, did distinctly hear upon a table in their chamber, as they stood by it, two several knocks, struck as it were with a cudgel—one of them before, and the other after, morning prayer—a little before dinner; which letter was shown by Mr Wood, senior (as the other knockings before the deaths of any that died were beforehand told), to several neighbouring gentlemen.[1]

APPARITION AT THE TIME OF DEATH.

"Some years since," writes a lady, "my husband being absent on business in the country, I thought it an excellent opportunity to have a juvenile party at our then residence, Belitha Villas, Barnsbury Park, London, and invited Mr and Mrs H——, the parents of two of the little people, to assist me in the entertainment.

"The table was spread, all things were ready, but we waited for one little girl who had not

[1] Copied from an old eighteenth-century document, without attestations, belonging to the family of Wood, printed in 1854 in the 'Bucks Herald.'

yet arrived; when hearing footsteps in the hall, I myself went up from the breakfast-room to greet the tardy comer.

"Instead of the expected guest, I found standing on the door-mat a very old friend of my husband's, who, in the earlier days of our married life, had been welcome to our house almost as a brother. Unfortunately his career became, from some unexplained cause, one which we could not approve, and we no longer received him under our roof.

"How and why, then, should he, after a lapse of seven years, be standing there on that door-mat, looking not one bit older, just as handsome, just as carefully attired, as in the early days of our friendship?

"Being astonished and somewhat startled by this unexpected appearance, I called Mr H—— from the breakfast-room, that he also might welcome an old friedd.

"Imagine my surprise, on turning my head round to the spot where my visitor, Mr G—— S——, had stood but a second before, to find it vacant! No sign, no indication of any kind, of the so recent visitation. Not a sound was heard, not a door had moved. He had been, and he was gone; but how and wherefore?

"For a moment I stood aghast; then, with an indescribable feeling, which I tried in vain to dispel, I descended to the breakfast-room to entertain my little party. But my heart was ill at ease, my mind preoccupied with my unexpected visitor, his mysterious coming and going; and I was scarcely surprised when I heard a knock at the hall-door, and the servant handed me a card, 'Mr G—— S——.'

"Entering the drawing-room with the expectation of meeting our old friend, I beheld in the only occupant of the room a gentleman quite unknown to me.

"'I expected to find Mr G—— S——,' I explained to the stranger.

"'I am poor George's cousin and namesake,' he replied. 'Remembering your husband's great kindness and friendship, I am come to ask advice and assistance about the funeral. I feel assured you will grieve to hear that George expired about an hour ago.'"

The following, by a writer in the 'Fortnightly Review,' records a similar remarkable appearance :—

In 1739, 'Mrs Birkbeck, wife of William Birkbeck, banker, of Settle, and a member of the Society of Friends, was taken ill and died at Cockermouth, while returning from a journey to Scotland, which she had undertaken alone—her husband and the three children, aged seven, five, and four years respectively, remaining at Settle. The friends at whose house the death occurred made notes of every circumstance attending Mrs Birkbeck's last hours, so that the accuracy of the several statements as to time as well as place was beyond the doubtfulness of man's memory, or of any even unconscious attempt to bring them into agreement with each other. One morning, between seven and eight o'clock, the relation to whom the care of the children at Settle had been intrusted, and who kept a minute journal of all that concerned them, went into their bedroom as usual, and found them all sitting up in their beds in great excitement and delight. "Mamma has been here!" they cried; and the little one said,

"She called, 'Come, Esther!'" Nothing could make them doubt the fact, and it was carefully noted down, to entertain the mother on her return home. That same morning, as their mother lay on her dying bed at Cockermouth, she said, "I should be ready to go, if I could but see my children." She then closed her eyes, to reopen them, as they thought, no more. But after ten minutes of perfect stillness, she looked up brightly, and said, "I am ready now—I have been with my children;" and then at once peacefully passed away. When the notes taken at the two places were compared, the day, hour, and minutes were the same.

One of the three children was my grandmother, *née* Sarah Birkbeck, afterwards the wife of Dr Fell, of Ulverstone. From her lips I heard the above almost literally as I have repeated it. The elder was Morris Birkbeck, afterwards of Guildford. Both these lived to old age, and retained to the last so solemn and reverential a remembrance of the circumstance, that they rarely would speak of it.

The well-known death-warning to a noble

Scotch family, is the subject of the following interesting narrative :—

The recent death of the head of the house has revived the story that impending disaster to the Airlie family is always preceded by the sound of a drum, beaten by an invisible drummer, and the tramp of invisible soldiers; and people still living have come forward to testify that they have actually heard the ghostly music on the eve of certain calamities.

For instance, Mrs Ann Day, of 81 Burgoyne Road, S.W., thus writes: Early in the year 1845, I went to Cortachy Castle in attendance upon Miss Margaret Dalrymple, who was paying a two days' visit to the Earl and Countess of Airlie. We arrived late in the evening, and Miss Dalrymple had only just time to dress for dinner.

As she rested for a few minutes on the sofa, however (this she told me some time after we had left the Castle), she heard distinctly, as if immediately beneath the floor, the sound of fifes, and afterwards the beating of a drum.

While at dinner, she remarked to Lord Airlie, who sat near her — "What is that strange music you have about the house? You assuredly have an excellent piper?"

Lord Airlie, without replying, dropped his knife and fork and retired from the dining-room.

Later in the evening the place seemed to be all in confusion, and I learned that Lord Airlie, after leaving the table, went to the library and dined in solitude.

The next morning, whilst the family were at breakfast, I was quite alone in Miss Dalrymple's room, and as I stood before the fire I heard, as I thought, a carriage drive up, and stop dead, directly under my feet. Immediately there followed the sound of another carriage driving up, and stopping in exactly the same manner. And then, as if following the vehicles, came the tramp, tramp, tramp of marching soldiers. Then I heard some shrill notes of the instrument so distinctly that I looked round instinctively, expecting to see the piper in the room. In another moment I was still more startled by the beating of a drum. About this there was something indescribably weird and disagreeable; it seemed as if the drummer were making his way through the floor.

Being a perfect stranger to the place, I thought there might be a coach-road and an entrance-door to the Castle, near the room in which I stood, and that some distinguished guests were arriving or departing.

On looking out of the window, however, I found there was no door nor coach-road near, and not a human being was to be seen. I concluded, therefore, that the sounds must have been echoed from a distance.

The next morning, before our departure, Lady Airlie came to the door of Miss Dalrymple's room, to give her a £5-note for an orphan school in which she was interested. Neither of us ever saw the Countess again. She was confined of twins at Brighton some months afterwards, and died. It was not until Miss Dalrymple, a few days after we left the Castle, asked me if I had heard "the strange music there," that I disclosed my experience; and then for the first time I learned from her the tradition about the Airlie drummer-boy. She told me that she herself had been totally in ignorance of it, until her allusion at the dinner-table to the music she had heard, elicited from another guest an explanation.

A remarkable personal warning, prior to a sudden death by accident, is now put on record :—

WARNING OF DEATH.[1]

A farmer's son in Buckinghamshire, a week before his accidental death, had a dream which he at once duly related in all its details to his mother. This is its brief record. He dreamt in short that he was out shooting, and was accidentally shot by his own gun. In the dream he beheld the first person who came to the spot and discovered him; and saw himself, as it were, carried to his own home and to his sorrowing parents; while his corpse was surrounded by sympathising friends, whose names he mentioned.

On the following Tuesday his dream actually was realised to the letter. He went out shooting. The trigger of his gun was cocked, and with this he too carelessly and hastily made his way through a thickset hedge. The trigger was thus accidentally pulled, the contents of the loaded barrel were lodged in

[1] Recorded in the 'Bucks Advertiser,' by Mr Joseph King of Quainton, County Bucks, and given to me by Mr Joseph Pickburne of Aylesbury.

his head, and he soon afterwards died. The other details of the dream were singularly enough almost literally fulfilled, more especially as to the persons who sympathised with his relatives, some of whom actually served as jurymen on the inquest.

Two somewhat similar instances are so well authenticated by a personal friend that they may now reasonably follow :—

"Mr E—— B——" writes : In the year 1851 I was a merchant in Calcutta. My wife and myself were in excellent health, and our letters to friends at home, up to the first mail thence, in April, testified to the abounding good spirits of a young and exceedingly happy couple. Two days after that mail's departure my wife was seized by cholera : the attack proving fatal within fourteen hours. In England, the latest news from us being of the brightest and most assuring complexion, my wife's sister—herself then in robust health—on the early morning of 9th April, about one o'clock, wide awake and unable to sleep, saw her married sister appear at her bedside, exactly in the apparel she wore in Calcutta, gaze earnestly at her for a few moments through the opened bed-curtains, and then vanish. She felt sure that her sister was dead. Pre-telegraphic times afforded but one communication — namely, the overland mail. The letter announcing my wife's death, arriving some weeks later, was addressed to an aunt of the two sisters, who immediately sought her niece, and very cautiously attempted to break the sad tidings to her. The good old lady was met at once by the calm remark, "I know what you are come to tell me; my sister is dead. I saw her on the 9th of April, about one o'clock in the morning, at my bedside." The death in Calcutta occurred in my presence, at about seven o'clock in the morning of that day, the time in each case, allowing for the difference of longitude, being about identical.

Permit me to add a further instance, also within the range of my personal experience :—

In the summer of 1857, the Mutiny year, I was at home from India for some few months, and at the country-house where I was then staying, on a calm warm night in July, dozing, neither asleep nor actively awake, I distinctly saw the coffin and in it the corpse of a valued friend of mine, lying in a bedroom of a bungalow at Muttra. The features of the dead were exactly in the condition that might be looked for after death by one who was an old friend, in whose memory his living countenance was enduringly familiar. He was an officer in the 9th Bengal Cavalry, and I had left him in India, in May, in good health. I now felt assured that he must have died; and my anxious glance at the 'Calcutta Englishman,' received by the next mail, revealed his name, rank, and date of decease at Muttra, in exact fulfilment of the preceding weird intimation.

Another correspondent, who still further illustrates and confirms the reality of death-warnings, thus writes :—

Returning from India in 1854, I resided for a few months at Dusseldorf, and there made the acquaintance of two well-known families—viz., those of Haskal and Flocke. Mr Haskal, a gentleman well known as the author of several works on Oriental Botany, held a high appointment under the Dutch Government in Batavia. His family, consisting of Mrs Haskal, several daughters, and Miss Anna Flocke as companion, had engaged their passage out in a large Dutch vessel, and had duly sailed from Amsterdam. One evening soon afterwards, when Mrs Flocke with the rest of her family were at tea, they all heard a loud cry of "Mother!" outside the window. They all recognised at once the voice of the eldest daughter, Anna Flocke, who had sailed with the Haskals. They rushed to the window, but saw nothing. Scarcely had they taken their seats again when a most agonising shriek was heard, and the word "Mother! mother!" was twice exclaimed in the same voice.

A few days later a report came that a large Dutch vessel had been wrecked. I had left for England, and was written to and asked to make inquiries at Lloyd's if there was any truth in this report. The answer I received was, that on that particular evening this unfortunate vessel was lost with every soul on board.

Another example, intimating by a distinct vision the death of a relative, has been given to me in the following terms :—

I was staying in Brighton with some friends who were about to proceed abroad. Two ladies, a cousin, and myself went out to dine at Kemp Town one evening, it being a most charming moonlight night. I told my friends I should prefer walking home to Brunswick Square (the other end of the town). I accordingly proceeded thither, on the sea-side of the Esplanade.

When just opposite the Bedford Hotel, a carriage and pair drew up alongside the rails, with two servants on the box, and an elderly lady inside. I was greatly startled as, on remarking the thing most acutely, I at once observed that the wheels made no noise.

All at once I took about half-a-dozen steps towards the carriage to see what it meant, when I distinctly recognised the occupant as my grandmother, whom I had left perfectly well at Cheltenham a few days before; also her coachman and footman on the box.

I at once vaulted over the rails opposite the

carriage. At the same moment it struck me as most out-of-the-way that an old lady of eighty-three should bring all her belongings from Cheltenham to Brighton, without informing her relatives of the move.

As I touched the ground, I made one step forward to greet her, when to my utter astonishment and horror the whole thing vanished.

When I recovered myself, I went straight home and told the exact circumstances of the case.

Of course every one laughed at me, and sarcastically remarked that it was fortunate there were witnesses who could speak of my perfect sobriety. I was very much put out, and hardly slept all night. Early next morning, however, we received a telegram that my grandmother had been found dead in her bed at half-past seven o'clock that morning.

The following example is not mainly interesting because the person warned took others, strangers, into his confidence before his death :—

A DEATH-WARNING FULFILLED.

A certain person named Houghton, known as a "flatman," who lived at Runcorn, went to the parish church of Warrington one morning, and asked to see a clergyman. The clerk, who was in attendance there, replied that just then "none of the clergy were about."[1] Houghton then proceeded to tell the clerk that he had had a most vivid and remarkable dream during the previous night, which had disturbed him greatly, in which he was authoritatively informed by one whom he had seen in the dream, that he would certainly die on that very day.

The clerk, who was a shrewd and sensible man—with little faith and less imagination—tried to persuade him that the dream was of no importance, but a mere fancy, and that the conviction was a pure delusion. To divert his attention a little, the clerk showed Houghton over the church. When inside the building, the latter at once made for the communion-rail, where, with some emotion,

[1] The Rev. William Queckett, M.A., was at the time in question Rector of Warrington.

he knelt down before the holy table, and burying his face in his hands, offered up an earnest audible prayer for the forgiveness of his sins, and for the mercy and pity of his Maker.

Subsequently the clerk, touched by his evident earnestness, took him to the rector, to whom he related his dream. The rector was interested, listened attentively, spoke kindly to him, and, as a matter of prudence, advised him to keep out of harm's way. The man thanked his reverence, and went off.

Here is the exact sequel: During the afternoon of the same day, he went to his "flat," which was lying at Howley Quay; and on reaching the river, a fellow-workman on the other side suddenly beckoned to Houghton to bring a boat across to take him on board. Houghton jumped into the boat, but, when sculling across the river, his oar slipped out of the rowlock into the water; and in his endeavour to reach it, he fell overboard. He was shortly afterwards rescued by his friends who had witnessed the accident. Restoratives were applied, and the man was taken home. He seemed to be in a fair way of recovery; but he kept on doggedly repeating his statement that he should not get better; and, to the surprise of his friends, died a few hours after his immersion.

The following remarkable dreams—one a distinct warning of death—are from the original record of the lady referred to therein :—

WARNINGS OF MISHAP AND DEATH.[1]

Mrs A., a mother, whose son was in India, dreamed this dream thus given in her own words :—

"I dreamed that I saw David, my son, on a boat of a strange shape. I appeared to be standing in the boat with him at the foot of a ladder, which led to an upper deck. My son looked extremely pale and worn, his eyes being very heavy. I said to him, 'Oh, darling, are you not sorry you went away?' He looked earnestly at me and replied, 'Mother, I have nowhere to sleep.'

"I awoke, anxious and uneasy, and wrote down the dream and date in a diary. My

[1] I am indebted for the above, and for the record immediately following it, to Mrs Eliza Ravenshaw of Malvern Link, Worcestershire.

friends shared with me the anxiety I felt for news of him.

"A letter arrived in due course, stating that on his voyage up an Indian river, a storm nearly swamped the boat. 'I send you a rough sketch,' he wrote, 'of the boat, different to any you have seen. A ladder leads to the upper deck. My bed in the cabin was soaked, the boat nearly wrecked. I wrapped myself in blankets, and sat on the upper deck, thinking much of you all. *I had nowhere to sleep.*' The mother had, before this letter came, written her dream to her son.

"In due time another letter came from him, 'I shall never laugh at you for being superstitious again, dear mother. The storm occurred at the exact date of your dream.'"

The same lady dreamed very vividly, early on a certain Sunday morning, that she saw her same son David, still in India. His forehead was sorely bruised, his eyes were so heavy that they seemed half closed, but gazing at her with a most loving, but sad, expression.

She rose, and went to early Holy Communion, earnestly praying for him and his temporal and spiritual welfare.

At breakfast she related her dream to her sister, who remarked : "Oh, you superstitious creature! now you will be fancying you will get bad news from India."

An indescribable and intolerable depression rested on Mrs A's. spirits. She was at that time moving from one house to another; and strange to say, on the day *before* her dream, had felt compelled to unpack a box of books left by her son, and to arrange them in the new house. Also, having dismantled his old sleeping-room, she had knelt by his old bed in his old room, and blessed God for the comfort her son had been, and expressed her thankfulness that no death had ever happened in the old house.

On the Wednesday after her dream, however, a telegram came, saying that David had been drowned on the very Sunday of her dream.

A sister of the present Dean of York (Dr Purey-Cust) sends me the following :—

ANGELIC WARNING OF A CHILD'S DEATH.[1]

The wife of a printer named Hempton of Fishamble Street, Dublin, is confined in a lunatic asylum, having lost her reason through a shock to her nerves caused by the accidental scalding of her child.

The printer himself recently lost another child, who died of consumption in the hospital for incurables. He had seen her in the hospital constantly, and the day before she passed away, had spent some time with her, having learnt that she was getting better, and some hope was given to him that she might eventually recover. The nurses attending her gave no indications of approaching dissolution.

However, on the night of this child's death, at 2 A.M. her younger sister, astonished, but not alarmed, went to her father's bedside, and told him she was perfectly sure her little sister was dead, for that she had just seen the figure of a young man all in white lead her away.

In the morning before the father had reached the hospital, a messenger came to inform him

[1] Communicated by Mrs Caldwell of New Grange Lodge, Bray, County Wicklow, Ireland.

of the death of his little one, and that it had taken place about two hours after midnight, exactly the time when the child's sister had had the vision and warning.

THE DREAM CONCERNING A WATCH.

Two ladies, sisters, had been for several days in attendance upon their brother, who was ill of a common sore throat, severe and protracted, but not considered as attended with danger. At the same time one of them had borrowed a watch from a female friend, in consequence of her own being under repair. This watch was one to which particular value was attached, on account of some family associations, and some anxiety was expressed that it might not meet with any injury. The sisters were sleeping together in a room communicating with that of their brother, when the elder of them awoke in a state of great agitation, and having roused the other, told her that she had had a frightful dream.

"I dreamed," she said, "that Mary's watch stopped, and that when I told you of the circumstance, you replied, much worse than that has happened, for ——'s breath has stopped also," naming their brother who was ill. To quiet her agitation, the younger sister immediately got up, and found the brother sleeping quietly, and the watch, which had been carefully put by in a drawer, going correctly.

The following night the very same dream occurred, followed by a similar agitation, which was again composed in a similar manner, the brother being again found in a quiet sleep, and the watch going well. On the following morning, soon after the family had breakfasted, one of the sisters was sitting by her brother, while the other was writing a note in the adjoining room. When her note was ready for being sealed, she was proceeding to take out for this purpose the watch alluded to, which had been put by in her writing-desk: she was astonished to find it had stopped. At the same instant she heard a scream of intense distress from her sister in the other room: their brother, who had still been considered as going on favourably, had been seized with a sudden fit of suffocation, and had just breathed his last.[1]

[1] 'Inquiries concerning Intellectual Powers and the Investigation of Truth.' J. Abercrombie, M.D., F.R.S.

For the following, the Author is indebted to a clergyman in the province of Canterbury, who himself has written on the Supernatural :—

A WARNING, A TRANCE, AND A DELIVERY.

Two clergymen at Oxford, in the early part of the present century, had agreed in writing that whichever died first should visit his friend (if such were permitted), in order to confirm his belief in the Unseen World. They were both devout believers in the intervention of angelic beings in the concerns of the present life; and had largely studied the literature of the Supernatural.

One of them, Dr W——, was a fellow of his college; the other, Mr P——, a bachelor, had taken a living about eighteen miles from Oxford, where he resided.

In the month of November 1815 or 1816 (for the exact date seems uncertain, owing to the deaths of those who themselves knew the circumstances), Dr W—— twice dreamt of his friend P——, who appeared to him in his dream, as pale and suffering great pain; and on the second appearance exclaimed, "W——, they are burying me!" So vivid an impression did this dream make, that he had almost resolved to ride over to the house of his friend on the morrow. However, some pressing work in college demanded his time and attention; so putting aside his half-formed resolution, he did not go, and the day passed.

In due course he retired to bed, had no dreams, and rose as usual the next morning.

He had breakfasted and was sitting near the fire reading a book, when he heard an ordinary knock at the door, such as his servant the scout usually gave, and at once, without looking round, mechanically responded "Come in."

Suddenly he seemed to hear a distinct and hollow whisper, in his friend P——'s voice, "W——, they are burying me!"

Starting up somewhat alarmed, he found no one in the room, and no one in his adjoining chambers. The servant, on inquiry, had not been in; and no one had entered the apartment.

Coupling this occurrence with his previous dreams, he resolved to go and see his friend at once, and immediately ordered his horse. After a hard ride he came up to the clergyman's house, where to his intense amazement he found the blinds of the windows down, and saw a plumed hearse and pair of horses waiting at the front door.

On inquiry he found that his friend had died very suddenly; that the coffin was being actually screwed down, that the mourners were in the house, and that the funeral was to take place at three in the afternoon.

Having earnestly appealed for one more sight of the features of his friend, the relatives consented to have the lid of the coffin unscrewed, when Dr W——, stooping down to kiss the forehead, fancied that there were signs of life. Putting his ear to the breast and face, he cried out, " P——, do you hear me? This is a trance! Surely he breathes! This is not death! He is not dead!"

A slight motion of the muscles at the corner of the mouth was the immediate response.

The body as a consequence was lifted out of the coffin and placed again in bed. Warm applications were made use of; the hands and feet were rubbed; and, though he still lay in a trance, the signs of life were unmistakable.

Three days afterwards Mr P—— regained

consciousness. In the earlier part of his illness (when the trance was upon him), as he asserted, he could hear the remarks of the attendants, but was wholly unable to stir. Subsequently he lost all consciousness; and by no mental effort could he remember anything.

He recovered his strength so far, as that he was able to get about again, but in enfeebled health; and resigning the active duties of his office, he lived until the spring of 1825 at Bath, where he then died. He was always extremely reticent as to the incident recorded. To a friend these were his words:—

"The voice of entreaty heard at Oxford may have been my spiritual voice. Of that I can say nothing, for I know nothing, . . . or it may have been the voice of my guardian angel—if so, *Laus Deo!*"

Another most remarkable warning of death—its time, circumstances, and certain other preliminary events—is set forth in the following authentic narrative:—

APPARITION OF JAMES POWER OF CURRAGHMORE, EARL OF TYRONE, GIVING WARNING OF DEATH.[1]

Lord Tyrone and Miss Hamilton were born in Ireland, and were left orphans in their infancy to the care of the same person, by whom they were both educated in the principles of deism. Their guardian dying when they were each of them about fourteen years of age, they fell into very different hands. The persons on whom the care of them now devolved, used every means to eradicate the erroneous principles they had imbibed, and to persuade them to embrace revealed religion; but in vain. Their arguments were insufficient to convince, though they were strong enough to stagger their former faith. Though separated from each other, their friendship was unalterable, and they continued to regard one another with a sincere and fraternal affection.

After some years were elapsed, and both were grown up, they made a solemn promise

[1] The Author is indebted for the above faithful, accurate, and authorised account to the Count de la Poer of Gurteen-la-Poer in Ireland.

to each other, that, whichever should die first, would, if permitted, appear to the other to declare what religion was most approved by the Supreme Being.

Miss Hamilton was shortly after addressed by Sir Tristram Beresford, to whom she was, after a few years, married; but a change of condition had no power to alter the friendship of Lord Tyrone and herself — the families visited each other, and often spent weeks together.

A short time after one of these visits, Sir Tristram remarked, that when his lady came down to breakfast, her countenance was disturbed, and inquiring of her health, she assured him she was quite well. He then asked her if she had hurt her wrist. "Have you sprained it?" said he, observing a black ribbon round it.

She answered in the negative, and added, "Let me conjure you, Sir Tristram, never to inquire the cause of my wearing this ribbon; you will never see me without it. If it concerned you as a husband to know, I would not for a moment conceal it. I never in my life denied you a request, but of this

I entreat you to forgive me the refusal, and never to urge me farther on the subject."

"Very well," said he, smiling, "since you beg me so earnestly, I will inquire no more."

The conversation here ended; but breakfast was scarce over when Lady Beresford eagerly inquired if the post was come in; she was told it was not. In a few minutes she rang again and repeated the inquiry; she was again answered as at first.

"Do you expect letters," said Sir Tristram, "that you are so anxious for the arrival of the post?"

"I do," she said; "I expect to hear that Lord Tyrone is dead: he died last Tuesday at four o'clock."

"I never in my life," said Sir Tristram, "believed you to be superstitious; some idle dream has surely thus alarmed you."

At that instant the servant entered and delivered to them a letter sealed with black.

"It is as I expected," exclaimed Lady Beresford; "Lord Tyrone is dead."

Sir Tristram opened the letter; it came from Lord Tyrone's steward, and contained the melancholy intelligence of his master's death, and on the very day and hour Lady Beresford had before specified.

Sir Tristram begged Lady Beresford to compose herself, and she assured him she felt much easier than she had for a long time, and added, "I can communicate intelligence to you which I know will prove welcome. I can assure you, beyond the possibility of a doubt, that I shall in some months present you with a son." Sir Tristram received this news with the greatest joy.

After some months Lady Beresford was delivered of a son (she had before been the mother of only two daughters). Sir Tristram survived the birth of his son little more than four years.

After his decease his widow seldom left home; she visited no family but that of a clergyman who resided in the same village; with them she frequently passed a few hours every day, the rest of her time was spent in solitude, and she appeared for ever to banish all other society. The clergyman's family consisted of himself, his wife, and one son, who at the time of Sir Tristram's death was quite a youth.

To this son, however, she was after a few years married, notwithstanding the disparity of years, and the manifest imprudence of a connection so unequal in every point of view.

Lady Beresford was treated by her young husband with contempt and cruelty; while, at the same time, his whole conduct evinced him to be the most abandoned libertine, utterly destitute of every principle of virtue and humanity. By this her second husband she had two daughters, after which, such was the baseness of his conduct that she insisted on a separation.

They parted for a few years, when so great was the contrition he expressed for his former conduct, that, won over by his supplications, promises, and entreaties, she was induced to pardon him, and once more to reside with him; and was in time the mother of a son.

The day on which she had lain in one month, it being the anniversary of her birthday, she sent for Lady Betty Cobbe (of whose friendship she had long been possessed) and a few other friends, to request them to spend the day with her.

About seven, the clergyman by whom she

had been christened, and with whom she had all her life been intimate, came into the room to inquire after her health. She told him she was perfectly well, and requested him to spend the day with them, "for," said she, "this is my birthday; I am forty-eight to-day."

"No, madam," answered the clergyman, "you are mistaken; your mother and myself have had many disputes concerning your age, and I have at last discovered that I am right. I happened to go last week into the parish where you were born. I was resolved to put an end to the dispute: I searched the register, and find that you are forty-seven this day."

"You have signed my death-warrant," she exclaimed. "I have then but a few hours to live; I must therefore entreat you to leave me immediately, as I have something of importance to settle before I die."

When the clergyman had left her, Lady Beresford sent to forbid the company coming, and at the same time to request Lady Betty Cobbe, and her son (of whom Sir Tristram was the father, and was then about twenty-two years of age), to come to her apartment immediately.

Upon their arrival, having ordered the attendants to quit the room, "I have something," she said, "of the greatest importance to communicate to you before I die, a period which is not far distant. You, Lady Betty, are no stranger to the friendship which subsisted between Lord Tyrone and myself: we were educated under the same roof, and in the same principles of deism. When the friends into whose hands we afterwards fell endeavoured to persuade us to embrace revealed religion, their arguments, though insufficient to convince, were powerful enough to stagger our former feelings, and leave us staggering between the two opinions. In this perplexing state of doubt and uncertainty we made a solemn promise to each other, that whichever died first should, if permitted, appear to the other and declare what religion was most acceptable to God.

"Accordingly one night, while Sir Tristram and myself were in bed, I suddenly awoke and discovered Lord Tyrone sitting by my bedside. I screamed out, and endeavoured to awake Sir Tristram.

"'For heaven's sake!' I exclaimed, 'Lord

Tyrone, by what means, or for what reason, come you hither at this time of the night?'

"'Have you, then, forgotten our promise?' said he. 'I died last Tuesday, at four o'clock, and have been permitted by the Supreme Being to appear to you, to assure you that the revealed religion is the only one by which we can be saved. I am further suffered to inform you, that you will produce a son, which, it is decreed, will marry my daughter. Not many years after his birth, Sir Tristram will die, and you will marry again, and to a man by whose ill-treatment you will be rendered miserable. You will have two daughters, and afterwards a son, in child-birth of whom you will die, in the forty-seventh year of your age.'

"'Just heavens!' I exclaimed, 'and cannot I prevent this?'

"'Undoubtedly you may,' returned the spectre; 'you are a free agent, and may prevent it all by resisting every temptation to a second marriage; but your passions are strong, you know not their power: hitherto you have had no trials. More I am not permitted to reveal; but if after this warning you persist in your infidelity, your lot in another world will be miserable indeed.'

"'May I not ask,' said I, 'if you are happy?'

"'Had I been otherwise,' he replied, 'I should not have been permitted to appear to you.'

"'I may then infer that you are happy?' He smiled.

"'But how,' said I, 'when morning comes, shall I know that your appearance to me has been real, and not the mere representation of my own imagination?'

"'Will not the news of my death convince you?'

"'No,' I returned; 'I might have had such a dream, and that dream accidentally come to pass. I will have some stronger proofs of its reality.'

"'You shall,' said he; and waving his hand, the bed-curtains, which were of crimson velvet, were instantly drawn through a large iron hoop, by which the tester of the bed was suspended.

"'In that,' said he, 'you cannot be mistaken; no mortal arm could have performed this.'

"'True,' said I; 'but while sleeping we are often possessed of far more strength than when awake; though waking I could not have done it, asleep I might, and I shall still doubt.'

"'Here is a pocket-book; in this,' said he, 'I will write my name with a pencil on one side of the leaves.'

"'Still,' said I, 'in the morning I may doubt; though waking I could not imitate your hand, asleep I might.'

"'You are hard of belief,' said he. 'It would injure you irreparably to touch you; it is not for spirits to touch mortal flesh.'

"'I do not,' said I, 'regard a slight blemish.'

"'You are a woman of courage,' replied he; 'hold out your hand.'

"I did; he struck my wrist,—his hand was cold as marble,—in a moment the sinews shrank up—every nerve withered.

"'Now,' said he, 'while you live, let no mortal eye behold that wrist: to see it is sacrilege.'

"He stopped.

"I turned to him again; he was gone.

"During the time I had conversed with him, my thoughts were perfectly calm and collected; but the moment he was gone I felt chilled with horror: the very bed moved under me. I endeavoured, but in vain, to awake Sir Tristram—all my attempts were ineffectual—and in this state of agitation and terror I lay for some time, when a shower of tears came to my relief, and I dropped asleep.

"In the morning Sir Tristram arose and dressed himself as usual, without perceiving the state the curtains remained in.

"When I awoke, I found Sir Tristram gone down. I arose, and having put on my clothes, went to the gallery adjoining the apartment, and took from thence a long broom (such as cornices are swept with), by the help of which I took down with some difficulty the curtains, as I imagined their extraordinary position might excite suspicion in the family. I then went to the bureau, took out my pocket-book, and bound a piece of black ribbon round my wrist.

"When I came down, the agitation of my mind had left an impression upon my countenance too visible to pass unobserved by my husband. He instantly remarked it, and asked the cause. I informed him that Lord Tyrone was no more; that he had died at the hour of four on the preceding Tuesday; and desired him never to question me more respecting the black ribbon, which he kindly desisted from after. You, my son, as had been foretold, I afterwards brought into the world; and in little more than four years after your birth, your lamented father expired in my arms.

"After this melancholy event, I determined, as the only probable chance to avoid the sequel of the prediction, for ever to abandon all society—to give up every pleasure resulting from it—and to pass the rest of my days in solitude and retirement. But few can long endure to exist in a state of perfect sequestration. I began an intimacy with a family, and one alone; nor could I then foresee the fatal consequences which afterwards resulted from it. Little did I think their son—their only son, then a mere youth—would form the person destined by fate to prove my destruction. In a few years I ceased to regard him with indifference. I endeavoured by every possible way to conquer a passion, the fatal effects of which

I too well knew. I had fondly imagined I had overcome its influence, when the evening of one fatal day terminated my fortitude, and plunged me, in a moment, down that abyss which I had so long been meditating how to shun.

"He had often solicited his parents for leave to go into the army, and at last obtained their permission; and came to bid me adieu before his departure. The instant he entered the room, he fell upon his knees at my feet—told me he was miserable, and that I alone was the cause.

"At that moment my fortitude forsook me; I gave myself up for lost; and, regarding my fate as inevitable, without farther hesitation consented to a union, the immediate result I knew to be misery, and its end death.

"The conduct of my husband after a few years justified a separation; and I hoped by this means to avoid the fatal sequel of the prophecy. But won over by his reiterated entreaties, I was prevailed upon to pardon, and once more to reside with him, though not till after I had, as I thought, passed my forty-seventh year.

"But, alas! I have heard from indisputable authority that I have hitherto lain under a mistake with regard to my age, and that I am but forty-seven to-day. Of the near approach of death, then, I entertain not the slightest doubt, but I do not dread its arrival: armed with the sacred precepts of Christianity, I can meet the king of terrors without dismay; and without fear, bid adieu to mortality for ever. When I am dead, as the necessity of concealment closes with my life, I could wish that you, Lady Betty, would unbind my wrist, take from thence the black ribbon, and let my son, with yourself, behold it."

Lady Beresford here paused for some time, but resuming the conversation, she entreated that her son would behave himself so as to merit the high honour he would in future receive from a union with the daughter of Lord Tyrone. Lady Beresford then expressed a wish to lie down on the bed, and endeavour to compose herself to sleep.

Lady Betty Cobbe and her son immediately called the domestics, and quitted the room, having first desired them to watch their mistress attentively, and if they observed the smallest change in her, to call them instantly. An hour passed, and all was quiet in the room. They listened at the door, and everything remained still; but in half an hour more, a bell rang violently. They flew immediately to her apartment, but before they reached the door they heard the servants exclaim, "Oh, she is dead!"

Lady Betty then bade the servants for a few minutes to quit the room, and herself, with Lady Beresford's son, approached the bed of his mother.

They knelt down by the side of it. Lady Betty then lifted up her hand, and untied the ribbon; the wrist was found exactly as Lady Beresford had described it — every sinew shrunk, every nerve withered. Lady Beresford's son, as had been predicted, is since married to Lord Tyrone's daughter. The black ribbon and pocket-book were formerly in the possession of Lady Betty Cobbe, of Marlborough Buildings, Bath, who during her long life was ever ready to attest the truth of this narration, as are to the present hour the whole of the Tyrone and Beresford families.

A DREAM-WARNING OF FIRE.

"A clergyman had come to this city from a short distance in the country, and was sleeping at an inn, when he dreamed of seeing a fire, and one of his children being in the midst of it. He awoke with the impression, and instantly left town on his return home. When he got within sight of his house he found it on fire, and got there in time to assist in saving one of his children, who, in the alarm and confusion, had been left in a situation of danger.

"Without calling in question the possibility of supernatural communication in such cases, this striking occurrence, of which we believe there is little reason to doubt the truth, may perhaps be accounted for on simple and natural principles.

"Let us suppose that the gentleman had a servant who had shown great carelessness with regard to fire, and had often given rise to [a thought in] his mind that she might set fire to the house. His anxiety might be increased by being from home, and the same circumstance might make the servant still more careless.

"Let us further suppose that the gentleman, before going to bed, had, in addition to this anxiety, suddenly recollected that there was on that day, in the neighbourhood of his house, some fair or periodical merrymaking, from which the servant was very likely to return home in a state of intoxication. It was most natural that these impressions should be embodied into a dream of his house on fire, and that the same circumstances might lead to the dream being fulfilled."[1]

[1] 'Inquiries concerning the Intellectual Powers, and the Investigation of Truth.' J. Abercrombie, M.D., F.R.S.

DISTURBANCES AMONGST THE DEAD, AND SECOND-SIGHT

CHAPTER III.

DISTURBANCES AMONGST THE DEAD, AND SECOND-SIGHT.

THE following singular narratives, which can scarcely be said to come under one common characteristic, or to belong especially to a single type of such records, had perhaps better be left to tell their own stories. It is certainly not easy, either for persons who look upon themselves as "scientists" or "philosophers,"[1] to explain away accounts of this kind, which appear to be duly substantiated, and which

[1] As an American onlooker, in American phraseology, remarks: "Take the philosophy of England to-day. The scientists, as a class, are drifting squarely into blank materialism, relegating this whole World to the domain of fixed material law. In so far as we come within the influence of this materialistic philosophy, and lose our grasp on the idea of spirit, on the thought of a personal God, we lose our power over ourselves and over others in religion."—Dr H. W. Thomas, of Aurora, in the United States.

certainly afford to ordinary people some food for reflection.

THE FLOATING COFFIN.

In the church of Quainton, County Bucks—where so many members of the old family of Dormer lie buried—is a marble monument on the floor commemorating "the virtuous and religious Susanna, Lady Dormer, who most piously left this transitory life the 24th day of February, *anno Domini* $167\frac{2}{3}$."

Tradition declares that the husband of this lady, Sir John Dormer, who after her death was sojourning at Leghorn in Italy, was again and again perturbed by a series of vivid dreams, in which he beheld his wife floating in water. These dreams exercised such an influence over him, that he resolved to come back from Leghorn to Quainton, in order to examine the resting-place of his departed lady. On so doing, it was found that the vault was two-thirds filled with water, and that the coffin was floating therein.

Local tradition directly bears out all this. The water in the vault was removed, and the coffin replaced in its original position. Sir

John himself returned to Italy, but died 7th Nov. 1675, and his own corpse was brought home and placed beside that of his wife on the 23d of February following. When the vault was opened again in 1791, the outer coffin of Lady Dormer was found to be wholly decayed, and the intact leaden coffin beneath exposed to view.[1]

The next record is curious, but by no means singular. Of the fact that the Spectral Bird is a reality and not a mere fancy on the part of the spectator, many who have seen it are prepared to testify.

In ancient writers on the subject of the supernatural, a common traditional opinion is admitted—viz., that the souls of those who commit suicide sometimes appear on earth in the likeness or form of a bird. The late Dr J. M. Neale preserved some examples;[2] while in

[1] Dr George Lipscombe, the Buckinghamshire historian, intentionally avoiding the point of the record, remarks, in his 'History of Buckinghamshire,' that the current and well-authenticated story "is wild enough, but not altogether improbable, as the soil is a tenacious clay."—'History of Buckinghamshire,' vol. i. p. 433. London: 1847.

[2] In his rare and readable book, 'The Unseen World,' pp. 87, 88, &c., 2d edition, 1853. See also Odoetus, 'Superstitions concerning Birds and Beasts,' translated by J. Vaughan. London: 1662.

Germany, Wales, and Norway the belief is very often found to be current and unquestioned.

THE SPECTRAL BIRD AT WEST DRAYTON.

In the middle of the last century, *circa* 1749, owing to several remarkable circumstances which had then recently occurred, a conviction became almost universal amongst the inhabitants of the village, that the vaults under the church of West Drayton, near Uxbridge, were haunted. Strange noises were heard in and about the sacred building, and the sexton of that day, a person utterly devoid of superstition, was on inquiry and examination compelled to admit that certain unaccountable occurrences in regard to the vault had taken place. There are, it is said, three large vaults under the chancel — in the chief of which, towards its eastern part, the ancient and noble family of Paget find their last resting-place. Two other vaults are situated near the west end of the choir, one of the De Burghs, a more ancient family still. From each of these, the most remarkable knockings were sometimes heard, commonly on Friday evenings as was said; and many curious people from the village used to come together to listen to them. They were never either explained or explained away. Some people affirmed that one person had secretly murdered another, then committed suicide, and that both the bodies had been buried side by side in the same grave. Others maintained that three persons from an adjacent mansion-house in company had gone to look through a grating in the side of the foundation of the church—for the ventilation of the vault, and from which screams and noises were heard constantly, and had there seen a very large black raven perched on one of the coffins. This strange bird was seen more than once by the then parish clerk pecking from within at the grating, and furiously fluttering about within the enclosed vault. On another occasion it was seen by other people in the body of the church itself. The wife of the parish clerk and her daughter often saw it. The local bell-ringers, who all professed to deny its existence and appearance, one evening, however, came together to ring a peal, when they were told by a youth that the big raven was flying about inside the chancel. Coming together into the church with sticks and stones and a lantern, four men and two boys found it fluttering about amongst the rafters. They gave chase to it, flinging at it, shouting at and endeavouring to catch it. Driven hither and thither for some time, and twice or thrice beaten with a stick, so that one of its wings seemed to have been thus broken and made to droop, the bird fell down wounded with expanded wings, screaming and fluttering into the eastern part of the chancel, when two of the men on rushing towards it to secure it, and driving it into a corner, vaulted over the communion-rails, and violently proceeded to seize it. As the account stands, it at once sank wounded and exhausted on to the floor, and as they believed in their certain grasp, but all of a moment—vanished![1]

[1] Mrs de Burgh, the wife of Mr R. L. de Burgh, sometime Vicar of West Drayton, writes thus to me:—

"*July* 16, 1883.

"Your question has aroused recollections of often hearing sounds in Drayton Church like the strong fluttering of a large bird. It was many years ago; and I had quite forgotten it until I got your note. I can remember feeling persuaded that a bird must have got into the family vault, and in going outside to look into it through the iron bars to try if anything could be seen there, the sounds were then always in the chancel in the same place. This is all I am afraid I

It is said to be constantly seen, from time to time, often perched on the communion-rails of the sanctuary, or heard fluttering violently within the vault beneath.

A curious story comes to me from the diocese of Carlisle :—

THE DISTURBED GRAVE.

It is recorded that a youth, by name Robert Baty, had often expressed a wish to be interred

can remember about it. I have not even thought of it for years past. JULIA DE BURGH."

A Mrs White, whose relations (gentleman-farmers in the village) lived at West Drayton from 1782 to 1818, tells me through a friend that thereabouts "the country folks always believed that the Spectral Bird which haunted Drayton Church was the restless and miserable spirit of a murderer who had committed suicide, and who, through family influence, instead of being put into a pit or hole, with a stake through his body at the cross-road by Harmondsworth, as was the sentence by law, had been buried in consecrated ground on the north side of the churchyard."

A lady and her sister—as I am informed (1878)—who on one Saturday afternoon in 1869 had gone into Drayton Church to place some vases of flowers upon the communion-table, on coming out, each saw a great Black Bird perched upon one of the pews,—which they believed must have escaped from the Zoological Gardens or some menagerie.

A gentleman who is well informed, thus writes:—

"The thoroughly sceptical tone of the newspapers is such that persons would be held up to scorn and ridicule who might have the hardihood to maintain the reality of any supernatural appearance or intervention. Though I *know* that Drayton Church is haunted by the spirit of a murderer, who appears as a very large raven, I do not add particulars and do not give name."

within the church of Arthuret, close to the Borders of Scotland, in which for some generations previously his mother's forefathers, the Grahams of Grahamshill, had been buried. He died accidentally by drowning, 12th August 1680, being a little more than twenty-three years of age. So strong had been his wish, again and again expressed, that he had laid an injunction upon his nearest kinsfolk to fulfil his directions. But circumstances prevented these directions being carried out, and he was buried at the west end of the churchyard. On the night after his funeral, his spirit appeared to his youngest sister Mary, and upbraided her with not having regarded his wishes. She, without fear, replied that the place of burial had not been chosen by her but by others. He threatened to molest those who had disregarded his wishes, and to apply to them until his coffin was removed into the church. His sister promised to further the object of the apparition.

On the morning succeeding to the following night, as some persons were passing through the churchyard to their labours in the adjacent fields, they found the grave disturbed, all the earth which covered the coffin thrown out, and the coffin itself exposed to view. The coffin is said to have been examined and both found intact and undamaged; and the earth was duly placed over it again. People were set to watch that no intruder (as some imagined) reopened the grave.

But this watching was of no avail. On two succeeding occasions the earth was thrown out of the grave and the coffin once again exposed to view. As a consequence, Mary Baty, much alarmed at what had occurred, made known the fact of her brother's apparition, repeated what he said, and implored her kinsfolk to regard and respect the dead man's desires. A faculty was obtained from the city of York, where the Archbishop's Court is held, authorising the removal of the corpse to the family vault within the church, which was done; after which Robert Baty appeared in a vision or dream to his sister Mary, and exclaimed several times, "In peace and at rest."[1] Thus may be said to have

[1] In 1759 a record of this exhumation appeared in the Register Book, ascribing it to supernatural intervention; but the record was ordered to be, and was, obliterated by the minister in the year mentioned.

been exemplified anew the truth—" The nearer to church, the nearer to God."

A WARNING UNHEEDED.[1]

" My grandfather had a favourite daughter. She was his youngest child, had been born about ten years after the birth of his youngest son, and to her he was devotedly attached. The loss of his wife when his youngest daughter was about sixteen years of age, seemed to deepen and strengthen the affectionate attachment in question.

" He himself is said to have been a very hard-headed, unromantic, anti-sentimental man, who had been largely influenced by the Scotch philosophers of the last century in rejecting the revealed religion of Christ; and during the latter part of his life, with a habit of sneering and cynicism, appears to have given up any belief in God, the soul, or immortality. He was, however, reputed to have been a person of great integrity and good principles; living an upright life, respected by his friends, and a good friend

[1] The Author is indebted for the above to a member of the old Buckinghamshire family of Hickman, some members of which lived at Aylesbury and Great Marlow.

as regards things temporal to his poorer neighbours.

"The daughter in question, going with others to an outdoor party in one of the most beautiful parts of Buckinghamshire, not far from Wendover, rambling far from headquarters, was with several others overtaken by a storm, caught a severe cold, went home, took to her bed, and in less than ten days was buried in the village churchyard.

"The young girl in question was very fair both in form and features; and friends who came to see her in her coffin said that she had never in all her life looked more beautiful. She was interred in the family vault amid the tears of her relations, and to the intense grief of her sorrowing parent.

"Her father was inconsolable at his loss, the more so as he knew nothing of the consolations of religion, having long ago rejected them, and fretted much at what he looked upon as the stern decrees of Fate.

"The night after the funeral he is said to have had a most vivid dream. He dreamt that his daughter was confined in a cold and narrow underground cell, and that two resolute jailers were slowly filling her mouth with small pieces of cotton wool, in order to forcibly suffocate her; but that in the greatest trouble and agony she continued to resist, and would not be suffocated.

"The dream disturbed him considerably; but, on waking and thinking over it, he acknowledged that his recent loss had no doubt served to disorganise his stomach, to confuse his brain, and to give rise to such fantastic fancies of the night.

"However, a similar dream was had on the following night, and a third to his great astonishment on the night succeeding. His mental anguish and distress became so great that, at sunrise on the third day he rose from his bed, and went off to the clergyman of the parish to narrate what had happened, and to ask his counsel.

"The clergyman, who had not then risen, surprised at being roused so early, came downstairs, listened to the curious and affecting narrative, and at once advised the immediate opening of the vault. This was done at once, and the coffin examined. Under further advice—that of a doctor from the county town, who was going his rounds to visit his patients —the coffin was opened, when, to the horror of all who witnessed what was then and there discovered, it seemed perfectly clear that the young girl had been buried alive. It was obvious that she had been put into the coffin in a state of suspended animation or trance, and that since the burial (for the body was turned and twisted, the hands compressed, the nails being dug into their palms, and the face fearfully contorted), the poor creature had died of suffocation.

"An inquiry which was held resulted in nothing that could either give consolation to the living or benefit to the dead. The bare and melancholy facts as here recorded were both undoubted and unquestioned.

"The father of the girl soon afterwards died of grief, wasted away from sorrowing; and, as some said, died of a broken heart."

Is it unreasonable to hold, it may be remarked, that the repeated dreams in question were, through the ministry of angels, providentially sent, in order that the sufferings of the poor entombed creature might be assuaged? Or is it at all irrational to acknowledge that the dreamer's scepticism as to a future life distinctly debarred him from regarding the warning, or co-operating with the ministrants? On the other hand, if the warning came from angelic messengers, why, if it proved ineffective with one person, was it not made to another? Here is one more mystery to add to an accumulation of mysteries.

ANTIPATHY AFTER DEATH: A LINCOLNSHIRE TRADITION.[1]

The following circumstance certainly occurred at H——k Hall, in Lincolnshire, in the middle of the eighteenth century, and was long the theme of conversation in the county.

At the time of which we are writing, the ancient line of the family which had so long resided there had dwindled down to two individuals, the old Squire at that time in possession, and his only brother and destined successor, who was unmarried, and very little younger than himself.

The Hall, which had once been so full of life and gaiety, had become the abode of sor-

[1] Contributed by Mrs Cracroft-Amcotts of Hackthorne, Lincolnshire, from an eighteenth-century MS.

row and gloom, in consequence of the early death of the Squire's youngest daughter, his only child, and sole heiress of all his possessions. This death, followed in less than a year by that of his wife, to whom he was deeply attached, had quite broken down the old Squire's health and happiness.

The lady and her daughter were deposited in the family vault amid the tears and regrets of the villagers, by whom they were much and deservedly beloved.

For years the Squire had had no intercourse whatever with his brother, between whom and the lady of the Hall there had been a life-long feud: the hatred on her part having been quite of a passive nature, as she was never heard to mention his name; but on his, of the most abusive and virulent kind, which made his exclusion from the Hall an absolute necessity.

When the old Squire, after his double bereavement, became almost heart-broken, the clergyman of the village, whose friendship with the family had existed for fifty years, effected a meeting and a thorough reconciliation between the long-estranged brothers, and the younger one took up his abode once more in the home of his ancestors.

One only condition was made—that the name of his deceased sister-in-law should never pass his lips.

A year passed away. The old Squire, soothed and comforted by the companionship of his early playfellow, began to recover both his health and his spirits; but at this time a malignant fever broke out in the village.

Among its victims was the Squire's brother, who during his whole life had known neither sickness nor disease. He was prostrated at once, and never rallied.

The clergyman before mentioned, who well knew the family history—unmoved by that fear of infection which made him a solitary watcher—took his stand by the bed of the dying man, and vainly endeavoured to draw his thoughts to the eternity which was fast opening before him. His pious words fell upon a dull, unlistening ear; but as he touched upon the duty both of repentance and of forgiveness, and cautiously alluded to his well-known hatred of the deceased Mrs H——, the effect was appalling. All apathy at once vanished, and though a few minutes before apparently past the power of speech, yet now the sick man broke out into fierce imprecations, and by a last supreme effort, raising himself up right in the bed, exclaimed—

"I know that I am dying; *but mark my last words: if, when I am dead, you dare to bury me in the same vault with that accursed woman, the living as well as the dead shall hear of me!*"

He fell back with a frightful imprecation on his lips, and then expired.

The horror-stricken clergyman kept close in his own breast this dreadful death of one whom he had known so long, and thought it more charitable, as well as more prudent, to keep the poor Squire in ignorance of his brother's last hours.

As was the invariable custom in the H—— family, the body, after lying in state for a time, was consigned with the accustomed ceremony to the family vault, and placed next to the coffins of the Squire's wife and daughter.

That very night, certain cottagers living near the churchyard were disturbed by doleful shrieks and piercing cries proceeding from the vault—a noise of strife, and struggling, and blows, as if of enemies engaged in close fight.

The next morning, at daylight, the strange tale was carried to the rectory, and the rector thought it best, under the circumstances, to disclose to the Squire his brother's last fearful words and threats, and to suggest the opening of the vault.

To this the Squire, greatly shocked, consented. The vault was consequently unlocked, and entered by various persons sent to examine into the cause of the strange noises heard the night before.

A scene perfectly inexplicable met their eyes. The coffins of the Squire's lady and daughter were lying in a far corner of the vault, the young girl's coffin across her mother's, as if to protect it. Close to them, standing, not as deposited, but erect and menacing, was the coffin of the Squire's brother, so recently and decorously placed upon black trestles.

Amazement seized the bystanders, but, under the superintendence of proper people, the coffins were restored to their original places, and the vault was again closed up.

At night the noises began again; the sound of blows, shrieks of pain, and a frightful contention of struggling enemies appalled the party of villagers set to watch the place, in order to prevent the possibility of deception.

The tale was whispered far beyond the precincts of the village, and *savants* from the neighbouring city of Lincoln, who laughed at the idea of anything supernatural, suggested that an explosion of gas from the foul air of the vault might have occasioned the displacement of the coffins.

The Squire was induced to have large ventilators constructed in the vault; but this did not in the least abate the nuisance, which to the terror of the village rather increased than diminished.

At length the Squire himself resolved that a strong brick wall should be built up in the vault, so as to separate effectually the coffins of those who, even in the solitude of the tomb, seemed to keep up their antagonism.

This had the desired effect; from that duly performed action all was quiet in the vault, and the noises were never heard again.

Second-sight—of which some notable examples of different periods must now be given—has been thus defined: "A singular faculty of seeing an otherwise invisible object, without any previous means used by the person who sees it for that end. The vision in question makes such a lively impression upon those who possess the gift, that they neither see nor hear anything else, except the vision and its details, so long as that vision continues."

Signs are beheld indicating future events. Crowds have been witnessed walking along steep crags where no mortals could walk. Armies in battle array have been beheld where none were. Graves and headstones have been distinctly distinguished where no churchyards nor burial-places had been. Voices, resembling those recognised of friends and enemies, have been heard in wild solitudes; and prophetical utterances, made as a consequence by the owners of the gift of second-sight, have certainly in many cases come to be fulfilled.

Dr Samuel Johnson, born as he was in a most sceptical and unbelieving age, was far too sagacious and wise a man to deny either the fact or power of second-sight, coming under his constant observation, as it did, during his tour in the north.

It is said by Cortesius that some weeks prior to her death, it had been reported that Queen Elizabeth beheld herself lying on a bed which she was to occupy, pallid, shrivelled, and wan; and that this admitted warning deepened her increasing melancholy, and added to the bitterness of her last miserable and melancholy days.

A somewhat similar vision was seen by Lady Diana Rich,[1] when walking in her father's garden at Kensington one day just before noon. She appeared to see herself walking, in exactly the same dress she was then wearing, and at a distance of about twenty feet in front of her. She was much impressed by the apparition; and—here is the notable consequence—about a month afterwards, she died of the small-pox.

[1] One of the daughters of Sir Henry Rich, K.B.—who was created Baron Kensington, 8th March 1622, and Earl of Holland two years afterwards—by Isabel, daughter of Sir Walter Cope, Knt. A similar instance is on record in reference to another daughter of this Earl—the Lady Frances Rich, who had married Sir James Thynne. The gift or property of second-sight may have belonged to her family.

Thus again, in this case we have a timely and beneficent warning of approaching death.

A VISION SEEN BY DR DONNE.[1]

Dr Donne and his wife lived for some time in London with Sir Robert Drury. Sir Robert having occasion to go to Paris, took the doctor along with him, whose wife was left big with child at Sir Robert's house. Two days after their arrival at Paris, Dr Donne was left alone in the room where Sir Robert and he, and some other friends, had dined together. Sir Robert returned in half an hour, and as he had left so he found the doctor, alone; but in such an ecstasy, and so altered in his looks, as amazed Sir Robert to behold. He inquired the cause; and after some time the doctor told him he had seen a dreadful vision. "I have seen," says he, "my dear wife pass twice by me, through this room, with her hair hanging about her shoulders, and a dead child in her arms."

A messenger was immediately despatched to England, to inquire after Mrs Donne; and

[1] The above is taken from an old MS. Commonplace-Book, mainly written in the early part of the last century. It is also given in Isaac Walton's 'Life of Doctor Donne.'

it appeared that she had been brought to bed of a dead child, after a long and dangerous labour, about the very hour that Dr Donne affirmed he saw her pass by him in his chamber at Paris.

Here is a case from Scotland, followed by certain remarks on the subject in general :—

AN EXAMPLE OF SECOND-SIGHT.[1]

"There lives at Glenelg a person commonly known by the name of Sergeant, a most remarkable seer, of whom I had many stories, from very good authors, of his prophetic talent. I will only mention one, which may serve as a sample of all the rest, and was delivered to me by Ensign MacLeod, who as he was travelling home under night, accompanied by the Sergeant, this seer, on the sudden, desired him to keep to a side, as there was a throng gathering of people coming on the direct path of the road, carrying a corpse on a litter. The Ensign having told him he had no faith in such discoveries, the seer replied, the vision in a

[1] 'A Treatise on the Second-Sight, Dreams, and Apparitions, &c.' By Theophilus Insularius, pp. 40-44. Edinburgh: 1763.

short time would be fulfilled, and thát the Ensign himself would be one of the company; and then named severals from the neighbouring countries, distinguishing them by their names, arms, and clothing, who were to assist at the interment; and pointed at particular passes, where such and such men were to relieve those who carried the bier. In some short time thereafter, a gentlewoman that was sister to the Ensign departed this life, at Myle in Glenmore: all the persons foretold were called and assisted at the interment, without the least variation from the scene, as above described, from the declarant's observation, who took notice of the particular circumstances communicated to him by the seer.

"And if any of the curious should wish for more instances of his predictions, he may apply to the Reverend Mr Donald Macleod, minister of Glenelg, who may furnish him with severals, as he has a throng collection of surprising narrations, delivered him by the Sergeant.

"I cannot here omit to observe, before I go further, that these visions, which are often fancied to be seen at night, though the figures represented should be material, and that the moon should shine in her full splendour (which often is not the case), it would be impossible for the strongest eye, with the utmost attention, exactly to distinguish colours, differences of faces, and other circumstances in their respective attitudes; and consequently, these scenes so minutely corresponding as they are foretold, must be communicated, not to the sight, but to the imagination, as is already observed. I know it is and will be objected by many, how seers can fully and minutely describe those representations that are exhibited to them in the second-sight, unless seen by the organ of the eye? But I beg leave to observe, that this very objection corroborates my opinion, that they see it only in imagination; for will any one say, when a person is in a dream, that those objects which are represented to his eyes, or heard by his ears, are farther real than in imagination? And yet, when he awakes, he can describe them as exactly as if they were real.

"Now, if the second-sight and dreams, according to their impression upon, or representation exhibited to, the imagination, had their full completion, agreeable to all circumstances prefigured in the said instances, it plainly follows that this vision, representation, or whatever name you please to give it, is not carried levity of mind to appear singular; is not the result of innate principles, nor from any intrinsic quality in matter, which undoubtedly is void of all intelligence, but is communicated from one spirit to another; though we cannot describe (as we know but little of spirit) the manner these notices are given. From the certainty of dreams, second-sight, and apparitions, follows the plain and natural consequence of the existence of spirits, immateriality and immortality of the soul: a truth that is acknowledged by the most barbarous nations, as well as by the most civilised, and carries its own conviction in every human breast; unless sensual appetites and rampant lusts sink the man, and make the brute predominant. Under which category we must always consider those adepts in science, that refine themselves into infidelity, are the nuisances of society, and the disgrace of human nature, who bring themselves on the level with the brute beasts that perish. Happy, indeed, were it for those abandoned profligates, could they succeed in that boasted metamorphosis! The astonishing numbers and gradations of corporeal beings, in the animal life, from the least insect to man, the uppermost of terrestrial creatures, and who seems placed in the middle state, leads us (as by a clue) to be persuaded that the same gradation arises from man to the highest rank and order of angels, who, though they are immaterial, yet, as cogitative, intelligent beings, can communicate in sleep, or awake to the imagination (from their extensive knowledge) such truths as are hid, and always must escape the knowledge of organised bodies; which all these instances condescended upon fully evince, to any under the government of reason, or who is not biassed with invincible ill habits, wrong principles, or vicious education. When we look up to the firmament, and behold these glorious bodies in the azure fields of æther, the sun, moon, and stars, with their daily and annual revolutions, in the self-same order of rotation, should we not rather go into the mythology of some of the ancients, who fancied these stupendous luminaries to be the tabernacles of certain intelligences, which animated these orbs, as the soul doth the body, than become so beastly stupid as to own no higher principle, either within or without us, than what is only corporeal? You are not to imagine, from the above paragraph, that I approve of the idolatrous errors of the Sabians; but that I think their mistake more pardonable than to own no higher principle beyond what is material, and liable to dissolution. If one was to view the earth on which we tread (in which there is not the leaf of a tree, or stone, without inhabitants) from the highest star visible to us, it would not appear bigger than an atom; and can we imagine those numberless systems that compose the universe to be void of inhabitants, endued with souls proper to their state and size, and only made for our sakes, that are so inconsiderable a part of the creation?"

The following further considerations on this detail of the subject will no doubt commend themselves to many:—

It will not seem strange that Deists and Freethinkers, who deny all revelation, should at the same time declare their reluctance to believe [in] apparitions, and to raise what dust they can to cloud and discredit it, as they are sensible their yielding this point would be urged against them with great propriety, to overthrow their false system of faith; but it is much more surprising, and indeed lamentable, that Christians, who profess to believe the sacred oracles as they are handed down to us in the Scriptures of the Old and New Testament, should discover any scruple to admit the truth of apparitions, which so powerfully prompt and enforce the important belief of revelation; yet, after all they can say, what does their opinion amount to in point of argument? If a few singular and extravagant persons are extremely confident that a thing does not exist, is that a proof against experience that it does really exist? Such as have this unhappy cast of mind, will please read over Gen. xvi., from verse 7 to the end, Gen. xviii., from the beginning to the end, Gen. xix. 1-18, Gen. xxi. 17, Gen. xxii. 11, Gen. xxxii. 1, 2, Exod. iii. 1, 2, Matt. i. 20, Luke i. 11 and 28, Luke ii. 8-18, and same chapter, verse 26; particularly Joel ii. 28, "And it shall come to pass afterward, that I will pour out my spirit upon all flesh; and your sons and your daughters shall prophesy, your old men shall dream dreams, your young men shall see visions." Verse 29, "And also upon the servants and upon the handmaids in those days will I pour out my spirit." Acts. ii. 17, "And it shall come to pass in the last days, saith God, I will pour out of my spirit upon all flesh: and your sons and your daughters shall prophesy, and your young men shall see visions, and your old men shall dream dreams." Verse 18, "And on my servants and on my handmaidens I will pour out in those days of my spirit; and they shall prophesy." These, of many that might be added from the Word of God, I presume, are sufficient to confirm those Christians who find themselves squeamish to believe [in] apparitions.

AN APPARITION TO CAPTAIN RIDD.

Lord Byron, the celebrated poet, used to relate the following strange story of Captain Ridd, with whom he sailed to Lisbon in 1809:—

This officer stated that being asleep one night in his berth, he was awakened by the pressure of something heavy on his limbs;

and there being a faint light in the cabin, could see distinctly, as he thought, the figure of his brother, who was at that time in the naval service in the East Indies, dressed in his uniform, and stretched across the bed. Concluding it to be an illusion of the senses, he shut his eyes, and made an effort to sleep; but still the same pressure continued, and still, as often as he ventured to take another look, he saw the figure lying across him in the same position. To add to the wonder, on putting his hand forth to touch this form, he found the uniform, in which it appeared to be clothed, dripping wet!

On the entrance of one of his brother officers, to whom he called out in alarm, the apparition vanished; but in a few months after, he received the startling intelligence that on that night his brother had been drowned in the Indian seas. Of the supernatural character of this appearance, Captain Ridd himself did not appear to have the slightest doubt.

The following is a remarkable and well-authenticated recent example of second-sight:—

THE SPECTRAL COFFIN.[1]

My brother was a merchant in Jamaica, and, at the period referred to, had resided there for nearly twenty years. We two, he and I, belong to the old family of Wyborne of Kent, now, I believe, almost extinct; or, at all events, so admittedly altered in social status, that, as I myself believe, all, save ourselves, have either left those parts where our ancestors once flourished, or have sunk into obscurity. In some branches of the family only married women have survived; the male portions of the race having, one after the other, died out. My brother and I had a joint interest in a mere remnant of the old property—all that was left; a kind of superior farmhouse, with about three hundred acres attached, no great distance from Dover. This latter was let to a yeoman who farmed it; but I resided in the house (now pulled down) in the year 1841, up to Christmas of the year 1847.

In the month of October, in the last-named

[1] The Author is indebted for the actual narrative above—which has only been altered in a few unimportant particulars, for the sake of brevity, with a few words here and there added—to the lady who penned it.

year, I was expecting the arrival of a visitor, a lady friend; and having directed my housekeeper, our old-fashioned faithful servant, to prepare a certain bedroom for my friend, I went up-stairs to see that the room was ready. This was about four of the clock upon a bright October afternoon. The room was at the end of a long passage, and a fire had been lit in the grate since the morning.

Upon entering I was all at once suddenly appalled by seeing a large oak coffin on trestles, half covered with a black velvet pall, standing at the foot of the bed. The pall was disarranged, and I at once read on a plate, as I approached the coffin, my own brother's name, and the words which follow:—

MATTHEW WYBORNE,
BORN, 7 DEC. 1788.
DIED———.

Here I fainted and fell. . . .

How long I remained in that state I know not. But in due course I recovered my senses; awoke, and found to my still greater astonishment, that neither coffin, inscription, pall, nor trestles were there.

I then and there mentioned the subject to

my housekeeper, but not as a reality; merely as a strange and unaccountable feature of my own active imagination, though, all the time, I frankly confess that I felt much perturbed and alarmed. She did not say much. I, in turn, however, made a memorandum of the vision; for, to say the truth, I was much impressed by it.

My visitor came and spent some weeks with me. I was anxious about my brother's health, of course; but this anxiety was removed by the fact that two long letters from him reached me shortly afterwards by different mails.

In due course my visitor left; and although I never entered the bedroom referred to without a secret fear of seeing the coffin again, I soon forgot how great had been my original trepidation; and the impression began to fade away.

In September 1848 my brother returned to England quite unexpectedly. Social and political changes in Jamaica had led him to withdraw from his once profitable occupation; and so he suddenly retired, realised his property there, and came back to England intending to settle near the city of Canterbury.

Within a month of that period he was on a visit to me; he became suddenly ill, and within a week died on the bed of that very chamber. I myself, in weak health, was confined to my own room, save when I went to bid him a long farewell, towards the last hours of his sickness.

The day before the burial I entered the chamber of death, when suddenly, with feelings that I cannot describe, I beheld in reality the very sight I had seen a year previously in a vision, every detail realised—the coffin, the pall, the trestles, and the inscription, now complete—

DIED, 11 OCTOBER 1848.

Such is the account of my instance of second-sight.

PRE-VISION OF A FUNERAL.[1]

The following is also a distinct case of second-sight:[2]—

[1] The Author is indebted for the above incident—the distinct fulfilment of a day-dream—to a member of the family of the lady's husband to whom the warning had been vouchsafed.

[2] "Barbara Macpherson, relict of the deceased Mr Alexander

A lady whom I once knew had a day-dream. She was perfectly awake, and was resting in a garden-chair in the sunshine. She thought she saw her own funeral—coffin, pall, clergyman, clerk, mourners, and grave-attendant. She was being buried, as she imagined, in a vault in the nave of a certain church, which was remarkable and probably unique in several of its internal features; and which church-interior she felt certain she had never previously anywhere seen, either in picture or reality.

Mentioning the subject to her husband and other friends, they endeavoured to pooh-pooh the notion; laughing at her fears and ridiculing what they described as her weak and foolish superstition.

However, a few years afterwards, she became sick and debilitated, so that her physician ordered her to go to a mild country, which advice was adopted. She was taken to the

MacLeod, late minister of St Kilda, informed me that the natives of that island have a particular kind of the second-sight, which is always a forerunner of their approaching end. Some months before they sicken they are haunted with an apparition resembling themselves in all respects as to their person, features, or clothing: this image (seemingly animated) walks with them in the fields in broad daylight."—'Treatise on the Second-Sight,' p. 8. Edinburgh: 1763.

house of a relation of her husband—a place to which she had never before gone.

On attending church the first Sunday of her arrival, she beheld in the sacred fabric itself the very place which she had beheld in her dream. After service she pointed out the spot where she had seen her own funeral. The pathway was covered with matting. Under it, however, was the family-vault of her husband's ancestors and kinsfolks. In their house she soon died: in that very vault she was soon actually interred.

Thus was her pre-vision realised. Thus—it may be most reasonably remarked—was a merciful warning given of approaching death.

A WARNING OF DEATH FULFILLED.[1]

A similar story is furnished to me from a reliable source:—

A lady, fond of a country life, had inherited amongst other property a certain extensive farm in Berkshire, and had an efficient bailiff to manage it for her. This man was engaged to be married to the dairymaid of the farm—

[1] A version of this incident, which took place in 1832, is given in Mr Barham's 'Journal.' I heard it related both by the late Sir George Bowyer and by Mr W. J. Bernhard-Smith.

a young woman of respectability and good character.

One morning her mistress noticing that her countenance and absent manner seemed to indicate great mental distress, earnestly asked her to indicate its cause. After some conversation she consented to do so; setting forth that she had had on the previous night a strange vision. Being awoke by a sudden noise, she sat up in her bed and beheld the man to whom she was engaged to be married, standing between her bed and the window. Believing that it was himself, she called out peremptorily to him to leave the room at once. He did not answer and he did not move, but continued to look at her with a strained and sorrowful countenance. She again bade him depart; but he continued perfectly motionless, and in a low clear voice told her that he had come to inform her that he would soon die, and would not, in fact, survive longer than that day six weeks. Very much terrified, she sat gazing at the form of the man, which at once began to grow dimmer and dimmer, and then entirely vanished away.

The morning light was breaking. She

therefore rose, and, after finding that the door of her sleeping-room was as usual locked from the inside, dressed herself, and going down-stairs found everything in its accustomed order. Most prudently she said nothing of what she had seen to any one—not even to the bailiff himself.

Her mistress commended her prudence and discretion, and succeeded in inducing her to believe that the apparition was the result of a fantastic imagination or unworthy fears.

Some weeks passed. On the morning of the day upon which the time mentioned would elapse, the mistress of the girl, in company with some other friends, found the girl perfectly cheerful, and recovered from her former fright and anxiety. The bailiff, as they learnt on inquiry, was in perfect health, and had gone to Wantage market with a load of cheeses.

In the afternoon, however, the dairymaid came running up to the mansion-house, in a state of great fear and trepidation. The bailiff had returned all well and sound from market; but, looking pale and tired, had gone up-stairs to rest for a while, while the farm-labourers went to their dinner.

Not coming down as was expected, his room was entered, and he was there found lying dead upon his own bed, having died almost suddenly of disease of the heart.

Thus the warning words of the strange apparition were exactly fulfilled, both as regards time and purpose.

CASE OF SECOND-SIGHT AT THAME.

A remarkable case of second-sight occurred at Thame in Oxfordshire on the night of Saturday, 25th October 1828, which is reported to have led to the conviction of a murderer. It appears that a certain gardener and nurseryman named Edden—who from his handsome face and fine form had obtained thereabouts the *sobriquet* of "Noble Edden"—was coming home from Aylesbury market late at night, when he was waylaid half-way between that town and Thame, near a hamlet called Gibraltar, and cruelly murdered. It was reasonably assumed that, as Edden was a strong and vigorous man, at least two persons must have had a hand in the foul deed.

Anyhow, Edden's wife, who was at her home engaged in ironing some linen clothes at the time of the murder, stated distinctly and categorically that she was suddenly overcome by a strange and almost indescribable sensation. She saw, as it were, her husband in a stooping position, trying to guard his head with an uplifted arm, rush past her, followed by a man with a raised bludgeon named Benjamin Tyler (whom she well knew), who seemed to be cruelly maltreating her husband.

She was so excited and affected that she at once left off her work, and telling some near neighbours of what she had just seen, started off on the road to Aylesbury, to endeavour to discover him. After walking several miles, and not finding him, she returned home thoroughly unnerved and exhausted.

Some hours afterwards she learnt her husband's fate. An inquest was held at the Cider House, Haddenham, when a verdict of "wilful murder" was returned against some person or persons unknown.

The body of the murdered man was brought to his cottage at Thame; and while it lay coffined, the wife of Edden did all in her power, both directly and indirectly, to induce Benjamin Tyler, the suspected murderer, to come and touch the corpse, — the woman strongly believing that such contact would at once make the blood flow from the stanched wounds, and prove the guilt of the supposed assailant. Tyler, however, directly refused this testing ordeal—which remarkably strengthened the woman's suspicion of his guilt.

Subsequently Tyler and a man named Sewell were arrested: the woman told her experience on the night of the murder before the local magistrates. Eventually the men were tried, convicted, sentenced, and executed,—one of the most remarkable and well-authenticated modern cases of Second-Sight, which indirectly led to such consequences.

A WOMAN CURED OF A CANCER BY A DREAM.[1]

Jane Cotteral, of L——, was afflicted with a cancer in her mouth for several years, and was brought very low both in body and mind and circumstances. Being in an agony of

[1] The above, which was originally printed in a chap-book, may be found set forth in Simpson's 'Treatise on Dreams.'

pain one day, while the surgeon was dressing the sore, she cried out in great earnestness, " My good God ! look down upon me in mercy, for Christ's sake."

The surgeon being angry, immediately left off dressing the wound, bid her go to the God she called upon, and see if He would help her, for he himself would have nothing more to say to her.

The poor afflicted woman was greatly shocked at his behaviour, and begged to know what he demanded for his attendance. His demand was exorbitant, and reduced her and her family almost to want. However, at last she paid all he required, and returned home with a light purse and a heavy heart.

Some little time after this, the poor woman dreamt three or four nights together, that she saw a man who made a perfect cure of her cancerous complaint. Upon this she greatly importuned her husband to take her to the place where she saw the man.

He, thinking it was nothing but a dream, in consequence of her suffering, begged her not to think of going again from home, so ill as she was. Persisting, however, in the thought of going to the place where she saw the man, her husband consented.

She went, and had not been long at the place before she saw the very person walk into the room that she had seen in her sleep. She immediately started up, thanked God, and running to the man, said, she was rejoiced to see him.

The man, surprised (having never seen the woman before), asked what she meant. "Oh, sir," said she, "you are the person who is to cure my cancer." "Good woman," said he, "I never cured a cancer in my life." At this reply the poor woman was cast down and cried out, "Then all is over."

The man, seeing the woman in such distress, and a deplorable object to look upon, asked her the cause of her applying to him. She told him all the particulars before related, and added, "If you can help me, do so." He then bid her be comforted, for he knew of something which had been of use, if she would try it.

"Anything, sir, you advise, I will most certainly try," said she.

He accordingly made up an application,

which she used; and in a little time she was quite cured of the cancer, and restored to perfect health.

This happened upwards of fifteen years ago. I could mention the surgeon's name who treated her with such inhumanity, if it were expedient. He was a noted Deist.

LORD VIVIAN'S DREAM.

In the year 1879, Lord Vivian wrote to the 'Daily Telegraph' the true account of a remarkable dream of his, to which the Editor of that newspaper had alluded, in connection with the name of General Richard Taylor. His lordship wrote:—

"I did dream on the morning of the race for the City and Suburban Handicap, that I had fallen asleep in the weighing-room of the stand at Epsom prior to that race, and that after it had been run, I was awakened by a gentleman—the owner of another horse in the race—who informed me that a horse called 'The Teacher' had won. Of this horse, so far as my recollection serves me, I had never before heard.

"On reaching Victoria Station, the first

person I saw was the gentleman who had appeared to me in my dream, and to him I mentioned it, observing that I could not find any horse so named in the race. He replied, 'There is a horse now called Aldrich, which was previously called The Teacher.'

"The dream had so vividly impressed me, that I declared my intention of backing Aldrich for £100, and was in course of doing this when I was questioned by his owner as to 'why I was backing his horse.' I replied, 'Because I dreamt he had won the race.' To this I was answered, 'As against your dream, I will tell you this fact: I tried the horse last week with a hurdle-jumper, and he was beaten a distance.' (I afterwards learned that the trial horse was Lowlander.) I thanked my informant and discontinued backing Aldrich. General Taylor, who had overheard what passed, asked me, if I did not intend backing the horse again for myself, to win him £1000 by him. This I did by taking for him 1000 to 30 about Aldrich."

This chapter may be properly brought to its close with the following pertinent remarks :—

"Those who amongst Christians deny predictions by dreams, second-sight, and apparitions, are not wholly aware how great a handle they give up to unbelievers. To question the credibility of the sacred oracles, wherein there are so many appeals, and much mention of intelligence conveyed this way; and if the intelligences we get in this hidden manner are, from innumerable examples, sacred and profane, proven to be authentic, will it be a good objection against such communications that we cannot conceive the manner in which they are carried on? Can we pretend to know exactly how the union betwixt our own souls and bodies exists and operates in all its circumstances? Much less can we comprehend by what means a spiritual intercourse is introduced by other intellectual beings; and yet, if we absolutely refuse that such scenes have existed, we sap the foundation of all religion, and may herd with the brutal part of creation." [1]

[1] 'A Treatise on the Second-Sight, Dreams, and Apparitions, &c.' By Theophilus Insularius, p. 132. Edinburgh: 1763.

REMARKABLE DREAMS AND SUPER-NATURAL OCCURRENCES

CHAPTER IV.

REMARKABLE DREAMS AND SUPERNATURAL OCCURRENCES.

It has been remarked by one of the most acute students of supernatural occurrences, that what is wanted for their due investigation is a plain statement of facts in regard to the same—facts set forth in simple language, and with the details given on credible authority. Obvious dissertations might be made on each one of the succeeding narratives; but such dissertations are left to the reader. Where, for example, a disembodied spirit is seen by one person, and a sound as of its voice heard contemporaneously by another, it is obvious that such independent testimony as to its appearance cannot be loftily and contemptuously put aside as the result of an overwrought brain, imagination, or fancy.

The following plain and well-authenticated record is full of interest and pathos :—

THE RETURN OF THE SAILOR-BOY.[1]

On Croom's Hill, Greenwich, there resided a friend of mine, Mr Hammond, a gentleman of great respectability, of varied attainments and of considerable mental ability, a student of literature, religion, and science. His position was that of an underwriter at Lloyd's, and in the society of his wife and children he enjoyed a wholesome domestic life. Among those persons engaged in this comfortable household in the year 1866, was a young widow named Potter, whose services were occasionally required for various periods as a needlewoman and general assistant. She had one son named Tom, a bright, handsome, delightful boy; he could sing and play; he was clever and accomplished; he excelled in any study to which he gave his attention, and though he was wayward and restless, was the favourite of every one who knew him. This brave and troublesome boy was provided with a home and edu-

[1] I am indebted to Mr Newton Crossland, of Blackheath, for the above remarkable narrative.

cated at the neighbouring Roman Catholic College, under the direction and mastership of an able and enlightened priest, the late Dr W. G. Todd. Those who knew this kind and estimable ecclesiastic will not require to be reminded of his many excellent qualities. His learning and intelligence, his affability and wide sympathy, his devotion to the cause of education and religion, and his high principles, endeared him to all those who were honoured with his friendship. His heart was as tender as his mind was acute and sagacious. You might impose upon his good looks, but not upon his intellect.

Tom Potter, the restless and impetuous scholar, caused many an anxious thought to his mother and her friends, and at last they raised a general chorus of "What shall we do with Tom Potter?" About the year 1863-64, when he was probably fourteen years of age, he was placed in a first-rate house in Manchester; but his vocation was evidently not in "dry goods;" he would not settle down to a mercantile life—he determined to go to sea; and at last his friends most reluctantly consented that his whim should be gratified, as they could make nothing of him on shore. He was placed on board a training-ship at Woolwich, and in due time drafted on board one of her Majesty's ships of war. After a voyage or two, Tom got tired of the navy and rebelled. In company with some other naughty boys, he deserted his ship, and after some disastrous adventures, returned in a piteous plight —weary, famished, and half-naked—to his Greenwich home.

The tables were soon turned upon the young and interesting truant; he became very ill, and a warrant was issued for his apprehension. His mother and his patrons immediately raised a despairing cry, and asked, with more emphasis than ever, "What shall we do with Tom Potter?" Dr Todd again intervened with his kind offices and intercession. The captain of the ship consented, with only a nominal punishment, to receive back again the irresistible and pardoned culprit; and at last Tom was fairly shipped off on board the Doris frigate, bound to the West Indies.

Tom's mother having thus provided for

him, left the Hammond family altogether; got married again, and became Mrs Cooper. After a time, a new servant, who had never heard of either Mrs Potter or Mrs Cooper, arrived, and filled the office of housemaid. This new servant we will call "Mary"; and so ends the first portion of my tale.

On the night of the 8th September 1866, Mrs Hammond's street-door bell was rung. Mary the housemaid answered it; the door was duly opened, and after a little confabulation, the door was shut again. Mrs Hammond, who was unwell, was in her bedroom, which commands a view of, and is within ear-shot of the entrance-hall. She listened, and distinctly identified the voice of Tom Potter. She was surprised, and called out, "Mary, who was that at the door?" The servant replied, "Oh, ma'am, it was a little sailor-boy; he wanted his mother. I told him I knew nothing of his mother, and sent him about his business."

Mrs Hammond, whose anxiety was aroused, asked the servant what the boy was like.

"Well, ma'am, he was a good-looking boy in sailor's clothes, and his feet were naked.

I should know him again anywhere. He looked very pale and in great distress; and when I told him his mother wasn't here, he put his hand to his forehead, and said, 'Oh dear, what shall I do?'"

Mrs Hammond told her husband what an unwelcome visitor had been to the house, and gave him the unpleasant intelligence that "she was sure Tom Potter had run away from his ship again." The family now laid their heads ominously together, and vexatiously exclaimed, "Goodness gracious! what shall we do with Tom Potter?"

They sent to make inquiries of the mother, but she had heard nothing of her son; then they thought he was lost, and they upbraided themselves for "turning him away from their door."

In their trouble they went to consult the genial Dr Todd, but his opinion only increased their perplexity and astonishment. He told them—"It is almost impossible Tom Potter can have deserted his ship. I had a letter from the boy himself only about two months ago, and then he was getting on capitally."

It was then arranged that Mary should have

an interview with Dr Todd and be examined by him. She was accordingly ushered into Dr Todd's presence and invited to take part in the council. Dr Todd had a store of photographs of many of his pupils, and among them was a *carte* of Tom Potter. He laid a number of these portraits before Mary, and requested her to pick out the one that resembled the boy she saw; at the same time, with the view of testing her accuracy to the utmost, he called her attention to one which was *not* a photograph of Tom Potter, and quietly remarked, "Do you think that is the boy? he was very likely to run away from his ship." "No," said Mary, positively, "that was not the boy I saw; this is the one"—at the same time pouncing upon the likeness of Tom Potter —"I could swear to him."

The mystery became more mysterious, but the only decision the conclave could wisely make, was to await the issue of events; in the meantime they could do nothing but patiently exercise their faculty of wonder. A solution of the mystery was at hand. In the next month of October, Dr Todd received a letter from the Admiralty, stating that they communicated with him because they did not know the address of Tom Potter's mother. The letter gave the sad intelligence that on the 6th September, just two days before he was seen at the door of Mr Hammond's house, Tom Potter breathed his last, in consequence of a dreadful accident on board the Doris frigate off Jamaica. He fell from the masthead on the 24th July 1866, and was frightfully injured. He lingered a few weeks, and died raving and calling for his mother.

It was at Mr Hammond's door that the ill-fated boy parted from his mother, and there saw her for the last time in life. This circumstance may account for the spirit of the boy having been mysteriously attracted to the spot where he left his mother, of whose departure he was not aware. Disembodied spirits only know what comes within the compass of their experience and capacity. Their intelligence and information are sometimes very limited. The facts of this story are certain and indisputable. I have taken great pains to verify them.

In the following narrative, an apparition of

a relative was beheld simultaneously by three persons, and, as it subsequently appeared, at the precise time at which he passed away in death :—

AN APPARITION SEEN SIMULTANEOUSLY BY THREE PERSONS.

Three sisters, maiden ladies, who lived together in a country town in Herefordshire, were, one evening in the month of October 1862, sitting in their drawing-room, which overlooked their garden, and the chief door in which opened into a breakfast-room, which itself had a door leading out on to the adjacent lawn. One of the sisters had been reading to the other two; but the twilight having deepened, and the candles not being then lit, each of them was sitting silent; when, as they each distinctly affirm, the figure of their absent brother, suddenly passing the window outside, opened the lawn door of the breakfast-room, making some noise in so doing, and was seen by each of them hurriedly passing through that room into the hall on the other side.

Two of the sisters—the eldest being infirm —at once rose, and rushing out into the hall through the breakfast-room, expected to greet their absent brother, who was supposed to have unexpectedly returned from Calcutta (where for several years he had been employed in the service of the British Government); but no brother was to be found high or low, and the door into the garden was found to have been locked.

This circumstance, in all its extraordinary details, struck them much and saddened them deeply. They at once made notes of the occurrence, and recorded the hour, day, and date of it. On that day, making allowance for the difference of time between that of Greenwich and Calcutta, it was subsequently found that the brother of these ladies had died suddenly at the last-named city, of sunstroke.

A DREAM FULFILLED.

The son of an emigrant gentleman in Queensland was made a bank clerk in Brisbane; and it often became a part of his duty to collect money in outlying places, and deposit it in the chief office in the city in question.

On one of these occasions he received a considerable sum in gold and cheques. These, as usual, he placed in an iron safe in the presence of two or three of his fellow-clerks. Having to meet some members of his family in the town, he then left the office in order to join them, and did not return until the following morning. On again opening the safe, he made the alarming discovery that the whole of the gold coin had been stolen. No suspicion whatsoever was attached to him, for his character was of the highest. Nevertheless the duty of inquiring and investigating was at once placed upon the police. No result followed — save that the money was never recovered nor the thief found out.

As a matter of consequence the young man's friends were very much distressed at the unpleasant and unfortunate circumstance—though of course no charge had been made against him.

Some months afterwards, however, the father of the bank clerk in question dreamed on three distinct occasions that the money stolen had been secreted under ground in a certain spot in the Botanical Gardens of the city of Brisbane—a spot which he had often visited and knew perfectly well.

For some time he feared to communicate with the bank authorities. Mixed motives seem to have been the cause of the delay. Soon, however, the mental worry he endured in consequence, becoming almost intolerable, he wrote down carefully what had occurred under the three dreams, and set off for Brisbane itself.

On arriving there he went to the bank house, where he learned from the authorities that four days previously one of the other clerks had confessed to having perpetrated the robbery; and that out of the thirteen hundred sovereigns which had been stolen, nine hundred had been found at the exact spot in the Botanical Gardens which had been seen in the dream.

The following beautiful and touching narrative[1] is from the pen of the Rev. W. J. Moser, Catholic priest of the cathedral city of Peterborough :—

A young servant, religiously brought up,

[1] The record above given, as Father Moser kindly informs me, is taken from a French book, 'Les Douleurs de la Vie, la Mort, la Purgatoire,' par M. L'Abbé V. Postel, D.D., Chanoine et Vicaire Général.

had adopted the pious practice of having a mass said each month for the souls in purgatory, making the customary alms from her very limited wages. Brought to Paris by her employers, she never failed to observe this work of charity, and she had always been accustomed to assist in person at the divine sacrifice which she had caused to be offered. Her intercession had for its more especial object the deliverance of the soul whose expiation had been nearly achieved. Soon God tried her by a long illness, which not only caused her to endure much bodily suffering, but which resulted in the loss of her situation, and she was reduced to her last resources. The day when she was able to leave the hospital, a single franc was all she possessed. She prayed to God with confidence for help, and went in quest of employment. She had been directed to a register office at the other end of the town, and thither she proceeded; but passing a church on the way, she entered it. The sight of a priest at the altar reminded her that she had omitted that month her ordinary devotion, and that this was precisely the day on which she had been accustomed to have mass said for the souls in purgatory. But what if she applied her last franc to that purpose! She would not have anything to provide herself with food. There was an inward conflict for a moment. "After all," she said to herself, "God knows that it is for Him, and therefore He will not forsake me." She entered the sacristy, made her offering, and assisted at the mass offered for her intention. Afterwards she proceeded on her journey, filled with anxiety, it is easy to imagine. Absolutely destitute, how was she to satisfy her wants for that day? She had nowhere to go. Just, however, as she was turning a corner into a street, a young man, pale, of slight build and gentlemanly appearance, approached her and said—

"Are you in quest of a situation?"

"Yes, sir."

"Very well; go into such a street, and to such a number, to Madame ——; I believe that you will suit her, and that you will be happy there."

He disappeared among the passengers without waiting to hear the thanks which the poor servant had commenced to address to him. She found the street, recognised the number, and ascended to the apartment of Madame ——. A servant was leaving the house carrying a bundle under her arm, and muttering words of anger.

"Can madame receive me?" asked the newcomer.

"Perhaps she can, perhaps she can't," replied the other, "what matter is it to me? Madame will tell you herself I have nothing to do with her; good morning," and she descended with her bundle.

Our heroine remained trembling where she was, when a sweet voice told her to advance, and she found herself in the presence of an aged lady of venerable appearance, who encouraged her to make known her errand.

"Madame," said the servant, "I have learnt a few moments ago that you required a housemaid, and I have come to offer myself to you. I was assured you would receive me with kindness."

"My child, what you tell me is very extraordinary. It is only half an hour ago I dismissed an insolent servant; and there is no other soul in the world beside myself who knows it; who, then, has sent you?"

"He was a gentleman, quite young, whom I met in the street; he stopped me to tell me. I have thanked God for it, as it is necessary that I should find a situation to-day; for I am entirely without money."

The old lady could not understand who the person could be, and she became lost in conjectures, when the servant, accidentally raising her eyes to look about the room, perceived a portrait. "There, madame," said she, "it is no longer a difficulty; that is exactly the face of the young man who spoke to me. It is at his instigation I have come."

At these words the lady uttered a cry and nearly fainted away. She made the girl tell her all her history, of her devotion to the suffering souls, the mass in the morning, and the meeting of the stranger. Then throwing herself on the neck of the young girl, she embraced her with tears, and said, "You shall not be my servant, but from this moment you are my daughter. It was my son, my only son, that you saw; my son, dead these two years, who owes his deliverance to you, and who has been permitted by God to send you here. Remain here, then, and be happy, and henceforth we will pray together for the suffering souls in purgatory that they may enter into a happy eternity."

Those who perform this charitable duty of assisting the holy souls in purgatory are not forgotten, but they will be remembered in an especial manner, and will themselves receive the benefit of such charitable aid when they shall be in need of it; that is to say, that God will not permit a soul to be neglected in purgatory who in life assisted the holy souls.

W. J. MOSER.

QUEEN STREET, PETERBOROUGH.

THE LADY ANNE GRIMSTON.

It was a current belief, and the belief is still existent, that the Lady Anne Grimston, one of the wives of Sir Samuel Grimston, the third baronet of that family, was a person who disbelieved wholly both in the existence of God and in the immortality of the soul.[1] Her con-

[1] The Lady Anne (daughter of John Tufton, 2d Earl of Thanet, by Lady Margaret Sackville, eldest daughter of Richard, 3d Earl of

viction on these points in her mental maturity was apparently both sincere and deep; and she never hesitated to avow the existence of such conviction.

It was also recorded that the slow approach of death (for she is said to have died after a lingering illness), had no effect whatsoever in altering her profound conviction. As she had latterly lived so she was prepared to die.

On her deathbed, however, she is said to have repeated her atheistic convictions more than once, with great energy and astonishing boldness. So determined was she in the re-iteration of this singular and foolish unbelief,

Dorset), married Samuel, eldest son and heir of Sir Harbottle Grimston, Bart., Master of the Rolls.

Much has been written both for and against this tradition. The late Dean Stanley—not, however, an over-trustworthy explorer or guide—took considerable pains to prove it to be a mere legend. But he was wholly unsuccessful, and evinced his annoyance at so being. The amount of independent evidence which still exists in the neighbourhood of Tewin, convinced him of the difficulty of crushing and destroying what no doubt is a well-grounded record of facts.

'The Seven Trees of Lady Grimston in the Churchyard of Tewin; or, the Atheist Confuted.' By Joseph Waye, Minister of the Word. London: John Paul, 1752. See also 'Flora Hertfordiensis,' 'The Hertford Times,' A.D. 1870-1873.

On the other hand, it is only right and fair to point out that the present Lord Verulam, who, admitting that "*it is difficult at such a distance of time to show what were her opinions,*" maintains that there is existing evidence to make his lordship believe that "Lady Anne Grimston was a religious woman."—'Notes and Queries,' Feb. 25, 1871.

that, shortly before she expired, she openly maintained that if there were a God, and she found in the future that her silly negations were false, *no less than seven ash-trees would grow out of her tomb.*

Whether these exact words were uttered or not, appears to rest mainly on ordinary tradition and current belief. Words identical with them were no doubt spoken. The tale is universally believed and often repeated; and no doubt is founded on a *substratum* of truth.

Anyhow it is an undoubted fact, that in the churchyard of Tewin, in the diocese of St Alban's, seven ash-trees *have* sprung up through the substantial and solid tomb, and have broken away the masonry, rendering the reading of the inscription a great difficulty, if not now an impossibility.

This was its text:—

Here lieth interred the Body of
THE RIGHT HONOURABLE LADY ANNE GRIMSTON,
Wife to SIR SAMUEL GRIMSTON, Bart. of Gorhambury,
in Hertfordshire,
Daughter to the late Right Honourable
EARL OF THANET,
Who departed this life Nov. 22, 1713,
in the Sixtieth year of her age.

And here follows a description of the present state of the table-monument :—

The masonry of the tomb—once firmly set, and bound with iron pins together—is now disjointed and displaced; not by time or decay, but by the irrepressible growth of trees never planted by human hands. The appearance which the tomb presents is most singular. Within, and interlacing the iron railing surrounding the tomb, are seven ash-trees connected at the root. Those trees, as they have daily grown, have heaved up the stonework of the tomb, forcing it outward for some distance, and entwined around the iron railings, which in some places are completely imbedded and hidden in the trunks of the trees. The trees at their base also pass through and clasp the stonework, as though it were a mass of earth.

The surrounding iron railings are firmly imbedded in the several trunks of the ash-trees, which are distinct and separate,—and the fulfilment of the dying utterance of this atheistic woman is very generally looked upon as a remarkable example of direct supernatural intervention.

A singular record by Mr Strutt is worthy of being here reproduced :—

THE DISCOVERY OF A MURDER.[1]

Some years ago, having occasion to be at Chelmsford, a very strange adventure happened to me. I arrived late in the evening, on my journey from Colchester; and after having inquired for the best inn, was recommended to the White Horse, which was at the other end of the town, facing the market, and adjoining to the churchyard.

In the morning I was desirous of seeing the church, a long, large, and stately edifice, and then just finished. After I had surveyed the buildings, I walked among the tombs in the churchyard, and the sexton was then digging a grave for a burial, which was to be made of a townsman that evening. I stood awhile to observe the man, who, without the least compunction or reflection, cast out from the earth the remains of his fellow-mortals, and whistled with indifference.

[1] A Singular History of a Murder, found out twenty-two years after it was perpetrated, in the Town of Chelmsford, and discovered by the late Mr Joseph Strutt, Author of 'The Dictionary of Engravers,' &c.

Amongst a variety of bones thrown out of the pit was a skull, which appeared whiter than ordinary; this induced me to take it up, and turning it about, I heard something rattle within it: upon examination, I found a large nail, covered with rust, full four inches long. It surprised me to find a nail in such a situation; and on turning the skull about, I found on the forehead a perforation, incrusted with the rust of the iron, and in which a part of the nail yet remained. This led me to suspect that the owner of the skull had been murdered: but without mentioning anything to my *grave* companion, I inquired if he knew to whom the bones he was now throwing out of the earth belonged.

"Yes, sir," said he, "and well, too; he was as hearty a cock as ever broke bread, and was the master of the White Horse two-and-twenty years ago."

"How came he by his death?"

"Oh, very suddenly! Alas! master, we are here to-day, and there to-morrow: Death, when he comes, will not be said nay. Would you believe it, I drank with him the night before, and he seemed as well in health as I;

but in the morning he was dead, and I buried him with my own hands in this grave."

"He died suddenly, you say?"

"He was dead, I tell you, the next morning."

"Was any cause assigned?"

"He died in a fit."

"And do you think this was his skull?"

"I'd not deceive you, sir; I am certain—*sure* of it."

"See then," said I, "the cause of his dying suddenly," showing him the nail rusted in the skull, and the remainder corroded and loose in the cavity. He seemed astonished.

"Had he no family?"

"No: he left a widow, the woman who at present keeps the inn; and before two months were past from the death of her husband, she married the ostler,—he is at present the master."

Without farther questioning the sexton, I inquired for the residence of the Justice, and taking the skull in my hand, I wrapped the end of my mantle about it, and went to him. I was readily admitted, and after apologising for my intrusion, told him the cause of my coming, and then showed him the skull.

He was struck in the same manner that I had been, that the owner of this skull had been murdered, and sent for the sexton, who confirmed what he had said to me, and declared he was ready to make oath to the identity of the skull.

The magistrate then sent for the woman by a verbal message, that no alarm might be given; she instantly attended. She seemed surprised at seeing me there. I smiled, and bid her good-morrow, said I had rested well, and had walked out for amusement; when, after some little extraneous conversation, the magistrate gave it a different turn, and, without any more previous introduction, began to question her concerning her first husband. She then affected to weep, and praised him for a paragon of kindness and virtue.

"But still, I hope you have no reason to complain of your present goodman?"

"Certainly not, your worship," said she, "not upon the whole; but he has not the learning and breeding of my dear, dear Gregory!"

"You married him, I understand, very soon after your dear Gregory's death?"

"Why, la! your worship, what could a poor woman do, left alone, as you may say, in a large inn, and all men-folk about her? Indeed I wept for Gregory, but I was obliged to think for myself."

"He died suddenly, I heard?"

"Ah, your worship, I was happy enough in the evening; and in the morning, your honour, I was a poor, miserable, lone woman! Indeed it is true, your honour!"

"Did you know the cause of his death?"

"Oh, he was taken in a fit of apoplexy, and fell back on his chair, and spoke no more! We put him to bed, chafed and rubbed him, but all to no purpose."

"What help did you call in? did you not send for the doctor?"

"Oh, your worship, it was to no purpose—he was stone dead."

"But bleeding is sometimes efficacious. Then you did not call in the doctor?"

"No, your honour, I was too much affrightened to think on't."

"You said *we* put him to bed; who was it that assisted you?"

"Robert, the ostler, for I could not lift him

by myself: but forsooth, your worship, we called in the gossips; they saw my dear husband's corpse, and helped to lay it out, too, therefore there was no need of the coroner's inquest; and he was buried, your honour, as a man (St Michael bless him!) should be buried, and holy mass said over him, or I should be much to blame, your honour."

"No doubt; but prithee, did he never complain previously of the headache?"

"Yes, your honour, after he had been mellow with his customers; for your honour must know, Gregory was a rare hand to make his customers drink."

"Yes; but immediately before his death," said the Justice, "did he not complain of the headache?"

"Not in the least, your honour; he had just drunk a cup of ale——"

"Well," said the magistrate, abruptly, "he complained not of the headache?"

"Not in the least."

"Why," said he, fixing his eyes full on her, "that is strange indeed! I think a nail half the length would have made me complain."

"Nail! your honour," said she, trembling,

—"nail! Oh, that is false! there was no nail!"

She then hesitated, and soon after recollecting herself, rejoined, "Forsooth, I do not know what your worship means by a nail!"

"Why, I'll tell you, good woman," said he, producing the skull, and the part of the nail found in it; "had such a nail as this been driven into my skull, it would also have prevented me from complaining."

The moment she saw the skull and the nail, she exclaimed, "Murder will out! Yes, Robert must die!" and immediately fainted away.

The Justice caused her to be removed into an inner room, and sent for the husband, who was at home, but excused himself, on account of his wife's being absent, and customers being in the house; but the constable told him the business was of consequence. He put on his hat, and went with him. When he entered, the Justice said—

"Pray, Mr Robert, excuse me sending for you in so peremptory a manner, but there is a question between this gentleman and me, which you can readily answer."

"Your worship knows you may command anything which is in my power," said Robert.

"Well then, tell me, without disguise, how long a man can live after a long nail has been driven into his skull?"

"On the sudden statement of this question, his courage forsook him, his knees knocked each other, and his teeth chattered in his head, and he exclaimed, "Why—why—why—your wor—ship—how should—I—I—kn—o—w?"

"What is it that frightens thee? Surely it is not the ghost of Gregory, thy master, which has occasioned this astonishment!"

"Oh, then," cried he out, "I see that my she-devil has betrayed me! but it was all her doings."

"What," cried the Justice—"what was her doings?"

"Ay," cried he, a little recollecting himself, "I want to know why your worship asks such strange questions. I am sure as how I do not know how to answer them; but your honour must know how I have got some horses from Thaxted fair coming home this morning, and I daresay they are home by now. I hope your honour will excuse me at present. If your worship is in this merry mood in the afternoon, I'll come and answer any of your honour's questions with all my heart."

"Stop, my friend," says the Justice, "we cannot part at present quite so easily; shut the door, there; and for the horses, your ostler, good Master Robert, must look after them. But you must know that you stand charged with murder: your wife has confessed you are the murderer."

"I—I—your honour?"

"Yes, of your master."

"Did she confess?"

"I tell you she did, and accuses you of doing the deed."

"Oh! 'tis false! she wants to get rid of me as she did of Gregory. She persuaded me, but I never did any such thing!"

"Look here, Robert," said the magistrate; "see this skull. It was thy master's—yes, 'tis Gregory's skull! See this nail found within it, corroded by age; see where the head remains still in the bone, and recollect at once your handiwork."

The sudden exposure of the skull, and the address, so worked upon the mind of the unfortunate culprit, that, aided by the terrors of a guilty conscience, it led him to a full confession. He and his wife were consequently committed to the prison. I was obliged to appear as an evidence at the yearly assizes held for the county, where various circumstances were adduced in proof of the murder; and they, being justly condemned, suffered condign punishment.

THE SELF-SCOURGER.[1]

It was in the early part of ——'s life that he attended a hunting club at their sport, when a stranger, of a genteel appearance, and well mounted, joined the chase, and was observed to ride with a degree of courage and address that called forth the utmost astonishment of every one present. The beast he rode was of amazing powers; nothing stopped them; the hounds could never escape them; and the huntsman, who was left far behind, swore that the man and his horse were *devils from hell.* When the sport was over, the company invited this extraordinary person to

[1] The above is taken from 'Letters by the late Lord Lyttleton,' vol. i. p. 141: London, 1787.

dinner; he accepted the invitation, and astonished the company as much by the powers of his conversation and the elegance of his manners, as by his equestrian prowess. He was an orator, a poet, a painter, a musician, a lawyer, a divine; in short, he was everything, and the magic of his discourse kept the drowsy sportsmen awake long after their usual hour. At length, however, wearied nature could be charmed no more, and the company began to steal away by degrees to their repose. On his observing the society diminish, he discovered manifest signs of uneasiness; he therefore gave new force to his spirits, and new charms to his conversation, in order to detain the remaining few some time longer. This had some little effect; but the period could not be long delayed when he was to be conducted to his chamber. The remains of the company retired also; but they had scarce closed their eyes, when the house was alarmed by the most terrible shrieks that were ever heard. Several persons were awakened by the noise; but its continuance being short, they concluded it to proceed from a dog who might be accidentally confined in some part of the house; they very soon, therefore, composed themselves to sleep, and were very soon awakened by shrieks and cries of still greater terror than the former. Alarmed at what they heard, several of them rang their bells, and when the servants came, they declared that the horrid sounds proceeded from the stranger's chamber. Some of the gentlemen immediately arose, to inquire into this extraordinary disturbance; and while they were dressing themselves for that purpose, deeper groans of despair, and shriller shrieks of agony, again astonished and terrified them. After knocking some time at the stranger's chamber-door, he answered them as one awakened from sleep, declared he had heard no noise, and, rather in an angry tone, desired he might not be again disturbed. Upon this they returned to one of their chambers, and had scarce begun to communicate their sentiments to each other, when their conversation was interrupted by a renewal of yells, screams, and shrieks, which, from the horror of them, seemed to issue from the throats of damned and tortured spirits. They immediately followed the sounds, and traced them to the stranger's chamber, the door of which they instantly burst open, and found him upon his knees in bed, in the act of scourging himself with the most unrelenting severity, his body streaming with blood. On their seizing his hand to stop the strokes, he begged them, in the most wringing tone of voice, as an act of mercy, that they would retire, assuring them that the cause of their disturbance was over, and that in the morning he would acquaint them with the reasons of the terrible cries they had heard, and the melancholy sight they saw. After a repetition of his entreaties they retired; and in the morning some of them went to his chamber, but he was not there; and on examining the bed, they found it to be one gore of blood. Upon further inquiry, the groom said that, as soon as it was light, the gentleman came to the stable booted and spurred, desired his horse might be immediately saddled, and appeared to be extremely impatient till it was done, when he vaulted instantly into the saddle, and rode out of the yard at full speed. Servants were immediately despatched into every part of the surrounding country, but not a single trace of him could be found: such a person had not been seen by any one, nor has he been since heard of.

PRESAGES OF DEATH.

The Duke of Buckingham being to take his leave of his Grace of Canterbury (Archbishop William Laud),—"My lord (says the duke), I know your lordship has great influence over the King our sovereign. Let me pray you to put his Majesty in mind to be good to my poor wife and children." At which words his Grace being troubled, he took the liberty to ask him if he had any secret foreboding in his mind. "No," replied the duke; "but I think some adventure may kill me, as well as another man."

The very next day before he was slain, feeling some indisposition of body, the King was pleased to honour him with a visit. The duke, at his Majesty's departure, embraced him in a very unusual and passionate manner, and likewise his friend the Earl of Holland, as if he had known he should see them no more.

On the day of his death, the Countess of

Denbigh (his sister) received a letter from him: who, while she was writing her answer, bedewed the paper with her tears; and after a bitter passion of sorrow (whereof she could yield no reason) fell down in a swoon. Her letter ended thus: "I will pray for your happy return, which I look at with a great cloud over my head, too heavy for my poor heart to bear without torment; but I hope the great God of heaven will bless you!"

The day following, the Bishop of Ely came to visit her; but hearing she was at rest, waited till she awoke, which she did in a great fright; for she had dreamt that her brother passed through a field with her in the coach, where hearing a sudden shout, and asking the reason, it was answered, the Duke of Buckingham was sick: which she had scarce related to her gentlewoman, before the Bishop entered into her bedchamber with an account of his death.

APPARITION AFTER DEATH.[1]

In the year 1848, my youngest sister, in

[1] The Author is indebted for the above, and the very interesting narrative immediately following, to a sister of one of the bishops of the province of Canterbury.

delicate health, left her home to go to Cheltenham for the winter.

Before she went away, our old nurse, a family retainer, who had seen three generations grow up, was greatly distressed by the idea that she might not live to see my sister return, being then more than eighty years of age.

My sister repeatedly assured her that, come what might, *she would see her again*, these being her parting words.

Some weeks afterwards, when we believed my sister to be fairly well, the nurse came down one morning, greatly agitated, saying she had seen in the night a vision or dream, most distinctly, of a beautiful young lady, all in white, who passed close by her—her garments seemed to touch her—as she was standing on a green plain, at the end of which was a garden wall, with a gate opening into a fair garden. She could not distinguish the features, as the figure swiftly glided by, but distinctly marked that upon her forehead was bound a chaplet of brilliant pearls or shining stones. The lady passed on to the garden, through the gate, and was no more seen.

We were all at a loss to know who was meant by the vision; but that evening news came that my sister, the night before, had been suddenly seized with an attack of heart disease so severe, that every moment her death was expected. She lingered a few days, and so far revived that she wrote a line saying that, while in that state, her mind was occupied with thankfulness to God that her dear old nurse was safe with me, which made her so happy; and soon after she suddenly passed away.

The most remarkable point of my narrative is, that after her death, my brother, who had lately returned from the Holy Land, wrote to me that he had then brought back a string of pearls which had been blessed by the Patriarch for her; adding, "And she now lies in her coffin, with the chaplet round her brow."

So as proving the identity of the vision, and that she had kept her promise to once more see her aged friend, this narrative is sent, adding another instance of an appearance after death, resembling that also represented at the time of death.

Before hearing of her decease, the greatest

impression appeared to have been made by the beautiful chaplet shining on her head, clearly visible to the aged eyes of her old friend; without which the identification would not have been so complete.

APPARITION OF A DEAD SON TO HIS FATHER.

On the 20th of May 1860, I parted with my eldest son, a boy of fifteen, who as midshipman was going his first voyage to India.

My last words, on parting with him at Gravesend, were, "You will not forget your promise to me to come and see me again before leaving this world?"

He replied, "If such things are allowed, I will come." And I went back satisfied, for I knew he always kept a promise.

I never heard him speak again. No news came of him till October the 5th or 6th, when, about midnight, I saw his young sister, who slept beside me, rise up in her bed, and hold out her hands as if wishing to go to some one near, and earnestly looking forward.

I asked her what she was looking at, but receiving no reply, inquired a second time, and she replied, trembling with agitation, "Oh, mamma, Edward is standing at the foot of the bed looking at you!"

I said, "Show me where," and she exclaimed, "Oh! he is gone now; when you spoke he went away."

The child, six years old, was much agitated, and, weeping bitterly, said that the boy was in his sailor's dress, and looked just as he had done when he had bidden her good-bye.

Next morning a letter came from the captain to the ship's owners, announcing the sudden death of my son on the 8th of July, by a fall from the mast, in a storm off the Cape of Good Hope.

Two nights after this, he again was seen by his father about midnight; while, as before, a night-light was burning in the room. My son had gone to sea against the express wish of his father, whose grief on hearing of his loss endangered his reason, remembering that many angry words had passed between them. I saw my husband distinctly bend forward in his chair and earnestly gaze at some object of interest; and I spoke to him twice before I could get any reply. At length he said, "Now I can be at rest, thank God. My boy has been allowed to come to show that he has forgiven me. He was there smiling on me, just as when alive." After this time my husband's mind became resigned to God's will.

In both these cases the look of delight and wonder, unmixed with fear, was very visible; and the happiness to me from my earnest prayer being granted was very great then and since.

For the following remarkable record of pre-vision, I am indebted to one of the sons of the late Very Rev. W. Weldon Champneys, sometime Dean of Lichfield, to whom the dream-warning of death occurred:—

My brother, the Rev. Charles Champneys, had left London for the country, to preach and speak on behalf of a certain Church Society, to which he was officially attached. He was in his usual health, and I was therefore in no special anxiety about him.

One night my wife woke me, finding that I was sobbing in my sleep, and asked me what it was. I said, "I have been to a strange place in my dream. It was a small village, and I went up to the door of an inn, if so it might be called, though it really was a decent public-house. A stout woman came to the door. I said to her, 'Is my brother here?'"

She replied, "No, sir; he is gone."

"Is his wife here?" I went on to inquire.

"No, sir; but his *widow* is."

Then the distressing thought rushed upon me that my brother was dead; and I awoke sobbing.

A few days after, I was summoned suddenly into the country. My brother returning from Huntingdon had been attacked with *angina pectoris;* and the pain was so intense that they had left him at Caxton (a small village in the diocese of Ely), to which place on the following day he summoned his wife; and the next day, while they were seated together, she heard a sigh and he was gone.

When I reached Caxton, it was the very same village to which I had gone in my dream. I went to the same house, was met and let in by the same woman, and found my brother dead, and his widow there.[1]

[1] I have been favoured with the following note from the Dean's son, whom I here thank for the same :—

"DEAR DR LEE,—I have often heard my father tell this story, always in the same form, and it left a profound impression, which lasted for the rest of his life.—I am sincerely yours,

"F. H. CHAMPNEYS, M.A.,
Brasenose College, Oxford, M.B.

"*September* 3, 1884."

WITCHCRAFT AND NECROMANCY

CHAPTER V.

WITCHCRAFT AND NECROMANCY.

DIABOLICAL magic, or witchcraft, consists in the invocation of fallen spirits or demons, with a view of securing their active aid in effecting, by co-operation with them, certain supernatural consequences, either for the temporal benefit of the operator, or for the harming of some enemy or opponent. Or, to quote an old English writer: "A witch is one that worketh by the devil, or by some devilish or curious art, either hurting or healing, revealing things secret or foretelling things to come, which the devil hath devised to entangle and snare men's souls withal unto damnation."[1] That such acts are certain and stern realities

[1] 'What a Witch is, and ye Antiquitie of Witchcrafte,' p. 4. (Without date or place). 1612.

has been the almost universal conviction of mankind—whatever may have been the detailed forms[1] which, in different countries and at various times, they may have taken. Witchcraft is one of these forms, and there are not a few who still believe it to have been no delusion whatsoever, but a reality and a very diabolical and dangerous practice.

The constant warnings against the sin of witchcraft in Holy Scripture are quite inconsistent with the idea that it was either an imposture or the mere result of a wild fancy.[2]

Under the law of Moses, a witch was not to be suffered to live.[3] Enchantments were

[1] "There can be no doubt that immense evil is being caused to innumerable persons by these occult arts and practices, which have always been condemned by the Church as identical with sorcery and witchcraft, but which in the present day are not only, as I have said, employed by numerous secret societies and associations, but are also more or less openly avowed and practised by persons to be met with in society—clergymen, doctors, &c., and even by strong-minded persons of the other sex."—'Published Letter of Anti-Mesmer,' dated 14th Sept. 1878.

[2] "No one with any insight into the awful mystery of the false worships of the world, but will believe that these symptoms were evidence and expression of an actual connection in which these persons [seers, magicians, witches, and others] stood to a spiritual world—a spiritual world indeed, which was not above them, but beneath.—'Synonyms of the New Testament,' by R. C. Trench, Archbishop of Dublin. Part I. p. 43.

[3] See Exod. xxii. 18; Levit. xix. 26 and 31; Deut. xviii. 9-12; 2 Chron. xxxiii. 6.

distinctly forbidden. Those who owned and used familiar spirits were to be disregarded and avoided. Wizards were never to be sought after. In fact, all diviners, enchanters, charmers, necromancers, and consulters of familiar spirits were looked upon both as disgraceful and abominable; and it was because such persons and practices had been so common and current among the Canaanitish nations, that these nations were cast out and destroyed by the Israelites at the Almighty's express command. In any reasonable consideration of the subject, therefore, the principle here embodied should never be lost sight of. To maintain that the principle in question is a delusion, is in the teeth of facts and historical records.

Many of the absurdities of witchcraft, apparently trivial enough and ridiculous—*e.g.*, the methods and instruments by which wizards and witches worked their purposes—have been dropped; but with the necromancers of the present day other methods better adapted to the tastes and predilections of moderns are adopted—methods not at all differing in principle from those used of old, but distinctly differing in taste and character. The principle, however, which underlies the actions of both, is essentially one and the same.

That the apostles,[1] the fathers of the Christian Church, the decrees of the Councils, the authority of recognised Patriarchs, and the orders and Injunctions of our own Church of England divines, acknowledged witchcraft to be a reality, there can be no reasonable doubt.[2]

It was believed by those who had patiently investigated facts, that the devil and his angels —potent beings of far greater intelligence and influence than man—after a formal compact had been entered into, bestowed certain supernatural powers upon those who thus voluntarily and purposely became their servants,—powers by which sensuality might be surfeited, and riches and abundance secured in abundance. A gift of predicting future events

[1] See Gal. v. 19, 21.

[2] See Ordination of an Exorcist in the Catholic Pontifical; the Greek form of Exorcism with anointing in the *Euchologion*, the Bull of Innocent VIII. issued A.D. 1484, the Act against Witchcraft, drawn up by Lord Bacon and Coke, and passed in England in 1604, together with the well-known opinions of Sir Matthew Hale and Sir Thomas Browne. The various diocesan "*Injunctions*" and "*Articles of Enquiry*" of the Anglican Bishops of the seventeenth century may also be consulted, on this point, for conclusive evidence.

was likewise claimed and practised; and a power of working mischief on men, women, children, cattle, and possessions, frequently exercised.

For throughout the long and varied records of Holy Scripture, there are two religions: one, the true, having God for its author—preserving the old traditions of a lost Paradise, bidding man look up to Heaven; the other false, from Satan, the enemy of God and man, urging men to selfishness and sin. Each was distinguished by mystical works, intercommunion with spirits; the one true and glorious, from above, the battalions of the living God; the others fallen, only servants of "the prince of the powers of the air," leading men to evil and tempting them to despair, from below.

A relation and intercourse with good angels was a benefit and blessing to the whole race of mankind. On the other hand, should fallen man willingly and duly communicate with the spirits of evil, for purposes forbidden—actively willing that such should help him, and give him what he specially needs,—he thus voluntarily and of purpose subjects his will—the most important part of his being—to lost and dark spirits.

On this subject the learned Sir William Blackstone thus wrote:—

"To deny the possibility, nay, actual existence of witchcraft and sorcery, is at once flatly to contradict the revealed Word of God, in various passages both of the Old and New Testament; and the thing itself is a truth to which every nation in the world hath in its turn become testimony, either by examples seemingly well attested or by prohibiting laws, which at least suppose the possibility of commerce with evil spirits."[1]

Our "scientific leaders," as they term themselves, however, love noise and love words. They attract disciples by being primarily very pompous. They talk to us of "osmosis," and "chlorophyll," and "protoplasm," so as to startle us into worshipful attention. "The being called 'Man,'" they assert, "is a concurrence of atoms, acted upon by a voltaic pile, and emitting sparks of thought." It is thus that they seek to raise our self-respect. They are credulous as to evolution, as to monkey-

[1] 'Commentaries,' Book IV., chap. iv. p. 51.

origin, as to materialism, but incredulous as to the interference of the First Cause, or the existence of the Supernatural. They are disposed to believe in anything but the living God. In truth, if Darwin's theory be true, then man is matter and God is nothing. They even resent as an impertinence the bare suggestion that the Creator has spoken to His own creatures since creation. It is just possible, though scarcely probable, that creation was created, and consequently, that there was once a Creator; but that there should be now a Creator, who cares to recognise His own creatures, is a supposition which is supremely unscientific, and contrary to the opinion of "great thinkers." "A miracle," as it is called, is an impossibility, because it implies that the Creator may still create. Whereas science points out that the Creator—if there ever was one—retired into obscurity after creation. This is one of the modern scientific theories. It is not stated in terms—for it is not stated at all, being altogether too idiotic for definition; but so far as argument is concerned, or the inferring effects from a cause, the god of the scientists is treated like the god Baal, who is on a journey, or, peradventure, who sleepeth.

Of course persons, whether actually "great thinkers," or only so styled by their friends and admirers, who deny that man has a soul, or that any God exists, endeavour to wipe out man's hope of immortality,[1] repudiate the existence of all mysteries, of everything supernatural; and, by consequence, deny that there are any spirits of any sort or kind, devils or angels, fallen or perfect; and repudiate with scorn the reality of witchcraft and necromancy, and all that flows therefrom. In fact, they look upon these notions as obsolete and ridiculous superstitions, and upon all persons who cling to the old convictions upon the subject as lunatics, trivial dreamers, superstitious, or fanatics.

That witchcraft and necromancy, however, are still very widely practised—as will be abun-

[1] "Men who, like the late Lord Amberley, deny the Supernatural, endeavour to blot out our hopes of immortality, and make an attempt to instil into the great heart of Humanity the cold, cheerless form of materialism, have, in the words of Mr Bayle St John, 'set up their pump by the margin of an ocean, into which the rivers and the torrents and the rains of heaven are perpetually pouring, in defiance of their puny industry, which, indeed, has nowhere to put what it takes away, and is compelled to send it back by other channels whence it came.'"—'Spiritualism and its Critics,' by G. Sexton, p. 30. London.

dantly shown further on,—is as certain as that our English laws against such evils were, in the face of many weighty protests, foolishly and short-sightedly repealed in 1736. Now, all modern wizards, witches, and necromancers—styled "mediums," "seers," "spiritualists," "clairvoyants," "thought-readers," and "mesmerisers"—are punished as mere impostors.

But to pass for a while to a consideration of a few details on the subject:—

"A witch," remarks the ancient writer already quoted, in quaint but forcible language,[1] "is one that worketh by the deuill, or by some deuillish or curious art, either hurting or healing, reuealing things secret or foretelling things to come, which the deuill hath deuised to entangle and snare men's soules withall unto damnation. The coniurer, the enchanter, the sorcerer, the deuiner, and whatsoever other sort there is, are indeed compassed within this circle. The deuill doth (no doubt) after diuers sorts, and diuers formes, deale in these: but no man is able to show an essentiall dif-

[1] 'What a Witch is, and ye Antiquitie of Witchcrafte.' London: 1612.

ference in each of them from the rest. I hold it no wisedome, or labour well spent, to trauell much therein ; one artificer hath deuised them all. They are all to one end and purpose, howsoever they much differ in outward rules for practice of them, that is little or nothing besides meere delusion. Every man will confesse that the Father of Lies is not to be trusted. Every man knowes that all his dooings are hidden vnder coulorable shewes. Shall we then seeke for steadfastnes in his wayes? Shall wee be so foolish as to imagine that things are effected by the vertue of words, gestures, figures, or suchlike? All those are doubtlesse but to deceiue and draw men forward, and to plunge them more deepely into sinnes and errors."

Their method of bewitching was various; by muttering imprecations and curses; by casting an evil eye; by fascination; by making figures or representations of the person to be acted upon in wax or clay, and then roasting these figures before a fire; by mixing magical ointments and applying them; as also by the use of potions and ingredients, and by *willing* and *wishing* them all kinds of evil, misery, and sorrow. All these aforesaid methods—some of which seem trivial enough—based on a system, were handed down by tradition and practised in accordance with acknowledged rules and regulations; but however absurd they may seem to the Cockney scribe or the self-styled "philosopher" of the present day, they evidently worked their purpose.[1]

A spot where four roads met, a blasted and desolate heath, a deserted mansion, the plateau of a rugged range of mountains, or a lonely spot within some secluded forest, were the places commonly selected for the gathering of the witches.

Here are further details:—

Agnes Sympson, a Scotch woman—providing details of the forbidden work in which she was engaged,—asserted that "she had been at church at eleven of the clock at night, with

[1] The curious reader, desiring fuller information on the subject, may consult Pneumatologia, by George Hammond: London, 1701. Jamblicus de Mysteriis Ægyptiorum, Chaldæorum, &c.: printed by Aldus, 1497. Merlin Revived in a Discourse of Prophecies, &c.: London, 1683. Thaumaturgia, or the Elucidations of the Marvellous: Oxford, 1835. The Question of Witchcraft Debated, by John Wagstaffe: London, 1669. The Question of Withcraft further Debated, by R. T.: London, 1679. Witches and Witchcraft, a Dialogue, by George Gifford: London, 1603. This last is an extremely rare and curious volume.

above a hundred other witches. They had black candles, she said, set round the pulpit, and the devil in a black gown and hat preached to them that they should keep his commandment of doing all the ill they could. Then they opened three graves, and took the fingers and toes and noses of the dead people; and she had a winding-sheet and two joints for her share.[1] . . . After that . . . they went home."[2] This and similar confessions, voluntarily made—all more or less alike, and evidently founded upon a common tradition—no doubt resulted in the passing of a special Act in the early part of the reign of James I.

On another point, an old author[3] has thus

[1] Here certain details of the narrative are intentionally omitted, not being suitable for publication.

[2] The special Act against witchcraft, approved by legal luminaries of high character and great learning, passed under James I. contained the following enactment :—

"If any person shall use any invocation or conjuration of any evil or wicked spirit, or shall commit, covenant with, entertain, employ, feed, or reward any evil or cursed spirit to or for any intent or purpose, or take up any dead man, woman, or child out of the grave—or the skin, bone, or any part of the dead person, to be employed or used in any manner of witchcraft, sorcery, charm or enchantment; or shall use, exercise or practise any sort of witchcraft, &c., whereby any person shall be destroyed, killed, wasted, consumed, pined or lamed in any part of the body: that every such person being convicted, shall suffer death."

[3] 'What a Witch is, and ye Antiquitie of Witchcrafte.' London: 1612.

written. His sentences are reproduced exactly as they were first printed :—

"Touching the Antiquity of Witchcraft, wee must needs confesse that it hath beene of very ancient time, because the Scriptures doe testifie so much, for in the time of Moses it was very rife in Egipt. Neither was it then newly sprong vp, beeing common, and growne vnto such ripenes among the Nations, that the Lord reconing by diuers kinds, saith that the Gentiles did commit such Abominations, for which he would cast them out before the Children of Israel. How long it was before that time cannot for certainty be discussed : sauing that (as is sayd) it was not young in those daies when Moses wrote. If wee maintaine that it was before the Flood, there is great reason to iustify the Assertion. Wee know that the Deuill was exceeding crafty from the beginning, alwaies laboring to seduce, and deceiue after the worst manner. If he fayled of his desire, it was because Men had not procured Gods displeasure to come upon them, to deliuer them ouer unto strange delusions ; but God complaineth, that men had wonderfully corrupted their waies, long before the Flood : God beeing then prouoked by the wickedness of the world, what should make us doubt but that through his Iust iudgement the Deuill had power giuen him and was let loose, that he might seduce, and lead the prophane Nations into the depth and gulfe of all abominable sinnes ?"

In further illustration of this, it may be recorded that the following confession was made by Jane Bosdeau, a person reputed to have been a witch, before the Chamber of Justice at Bordeaux, that a certain Italian "carried her at midnight on the Eve of St John into a field, where, after he had made a circle and read out of a black book, there appeared a great black goat with a candle between his horns, and two women, and a man habited as a priest. She gave the goat a lock of her hair, and made the sign of the cross with her left hand in token that she was the Devil's. . . . After this, every Wednesday and Friday she met a rendezvous of above sixty witches at Prez de Dome. The black goat carried a lighted candle, . . . and they danced in a circle back to back. They had a mock and most profane sacrament, and mock holy water. . . . [Here the details are not fit for print.] She confessed all this and many other particulars freely, without torture, and was clear and constant in maintaining the aforementioned to be true."

Details such as these, from before which the veil cannot be drawn, abundantly serve to show the state of degradation to which such principles and practices led. Man, illuminated by divine revelation, and having lost the traditions of original natural religion—the traditions of our first parents and the patriarchs—became corrupt like the Canaanites, and often practised these abominations.[1] Those who indulged in them were guided onwards step by step to a deeper state of degradation. "If one link of a chain be drawn in," as an old and wise writer remarked, "another followeth, and is by-and-by in sight, which draweth we know not how many after it, until we see the last." And this is precisely the case, as with the old, so with the modern, system of witchcraft and necromancy. People begin by adopting trivial and almost ridiculous prac-

[1] The connection between gross sins of the flesh and necromancy has been pointed out of old, and is perfectly acknowledged in regard to the same evil in its revised forms now.

tices; but are led on step by step, until the whole system in its completeness is unfolded, and they are securely entangled in a net of difficulties.

The following account of a case of bewitchment is from a publication[1] which had an enormous circulation in the latter part of the seventeenth century, when first it was issued :—

"The story is this. At *Welton*, within a mile of *Daventry in Northamptonshire*, where live together *Widdow Cowley* the grandmother, *Widdow Stiff* the mother, and her two daughters. At the next house but one, live another *Widdow Cowley*, sister to the former *Widdow Cowley*, *Moses Cowley*, my acquaintance, her son, and *Moses* his wife, having a good estate in land of their own, and very civil and orderly people. These three told me, that the younger of the two daughters, ten years of age, vomited in less than three days, three gallons of water, to their great admiration. After this the elder wench comes running, and tells them that now

[1] 'Relation of a Wonderful Piece of Witchcraft, contained in a Letter of Master G. Clark to Mr M. T., touching a House that is Haunted nigh unto Daventree.' No date.

her sister begins to vomit stones and coals. They went and were eyewitnesses, told them till they came to five hundred. Some weighed a quarter of a pound, and were so big, as they had enough to do to get them out of her mouth, and he professed to me that he could scarce get the like into his mouth; and I do not know how any one should, if they were so big as he showed the like to me. I have sent you one, but not a quarter so big as some of them were. It was one of the biggest of them that were left and kept in a bag. This vomiting lasted about a fortnight, and hath witnesses good store.

" In the meantime they threw hards of flax upon the fire, which would not blaze, though blown, but dwindled away. The bed-clothes would be thrown off the bed. *Moses Cowley* told me that he laid them on again several times, they all coming out of the room, and go but into the parlour again, and they were off again. And a strike of wheat standing at the bed's feet, set it how they would, it would be thrown down again. Once the coffers and things were so transposed, as they could scarce stir about the room. Once he laid the Bible upon the bed, but the clothes were thrown off again, and the Bible hid in another bed. And when they were all gone into the parlour, as they used to go together, then things would be transposed in the hall, their wheel taken in pieces, and part of it thrown under the table. In their buttery the milk would be taken off the table and set on the ground, and once one panchion was broken, and the milk spilt. A seven-pound weight with a ring was hung upon the spigot, and the beer mingled with sand and all spoiled, their salt mingled most perfectly with bran."

Many of the details of these occurrences, set forth in similar once popular fly-leaves and now rare publications, are, it must be acknowledged, exceedingly trivial, yet it can hardly be conceived that it was a case of imposture; or, as in other examples, that many persons, unable to explain what they saw, would press forward to give evidence on the subject, and to maintain the accuracy of the recorded accounts, unless they had had their foundation in fact.

Current traditions on the momentous subjects of this chapter are almost universal; and when faithfully considered, bear out the fact that the principles underlying these subjects are perfectly uniform and verily stern realities.

From the period of the ancient oracles, I pass to what was believed and practised in England during the seventeenth century.

INTERCOURSE WITH EVIL SPIRITS.

The record which follows is a notable account of a certain person's conversation and intercourse with evil spirits, to his own ruin, in a letter sent to the Bishop of Gloucester, by the Rev. Mr Arthur Bedford, Minister of Temple parish, in Bristol :—

"BRISTOL, *Aug.* 2.

"MY LORD,—Being informed by Mr Shutes of your lordship's desire that I should communicate to you what I had known concerning a person who was acquainted with spirits to his own destruction, I have made bold to give you the trouble of this letter — hoping my design to gratify your lordship in every particular may be an apology for the length hereof. I had formerly given an account to the late Bishop of Hereford, in which there may be some things contained, which, if your lordship could procure from his lady, who now lives near Gloucester, would be more authentic.

"Whilst I was curate to Dr Read, rector of St Nicholas, in this city, I began to be acquainted with one Thomas Parkes, a young man about twenty years of age, who lived with his father at Mangotsfield, in Gloucestershire, and by trade a gunsmith, with whom I contracted an intimate acquaintance; he being not only a good-tempered man, but extremely well skilled in the mathematical studies, which was his constant delight—viz., arithmetic, geometry, gauging, surveying, astronomy, and algebra. He gave himself up to astronomy so far that he could not only calculate the motions of the planets, but an eclipse also, and demonstrate also every problem in spherical trigonometry from mathematical principles, in which he would discover a clear force of reason. When Mr Bailey, minister of St James', in the city, endeavoured to set up a mathematical academy, I advised him to this Thomas Parkes, as an acquaintance, in whom, as he told me, he found greater proficiency in those studies than he expected, or could imagine. After this he applied himself to astrology, and would sometimes calculate nativities, and resolve horary questions, which he told me oftentimes proved true; but he was not satisfied with it, because there was nothing in it which tended to mathematical demonstration.

"When by the providence of God I was settled in Temple parish, and having not seen him for some time, he came to me, and we being in private, he asked my opinion very seriously concerning the lawfulness of conversing with spirits. After I had given my thoughts in the negative, and confirmed them with the best reasons I could, he told me he had considered all those arguments, and believed they only related to conjuration; but that there was an innocent society with them which a man might use, if he made no compact with them, did no harm by their means, and was not curious in prying into hidden things; and that he himself had discoursed with them, and heard them sing to his great satisfaction. He gave an offer to me at one time, to Mr Bailey at another, that if we would go with him one night to Kingswood, we should see them, hear them talk and sing, and talk with them whatsoever we had a mind to, and we should return very safe; but neither of us had the courage to venture. I told him of the subtilty of the Devil to deceive mankind, and to transform himself into an angel of light; but he could not believe it was the Devil. I proposed to try him a question in astronomy relating to the projection of the sphere, which he projected and resolved; and afterwards did so demonstrate from the mathematics, as to demonstrate that his brain was free from the least tincture of madness and distraction. I asked him several particulars concerning the method he used, and the discourse he had with the spirits he conversed with. He told me he had a book where there was the directions he followed. Accordingly, in the dead time of the night he went into a causeway with candle and lanthorn, which was consecrated for the purpose with incantations. He had also consecrated chalk, consisting of several mixtures, with which he used to make a circle of what distance he thought fit, within which no spirit had power to enter. After he invoked the spirit by several forms of words, some of which he told me were taken from the Holy Scripture, and therefore he thought them lawful; without considering that they might, as the apostle saith, 'be wrested to his own destruction' (2 Pet. iii. 16). Accordingly, the spirits for which he called appeared to him in the shape of little girls, about a foot and a half high, and played about the circle. At first he was affrighted, but after some small acquaintance this antipathy in nature wore off, and he became pleased with their company. He told me they spake with a shrill voice, like an ancient woman.

"He asked them if there was a God; they told him there was. He asked them if there was a Heaven and Hell; they said there was. He asked what sort of place heaven was; which they described as a place of glory and happiness. He asked what place hell was; and they bid him ask no questions of that nature, for it was a dreadful thing to relate. 'The devils believe and tremble.' He asked what method or order they had among themselves; they told him they were divided into three orders: that their chief had his residence in the air—that he had several counsellors, which were placed by him in form of a globe. Another order, they said, is employed in going to and fro from thence to the earth to carry intelligence from those lower spirits. And a third order was in the earth, according to the directions they received from those in the air. This description was very surprising; but being contrary to the account we have in Scripture hierarchy of the blessed angels, made me conclude they were devils; but I could not convince him thereof. He told me he had desired them to sing, and they went to some distance behind a bush, from whence he heard a perfect concert of such music, the like he never heard; and in the upper part he could hear something very harsh and shrill like a reed, but as it was managed it came with particular grace.

"About a quarter of a year after he came to me again, and said, he wished he had taken my advice; for he thought he had done that which would cost him his life, and which he did heartily repent of. He appeared to me as if he had been in great trouble, as his countenance was very much altered. I asked him what he had done: he told me that, being bewitched to his acquaintance, he resolved to proceed further in the art, and to have a familiar spirit at his command, according to the directions of his book; which was to have a book of virgin parchment, consecrated with several incantations; as also a particular inkhorn, ink, and pen. With those he was to go out as usual to a cross-way, and call up a spirit, and ask him his name, which he was to put in the first page of his book; and this was to be his familiar spirit. Thus he was to do by as many as he pleased, writing their names in distinct pages, only one in a leaf; and then, whenever he took the book and opened it, this spirit whose name appeared should appear also. The familiar spirit he had was called Malachi—*i. e.*, my king; an Hebrew name of an evil signification to him —*i.e.*, that an evil spirit was become his king. After this they appeared faster than he wished them, and in most dreadful shapes—like serpents, lions, bears, &c., hissing at him, which did very much affright him; and the more so when he found it was not in his power to lay them, expecting every moment to be torn in pieces. This was in December, about midnight, when he continued there in a great sweat; and from that time he was never well so long as he lived. In the course of his sickness he often came to Mr ——, the apothecary, in Broad Street, concerning a cure; but I know not whether he told him the original cause or not. He also came to me at the same time, and owned every matter as fact, which he had told before unto the last; and insisted that whenever he did anything of that nature, he was deluded in his conscience to think it lawful; but that he was since convinced to the contrary. But still asserted he made no compact with those spirits, never did harm to others by their means, nor ever pryed into the future fortune of himself or others: he expressed a hearty repentance for, and detestation of, his sins; so that though these matters cost him his life, yet I have room to believe him happy in the other world. I am not certain whether he gave this account to any other but myself, though he did relate something of it to Mr Bailey, minister of St James', in the city. Perhaps your lordship may be further informed by his relations and neighbours of

Mangotsfield, which is not above a mile out of the road to Bath. I have often told the story, but never mentioned his name before; and therefore if your lordship has a mind to print such accounts as these, I beg it might be with such tenderness to his memory as he deserved; and so it may not be the least prejudice to his relations, who have the deserved character of honest, sober people.—I am, with due respects, your lordship's son and servant,

"ARTHUR BEDFORD."

A few years ago—to note one out of several scores of quite recent examples—James Haywood, an old labouring man of Long Compton, in South Warwickshire, was indicted for the murder of Ann Tennant, an old woman of eighty years of age. It appeared in evidence that a general belief existed in the village that there were sixteen or eighteen witches living thereabouts, she being the chief; and Haywood maintaining that Tennant had "overlooked" or bewitched him, as she had also betwitched other people—and that three or four evil spirits "had been in him," by her instrumentality—struck her on the leg with a fork with which he had been working, making several wounds, in order "to draw blood and break the spell," from the effects of which she died the following day. As to the facts of a belief in witchcraft and its consequences, the evidence was conclusive. But the jury found the accused to be a lunatic, and he was detained during her Majesty's pleasure.

However, examples of affairs like this are very numerous, constantly occurring, and bear a striking likeness, either to other, in their leading features and characteristics. The case of the haunted house at Tedworth, in Wiltshire, the experiences of the Wesley family, and several examples which have been frequently printed, will readily occur to the general reader.

At the same time, it may be well to provide accounts of two most remarkable cases of a similar character, to which reference has been made in the public prints, so that the past and present examples of such occurrences may be duly compared by the reader:—

MYSTERIOUS AFFAIR AT WORKSOP.[1]

The town of Worksop was in an uproar on Saturday (March 3, 1883), consequent on the circulation of a report that the household goods of a man named Joseph White, a well-known dealer, were being smashed and removed by some unseen agency. All day long crowds of excited people wended their way towards the New Building Ground, where White's semi-detached house stands, drawn thither by the exaggerated accounts of the mysterious occurrences said to have been witnessed by the inmates and others. . . . As I entered the door I myself saw an Oxford frame slip out of the rocking-chair. I told the boy to pick it up; and he said he dare not. After hearing what the folks had to say, I was joining in the conversation, when a basin which had stood on the meal-bin suddenly began to rise in a slanting direction over my head and then fell at my feet, smashing into bits. I then left, thinking the affair very strange. I had not the slightest belief in the

[1] The above account is abridged from the 'Retford, Worksop, and Gainsborough News' of March 10, 1883.

supernatural. I cannot account for what I saw. No one was nearer to the basin than myself, and, as far as I saw, there was no cause for the phenomenon.[1] The room was dimly lighted by a candle. . . . We were talking about the things, and the doctor was saying, " It's a very mysterious thing," with his back turned to the flour-bin, when a basin which stood on the bin suddenly flew up slantingly over the doctor's head, to where some bacon was hanging on some hooks, and fell straight down and smashed at his feet. The doctor looked in the bin and found nothing, and thinking the devil was in the place, he left and went home. I stayed a short time longer, but nothing further occurred. About half-a-dozen persons were in the room whilst these things happened. As far as I saw, no human agency caused the articles to move and knock about. I have not the slightest belief in anything appertaining to the supernatural. . . . White and I went in ; I followed him into the front room ; and he called my attention to the bare walls, saying that everything except the

[1] The above is a fair specimen of the ordinary reporter's logic, method, and conclusions.

clock and a stuffed pigeon in a glass case, which remained on their respective nails, had been dashed to the ground and broken. The clock hung over the bed, which was right up in the corner of the room, with the head and one side close to the walls. While White was telling me that the chest of drawers before us had been turned topsy-turvy, we heard a smash, and on turning my head I saw the clock in the middle of the floor, with its end knocked out. It had cleared the bed, and was nearer the fireplace on the opposite side of the room. I was the nearest person to the clock when it hung on the wall. The servant girl opened the door of the room, and came inside just as the clock left the wall. If White or the servant had been instrumental in throwing the clock down, I could not have failed to have detected them. We went back into the kitchen, and as I stood looking towards the fire, with the girl on my left hand engaged in some household duty, and White on my right hand, I saw a pot-dog ornament, such a one as you see in old people's houses, smash on the floor in front of me. It had come off the mantelpiece, but I did not see it leave the mantelpiece. The things seemed to fly like lightning, and you only knew they were gone when you saw them broken on the floor. I picked up the broken dog, and closely examined it; but I saw no string nor spring on it, or on or near the mantelpiece or fireplace. Then I saw a cream-jug, which had stood on the table, jump to the floor and smash. I cannot account for the occurrences; and if I had not seen for myself I should not have believed that the removal of articles could have taken place in the way it did. . . . White and his family, with the exception of his wife, agree in laying all the blame on the shoulders of the unfortunate girl, alleging that she had 'overlooked' the house; but all agree in attributing the spiritual demonstration to powers higher than human. . . . Our representative on Monday evening interviewed the girl Rose. She says she is eighteen years old; but she is very small, and looks to be not more than fifteen, while physically she appears quite incapable of being the cause of the extraordinary occurrences which took place; nor is there anything in her manner which would induce any one to think she could concoct and carry out such trickery. . . . About half-past eleven o'clock things in the house began to knock up and down and break themselves without anybody touching them. A pot-dog (*i.e.*, an ornament in shape like a dog, but also a vase) flew off the chimney-piece towards the door. Mrs White picked it up and put it back, when it flew off again and was broken. The girl was then at the bin, washing up pots, and Mrs White was finishing baking, and there was no one in the room besides Mr White, Mrs White, and the girl. The brass candlesticks next flew off the mantelpiece, going towards the back-door. Everything flew towards that door. . . . All sorts of theories are put forward to account for the occurrences—galvanic batteries, animal magnetism; while some incomprehensible mediums are mentioned as causes by the ignorant, who know not that glass and earthenware are non-conductors of electricity.

The following is another case, which also occurred quite recently:—

REMARKABLE OCCURRENCES NEAR ELLESMERE.

A series of remarkable occurrences, which have caused great excitement in the whole neighbourhood between Ellesmere, Wem, and Shrewsbury, are said to have taken place in October 1883, at a farm called "The Woods," where a farmer named Mr John Hampson resides. "The Woods" is situated about five miles from Welshampton, a mile and a half from Loppington, and nine or ten miles from Shrewsbury. With the exception of a farm about one hundred yards distant, there is no house within half a mile. It appears that just as dusk was closing in on Thursday, Mrs Hampson was about to get tea ready, and put a saucepan of water on the fire for the purpose of boiling an egg. When the water began to boil Mrs Hampson placed the egg in, as usual; but the saucepan suddenly "shot," as the servants declare, off the fire into the middle of the kitchen. The cups and saucers had been arranged on the table, and one of them fell on to the floor and smashed. Of course Mrs Hampson was a little surprised at this; but directly afterwards, when she saw the table partially turn over, apparently without being touched, and all the cups fall, she was thoroughly frightened, and ran up to Mr Lea's farm. Mr Hampson had not at this time returned home from Bagley Coursing Meeting. Mr Lea at once went down, and when he arrived near the house he saw, as he describes it, "a light in all the upper windows, just as if the house was on fire," but on entering the front door and going up the stairs all was dark. Meanwhile something had set fire to some clothes in the kitchen, and Mr Lea went in to try and put out the flames. Just then there was a noise like the report of a pistol, and the furniture and other things in the kitchen began to jump about in a manner which seemed altogether inexplicable. One of the farm-servants says: "The things began to fly about smick, smack, the very same as if there was war!" Mr Lea decided to get some of the things outside, as they were being damaged, and accordingly he took hold of a barometer and carried it out. He returned, and was in the act of reaching the gun, when he was struck by a loaf of bread;

and at the request of his wife he left the house. A little cupboard in the kitchen burst open, and a bar of salt was thrown out of it on to the middle of the dairy floor. A small timepiece which stood on the mantel-shelf was thrown on the ground near the door. When Mr Hampson came home, finding it there, he placed it on a chair; and one of the servants afterwards placed it where it had stood before; and after being knocked about in this fashion it is asserted that it was not damaged, and that it did not stop. Mr Lea, with assistance, succeeded in getting a number of articles out of the house; and once, when he was coming out, a large kitchen table which stood under the window followed him to the door, and it probably would have gone further if the width of the door would have allowed it. On the table there stood a double-wick paraffin-lamp with a globe on it, and the globe was "lifted" off and thrown across the room, and the other part of the lamp was left standing on the table. Meanwhile things in the parlour had been taking pretty much the same course, for a volume of the 'Pilgrim's Progress' came flying through the parlour door and out to the walk opposite the front door; whence, after lying there a short time, it jumped up on the window-sill!

When the mysterious affair began, a little servant girl, aged thirteen or fourteen, whose home is at Weston, near Baschurch, was in the kitchen taking care of the child. Their clothes immediately began to singe and smoulder in patches, and the child's face and arms were burnt. The fire in the clothes of both the girl and the child was extinguished, and they set off for Mr Lea's farm; the girl taking with her two shawls which also had been burning. When she reached the farm her clothes broke out into a mass of flame, and they were torn from her body by Mrs Lea. The clothes of the child also took fire again, but it was soon put out. The two shawls began to burn again, and they were placed by some one in a small tub which was about half full of water; but they immediately sprang out again, and were eventually kept in the tub by the weight of a pan-mug. Mrs Lea was carrying a cream-jug which Mr Hampson had won in a cavalry competition, when it suddenly leapt from her hand on to the causeway.

Strange occurrences are said to have taken place at the neighbour's house during the evening. A plate she touched while eating her supper was apparently thrown on the floor, and the pieces were picked up by some unseen agency, and placed in the centre of the table! The flower-pots were carried out of Mr Hampson's house, and being placed on the grass-plot they all began to move and jostle against each other. During the evening Mrs Lea went down to the house to fetch a bottle of brandy, which Mrs Hampson told her she would find in a certain cupboard; and immediately she opened the door a large dish was hurled out into the centre of the kitchen. Mrs Lea having got the bottle, at once shut the cupboard door, for, as she says, "the other things were clattering." Other pieces of furniture were hurled into most curious places, and a pepper-box was found the next morning on the top of the clock; while a large sewing-machine in the parlour was found very much damaged, at the opposite end of the room to that in which it formerly stood. About the time of the disturbance one of the inmates of the house was kneading some dough for baking purposes, and when things had settled a little, she was taking it to the oven, when some of the loaves were suddenly removed from the tray.

A policeman subsequently arrived and stayed with Mr Hampson at the house all night. On Friday a large number of persons paid a visit to the house, and four policemen were there during the day, making full inquiries. Thinking there might be some kind of explosive material in the coal, they ordered it to be consumed in the open air; but it burned quietly away.

On Saturday, just about dinner-time, the servant girl threw some coal on the boiler fire in the dairy, when it was all thrown back again on the floor. Thomas Williams, a young farm-servant, then went to replace it, when a brick flew out from the back of the grate right across the dairy.

The place was visited by scores of persons on Sunday.

When our reporter visited the place yesterday it was deserted by the family, and paperhangers were busy in the kitchen. The front windows were all broken, and there was a heap of broken pitchers and glass in the yard. Mrs Hampson and the children are staying with a relative.

No one can explain the cause of the occurrences, and they all seem to tell a very straightforward story. The people in the neighbourhood do not appear to attribute the affair to a supernatural cause so much as might have been expected in a quiet country locality; but still they do not know how to explain it, and it is the almost only topic of conversation.

For myself, after due remark and examination, I believe firmly that witchcraft, necromancy, table-turning, using spells and charms, spiritualism (or as some prefer to term it, "spiritism"), and the invocation and service of evil spirits in any form, each and all belong to one uniform dark and unlawful system; and that to treat that system as nothing but an imposture is at once unphilosophical, short-sighted, shallow, and futile.

Moreover, such a position distinctly implies that all the Mosaic laws against divination, the having and consulting a familiar spirit, or witchcraft, and similar abominations, were founded on error, and were at once superfluous and absurd—which of course they were, if witchcraft and necromancy were mere delusions, and such evils and sins had no real existence.

Yet, since the repeal of the English laws against witchcraft, as is notorious, a policy has been necessarily adopted by judges, magistrates, and those in authority, by which the foolish delusions, only acknowledged by the shallow and uninformed, that all necromancers are impostors, has been fostered. Human knowledge and experience, however, combined with a belief in God's revelation and the truths of the sacred Scriptures, are far too strong at present for such a worthless theory—however be-lauded and propped up by worm-eaten props—to have much weight.

The remarks of Mr Flowers, the London police magistrate, when, under the Vagrancy Act, he condemned Dr Slade the spiritualistic medium to three months' imprisonment for having practised modern necromancy, are an excellent specimen of modern credulity, and exactly express the sentiments of those who altogether deny the Supernatural; and as such, are curious sentiments, worthy of being here preserved.

"First," asked Mr Flowers, in giving judgment, "Do the facts alleged constitute an offence under the Vagrancy Act? and, secondly, Did Slade do what he is alleged to have done? The offence defined by the Vagrancy Act is 'professing or pretending to tell fortunes, or using any subtle craft, means, or device, by palmistry or otherwise, to deceive and impose on any of her Majesty's subjects.' I maintain that in order to constitute this offence, two things are necessary—'using some subtle craft, means, or device' like palmistry, and 'an attempt to deceive or impose on some person.' Palmistry is defined in Richardson's 'Dictionary' thus:—

"'Divination by inspection of the hands, from the roguish tricks of the pretenders to this art; to palm; to trick, or play a trick; to impose upon, or practise a trick, imposition, or delusion; more restrictedly, to palm is to hold and keep in the palm, to touch with the palm, to handle.'

"The definitions given by Johnson and Webster are very similar.

"Now the trick imputed to Slade consists in falsely pretending to procure from spirits messages written by such spirits upon a slate held under the table by Slade for the purpose; such messages having previously been written by himself. Such a trick seems to me to be 'a subtle craft, means, or device' of the same kind as fortune-telling. In each case the impostor pretends[1] to practise a magical, or at least an occult art.

"I am confirmed in this view by the language of another statute to which reference has been made in the course of these proceedings—viz., the 9th George II. c. 5. This Act repealed that of James I. c. 12, by which witchcraft was made felony, and prohibited prosecutions for the offence of 'witchcraft, sorcery, enchantment, and conjuration,' which, apart from the statute of James, was punishable by the ecclesiastical courts, and perhaps at common law. It then enacts, that for the more effectual preventing and punishing any pretences to

[1] Of course the point consists in whether any accused person "pretends" or not.

such arts or powers as are before-mentioned, whereby ignorant persons are frequently deluded and defrauded, or if any person pretended to exercise or use any kind of witchcraft, sorcery, enchantment, or conjuration, or undertook to tell fortunes, or pretended, from his or her skill or knowledge in any occult or crafty science, to discover goods supposed to be lost or stolen, he shall upon conviction or an indictment, be liable to a year's imprisonment, and be set in the pillory four times.

"The punishment of the pillory is abolished, but the rest of the section remains in force, and I refer to it only to illustrate the meaning of the Vagrancy Act.

"It seems to me that the statute in question forbids substantially the same thing: 'The practice of occult and crafty sciences,' to use the words of the Act of George II.; 'subtle, crafty means or devices, by palmistry or otherwise,' to use the words of the Act of George IV.

"For these reasons I hold that if, by the trick I have described, Slade tried to impose on Professor Lankester and Dr Donkin, he committed an offence against the Vagrancy Act.

"And this brings me to the second question. Did he do so or not? a question which lies in a narrow compass, though much time has been occupied in its discussion.

"I was unwilling to exclude evidence to which the parties attached importance, and I accordingly admitted a good deal which, when given, appeared to me at the time, and still appears to me, irrelevant.

"On the other hand, I attach no importance to the evidence of Mr Maskelyne, given on the summons for conspiracy, because it proves what no one can doubt—namely, that some things done by Slade might be done by a conjuror; neither can I do so to the testimony of the witnesses for the defence, because they can only prove that on other occasions strange—if you please, very strange—things happened in Slade's presence, and that they did not perceive that he caused them.

"I forbear, however, to speculate on these matters, and confine myself to what happened between Slade, Lankester, and Donkin. The whole case turns upon the evidence of the two last-named persons, which, in a few words, is to the effect that they saw Slade's hands move as if he was writing, and that on snatching the slate from him immediately afterwards, before it was placed in the position in which the spirits were to act, and without any sound as if of writing, they found words upon it.

"Now, if this be true, it involves the inference that Slade produced the letters himself, and that therefore he could not think the spirit of his wife had written them. I must decide according to the well-known course of nature; and if it be true that the two witnesses saw the motions which they describe, and found the writing on the slate immediately afterwards, it is impossible for me to doubt, whatever happened on other occasions, Slade did on that occasion write those words on that slate in order to cheat Professor Lankester and Dr Donkin. It is true that Simmons said there was nothing to pay, as Lankester and Donkin were not satisfied; but the question is, whether 'subtle craft, means, or device' was used to impose on these gentlemen; and it clearly was, as the money would have been paid if the trick had not been discovered.

"Upon the whole, therefore, I hold that an

offence against the Vagrancy Act has been proved; and considering the grave mischiefs likely to result from such practices—mischiefs which those who remember the case of Home, also a professional medium, cannot consider unsubstantial—I feel that I cannot mitigate the punishment which the law imposes; and therefore I sentence the defendant to three months' imprisonment with hard labour in the house of correction."

But let it be assumed, for the sake of argument, that all such sorcerers and wizards—all table-turners, thought-readers, and diviners—are impostors; that their witnesses, who maintain that they have seen these wonders, are both impostors and liars, or that these witnesses are deceived by credulity or imagination. If they are impostors, what can be their object? The three principal objects of the corrupt human mind are power, money, and sensuality. As a rule, however, the so-called "wizards" are not reported to gain money, nor any other such possession or gain by their operations. Moreover, if they are impostors, how do country people, —sometimes mere ignorant and decrepit old men and women,[1] — learn so perfectly and successfully to juggle and perform tricks—as credible and competent witnesses admit and aver—without the aid of any apparatus, and often far more remarkable ones than those of the most dexterous professional conjurors?

Call them "wizards," "witches," "sorcerers," or what we will, they either possess superhuman powers, derived apparently from Satan and his angels, or they are plainly impostors; while the witnesses who relate their acts, and testify to the reality of their deeds, are likewise both impostors and liars.

Now, as a rule, it may be assumed that there have been in the past many pretended sorcerers. The theory, therefore, that all witnesses are impostors, may be at once dismissed. Such persons, at all events, may have seen the acts and deeds of pretended sorcerers. More-

[1] "Now mediums are not conjurors; *they are, as a rule, persons whose past life has been very unfavourable to learning the mysteries of this, or indeed of any other art.* They are frequently ignorant, uneducated, and withal most diffident and modest. When we see certain phenomena taking place in their presence, we are perfectly sure that they could not have produced them; first, because to do so would require mechanical contrivances which we know are not present; and secondly, that were such apparatus there, the medium would be utterly ignorant of its use."—'Spirit Mediums and Conjurors,' by George Sexton, LL.D., pp. 8, 9. London: 1873.

over, such witnesses should be examined as to what they may have seen and heard; and on the theory of deception by "natural magic" and trickery, their evidence carefully sifted and examined.

How is it, furthermore, that there notoriously exists amongst mankind in general a *consensus* of ancient and modern tradition respecting the existence of supernatural agents, and the ruler of them, the prince of the powers of the air; [1] and that even at the point of death prophets of future events,[2] wizards, and witches have confessed to evil deeds, attributing the same to Satanic origin?

If witnesses be impostors and liars, they must evidently have some object in view.

[1] "Amongst uncivilised people, moreover, there were various traditions respecting a Tree of Life, Paradise, a universal Deluge, and the Devil."—"Primitive Traditions as to Paradise:" a Paper read at the Meeting of the British Association at Southport, in September 1883.

[2] The late Dr Livingstone testified to the fact of the following apparitions and gift of prophecy in one of his most interesting books: "Suleiman-ben-Juma lived on the mainland, Mosesessami, opposite Zanzibar. *It is impossible to deny his power of foresight except by rejecting all evidence;* for he frequently foretold the deaths of great men amongst the Arabs; and he was pre-eminently a good man, upright, and sincere. . . . He said that two middle-sized white men, with straight noses and flowing hair down to the girdle behind, came at times and told him things to come. He died twelve years ago, and left no successor: he foretold his own decease three days beforehand, by cholera."—Livingstone's 'Journals,' vol. ii. p. 86.

People do not tell a series of deliberate lies, and persist in carefully and artfully repeating them, for no purpose. What, then, can the purpose be? Moreover, if the narrators of supernatural deeds be impostors and liars, in many cases there must have been not only a combination and co-operation of several liars to deceive and mislead, but there must have been amongst such a common object in view. What, then, is that object?

Such relators of these occurrences—persons often unacquainted with each other, and living at a distance,—most notoriously have laid themselves open to ridicule from all disbelievers in the Supernatural; making themselves objects of contempt and scorn, instead of subjects of fame and good report.

And if it be assumed that witnesses of such cases be credulous and open to deception, it follows that such do not necessarily speak falsely when they only affirm that they believe themselves to have seen or heard certain things. For credulity and imagination do not invariably affect several independent persons at the same time, at the same place, and exactly in the same manner.

Hence it may be reasonably and properly concluded that witchcraft is not a delusion, but a reality, and that it has not now ceased to exist, but is largely practised—not exactly by the same methods as of old—but still unquestionably and undoubtedly practised.

MESMERISM, CLAIRVOYANCE, AND SPIRITUALISM

CHAPTER VI.

MESMERISM, CLAIRVOYANCE, AND SPIRITUALISM.

MESMER, the author of the system which is called after his name, was born at Mersburg in Swabia, on 23d May 1734, and studied medicine at Vienna. In 1766 he received his degree of M.D. He had long been a proficient in astrology—like Mead, Richter, Balfour and Murat—and in the face both of prejudice and ignorance, maintained the influence of the planets on the human body.[1] He was a man with a sensitive organisation, of rapid perception, great imagination, considerable zeal, and was eminently persevering. Nor were his literary abilities mean. In a public dissertation he maintained that the sun, moon,

[1] This influence is even now allowed and admitted by many learned men.

and fixed stars mutually affect each other in their orbits; that they cause and direct on the earth a flux and reflux, and this not only in the sea, but in the atmosphere, and directly affect in a similar manner all organised bodies, through the medium of a subtile and mobile fluid which, he maintained, pervaded the whole universe, and in a wonderful manner associated all things together in mutual intercourse and harmony. Such was his theory. After first using magnetic plates, he subsequently by his own will and mental resolution produced remarkable effects by mere motions and passings of his hands from the head downwards towards the feet of the patient: and this even at a distance from the body. Such occurred in 1773. By his new principle and powers he worked cures, and did several wonderful deeds,—often obtaining astonishing influence over those upon whom he operated, and who, at his direction, readily gave up their wills to him during the process of being operated upon. Mesmer died on the 5th of March 1815, aged eighty-one.

In France the discovery created singular interest. Commissioners, specially appointed by King Louis XVI. to examine and report on the subject of Mesmerism, proceeded to inquire into the being, nature, and character of the fluid which Mesmer asserted to exist and had described; but of course it escaped all their researches. In 1784, Lavoisier, Bailly, and Jussieu, three learned men, a little over-confident, looked for it in vain. They could not discover it either by sight, touch, or taste. They were unable to collect it in masses, or to subject it to any tests of weight or measurement. They therefore, somewhat illogically, came to the conclusion that animal magnetism or mesmerism did not exist at all; and that the remarkable facts of which they had been eye-witnesses—and which it was impossible for them to have denied—were occasioned only by imagination, imitation, and manual contact.

On the other hand, amongst many more, the French *savants* Ampère, Cuvier, and La Place, together with Archbishop Whately in later times,[1] respectively examined the facts of

[1] "I myself was for many years reluctant to believe in mesmerism; but I was at length overcome by facts. Any amount of detected mistake or imposture will no more go to disprove a well-established fact than the detection of a number of pieces of counterfeit coins will prove a genuine shilling and sovereign not to be genuine silver and gold. To suppose that we are all so mad as to believe that things

mesmerism, and pronounced in their favour. In somewhat dogmatic terms Lessing thus wrote: "I am persuaded that animal magnetism—that active principle which we possess within us, and which, under the energy of our determined volition, manifests itself by the remarkable effects it visibly induces, does possess fixed and constant laws, which the progress of knowledge will eventually reveal to us."

The following was the method of action ordinarily recommended:—

Prepare yourself so as to be neither too warm nor too cold, and to enjoy perfect freedom in your gestures; you should also take your precautions not to be interrupted during the sitting. These preliminaries arranged,

are taking place before our eyes which do not, and all mad in the same way, is utterly incredible. No one, I am convinced, who has seen what I have seen, or the half of it, can remain unconvinced that mesmerism is a real and powerful agent. Those who profess complete disbelief, therefore, must belong, I conceive, to one of two classes: first, those who have made but a slight and scanty inquiry or none at all, and shun full investigation, lest they should be convinced—which is what they do not wish; and secondly, those who have inquired more fully and really are convinced, but are afraid to own it, for fear of being laughed at, or of being sent to Coventry by a kind of trades-union conspiracy."—Richard Whately, D.D., sometime Archbishop of Dublin.

seat your patient as conveniently as possible, and place yourself opposite to him, on a seat rather more elevated than his, so as to hold his knees between yours, and to touch your feet with his own. Request him to give himself up, to think of nothing, and not to distract his attention by examining the effects he may experience; to be full of hope, and not to be uneasy or alarmed, should the magnetic influence produce in him momentary pains. After having composed yourself, hold his thumbs between your fingers, so that the inside of your thumbs may touch the inside of his, and fix your eyes upon him. You may remain from two to five minutes in this position, or until you feel that your thumbs and his are at the same temperature. This being done, you must withdraw your hands, by moving them outwardly right and left, so that the inward surface be turned outwards, and raise them as high as the head; you must then lay them on both shoulders, and leave them there for about one minute; then bring them down along the arms to the extremity of the fingers, touching slightly all the way. You will repeat this manipulation five or six times, keeping your hands off the body when you raise them. You will then hold your hands above the head for a moment, and draw them down before the face, at a distance of about two inches, as low as the pit of the stomach. Here you will stop again for about two minutes, laying your thumbs on the pit of the stomach, and your fingers under the ribs. You will then slowly come down the body as low as the knees. These manipulations should be repeated during the greater part of the sitting. You will also occasionally come nearer to the patient, so as to lay your hands behind his shoulders, and bring them slowly down the spine, and thence over the hips and along the thighs, down to the knees or to the feet. When you wish to bring the sitting to a close, you must take care to draw the magnetic fluid to the extremities of the hands and feet, by lengthening your time of motion beyond these extremities, each time shaking your fingers. Lastly, you will make before the face, and even before the breast, a few transverse manipulations, at a distance of three or four inches. It is essential to magnetise invariably downwards from the head toward the extremities, and never upwards from the extremities towards the head. The downward manipulations are magnetic—that is, they are accompanied with the intention of magnetising. The movements upwards are not so. When the magnetiser operates upon the magnetisee, they are said to be *en rapport*—which means a peculiar and acquired disposition, by virtue of which the magnetiser exerts an influence upon the magnetisee: in other words, a communication of vital principle is established between them; and when this has once taken place, the magnetic action is renewed at every subsequent sitting, the instant the operation begins.

Dr Ashburner, in a note to his translation of Reichenbach's 'Researches in Magnetism,' p. 46—and to this statement particular attention should be directed—declares of persons thus deliberately placed in a state of mesmeric influence: "A man may be quite conscious and be unable to exercise will; or the organs of the brain, influenced by a force analogous to the magnetic power, may be placed in a condition such as that the individual is unable to act except at the bidding of another." And in his own treatise, 'Animal Magnetism and Spiritualism' (p. 293), he again and again asserts that magnetic operators can make their subjects "perform acts to which they are urged by the silent power of our will." And furthermore (on p. 137), he writes thus: "Many a time have I made persons travel considerable distances when desired to do so by the force of my silent will. Many a time have I in public carriages obliged persons I never saw before in my life to place their hands in mine, or to take hold of my shoulders, or my elbow, or my knee. Of course, not being aware of the cause which influenced them, they have either looked uncommonly awkward, or have sometimes fallen asleep under the powerful attractive agency of the force."

Further on, examples of experiments of the most dangerous nature are set forth, showing the obvious all-powerful influence of the will of a strong operator over the weaker will of a person operated upon.[1] And here is the

[1] Deleuze, in his treatise on the subject, its origin and nature, asserts that the first preliminary condition, without which little or nothing can be effected, is the consent of the will—a perfect implicit submission to the will of the operator being essential to success. If this be refused, the effect, as he points out, is sometimes partial and sometimes *nil*.

writer's comment thereupon : "Here is a man endowed or gifted with an extraordinary power of clear will, able to influence the phrenological organs of his neighbour, so as to excite his amorous feelings, and cause him to suspend his sense of moral duty; and the next minute lead him, by exerting spiritual force on the organs of conscientiousness, to produce remorse and melancholy; and the philosophic World of Science is to gape and wonder, or to deny boldly and flatly truths as sacred as any that God has ever poured out to man's cognizance." The crucial point on the part of the person operated upon evidently consists in giving up the will.

In the peculiar state of sleep which is developed in the person mesmerised—I write with hundreds of reported cases before me—the surface of the body is sometimes acutely sensible; but more frequently the ordinary sense of feeling is absolutely annihilated.[1] The jaws are firmly locked, and resist every

[1] The actual tests of this kind, very often cruel, repulsive, and disgusting, which have been made use of, and which are distinctly set forth in the numerous reports of disbelieving physicians and sceptical *savants*, more than cover every statement and detail in the test above. To certain tests—of a most offensive nature—reference can only be made in the most general terms.

method to wrench them open; the joints are often rigid, and the limbs inflexible; and not only is the sense of feeling, but the senses of smell, hearing, and sight also, are so deadened to all external impressions, that no pungent odour, loud report, nor glare of light can excite them in the smallest or slightest degree. The body may be pricked, pinched, lacerated, or burned; fumes of concentrated liquid ammonia may be passed up the nostrils; the loudest reports made suddenly close upon the ear; dazzling and intense light may be thrown upon the pupil of the eye; yet so profound is the physical state of lethargy that the sleeper will remain undisturbed and insensible to tortures which, in the waking state, would be simply intolerable.

Unconscious patients, in several cases of special experiments, have been subjected to the following trials: their lips and nostrils were tickled with feathers; their skin was pinched until bruises were produced; fired tow and burning flax were applied to the tenderest parts; smoke was introduced into the nostrils; and the feet of one female were plunged into a strong infusion of mustard seed at a high temperature. But not the slightest sign of pain did they evince. The expression of the countenance remained unchanged, nor was the pulse in any degree affected. On being awakened, however, out of the magnetic sleep, they all experienced the pain usually attendant upon such applications, and were, reasonably enough, exceedingly angry at the treatment they had received.

It has been asserted that persons in a state of mesmerism are so divested of all gross and sensual qualities that the slightest notions of impurity are recoiled from by them with horror. On the other hand, it is evident from printed examples of "test-cases" that the reverse is sometimes the case; and, moreover, that the very circumstances admit of much which it is painful to contemplate. "I myself was present," writes a German doctor named Loewe, "when a magnetised person said to the magnetiser, 'No, doctor, you have impure ideas. I beg you will renounce them, as you give me much pain.'"

There can be little doubt that the Munster Anabaptists, the Fifth Monarchy men, the English Puritans in their maddest phases of delusion, and the dancing lunatics and other similar fanatics of the middle and later ages, were possessed by evil spirits. Hecker, a German writer, has thus described the convulsed fanatics.[1] His account is here paraphrased rather than reproduced *verbatim* :—"They wandered in bands through country towns and villages, taking possession, wherever they went, of the religious houses, with the view of annoying the clergy, against whom their revilings were specially directed. . . . Children left their parents, servants their masters, mechanics their workshops, and housewives their domestic duties, to partake in this disorder. . . . The fury of some was so great that they would dash their brains out against the walls and corners of buildings, or rush

[1] It appears extremely probable that the doings and sayings of certain modern fanatics, who perambulate the country, are directly inspired from below. To write of such profane and repulsive exhibitions as "religious" in any sense of the word, is to misuse terms and to degrade the English language. Here is one account: "At the service in Wesley Chapel, two of the Hallelujah preachers, Happy Jack and Happy Tom, conducted the services, such as they were. They waved their hands, bellowed until they were hoarse, distorting their bodies in inconceivable forms, opened their mouths simultaneously, and shouted 'Glory' six consecutive times, and in appearance resembled dangerous maniacs. . . . The address of Miss Shepherd was listened to with rapt attention. One of the hearers remarked, 'Yes, it is wonderful, devilish wonderful. I believe that Miss Shepherd do mesmerise them all.'"

headlong into rapid rivers, where they were drowned. Roaring and foaming at the mouth as they rose, the bystanders could only succeed in restraining them by placing benches and chairs in their way, so that by taking high leaps, their strength might be sooner exhausted. Many, after wearying themselves out, would revive in a certain time, and join once more the frantic revel." These kinds of exhibitions of frantic fanaticism and heresy in action, of experimentalists in spiritualism and magnetism, prove the existence of a direct supernatural influence.

Many persons are fascinated by their relation to and connection with the spirits of the world unseen, and readily give themselves up to intercourse with such spirits. "Why," asks a writer from whose books quotations have already been made,—"why should we doubt of the existence of invisible beings in the air, who are constantly engaged in works of good or evil?" "Why, indeed!" I reply. But who is to judge which are good and which are evil? Experimenters are often completely at the mercy of the latter; while persons experimented upon become first their dupes, and subsequently their slaves. Some public exhibitions of spiritualism at Glasgow—where, as the promoters admitted, evil spirits secured the upper hand, to the manifest alarm and horror of the assembly—were brought to a sudden termination in consequence. In certain cases lunacy and suicide have directly followed the practice of invoking spirits at formal *séances;* and some scores of "spiritualists" are now confined in madhouses.

Dr Arndt, the eminent German physician, relates, that being one day seated near the bed of one of his somnambulists, on a sudden she became agitated, uttered sighs, and, as if tormented by some vision, exclaimed, "O heavens! my father! he is dying!" A few moments afterwards she awoke, seemed quite cheerful, and recollected nothing of the anxiety she had so recently manifested. She again relapsed twice into the same state of magnetic sleep, and each time she was tormented by the same vision. Being asked what had happened to her father, she answered, "He is bathed in blood—he is dying." Soon afterwards she awoke, became composed, and the scene finished. Some weeks afterwards, Dr Arndt found this lady pensive and sorrowful. She had just received from her father, who was at a distance of some hundred miles, an account of a serious accident which had befallen him. In ascending the stair of his cellar, the door had fallen upon his breast,—a considerable hæmorrhage ensued, and the physicians despaired of his life. Dr Arndt, who had marked the precise time of the preceding scene of the somnambulism of this lady, found that it was exactly on the day, and at the hour, when the accident happened to her father. "This," observes the doctor, "could not have been the mere effect of chance; and, assuredly, there was no concert nor deceit on the part of the observer."

There are several reasons for believing, it should be here remarked, that divers of the mysteries which are gathered round pagan worship, oriental magic, the operations of the old oracles, witchcraft, and necromancy—remarked by many, but amply explained by none—are in some obvious, but as yet unknown, way bound together by the principle of action underlying modern Mesmerism, Clairvoyance, and Spiritualism—which principle, whatever it be (and whatever else it may be presumed to teach), serves abundantly to demonstrate the inherent absurdity of mere Materialism and scientific Atheism. The faculty of clear-sightedness, or *clairvoyance*, by which is signified an interior power of seeing events passing at a distance, or of perceiving events about to occur in the future, is extremely like the property which—as I have already pointed out—is notoriously existent in Scotland and elsewhere. In ancient history numerous examples have been recorded. They occur in the records of the children of Israel, of Greece and Rome; in the writings of the Christian Fathers, as well as in the numerous published works which have been issued concerning the Supernatural during the last four centuries. Those who reasonably believe that the utterances of the possessed women and inspired priestesses of the Ancient Oracles had a *substratum* of truth in them,—and there are many such reasonable persons, even in these days of arrogant scepticism,—hold that clairvoyance was often the method in use.

There can be little doubt, it may be further pointed out, that the various ancient pagan oracles were inspired by demons, more especially when the old traditions of a true primitive religion had become obscured, and in regard to many nations the Evil One had usurped the place of the Living God.

Certain of the false gods of the heathens, when not deified men, were probably fallen angels who guided and directed the priestesses when speaking the will of their superior, or directing the applicant for advice and warning. At Delphi, for example, before the golden statue of Apollo, on an altar burnt the sacred fire. This was the most celebrated and renowned Oracle of old. In the centre of the floor of its innermost sanctuary was a fissure or chasm in the earth, from which from time to time rose an intoxicating smoke.[1] Whether this was natural or artificial remains uncertain. Over this stood the tripod, on which the Pythia or priestess took her place whenever the Oracle was to be consulted. It is recorded that the smoke from below so affected her brain that she passed into a state of mental intoxication,

[1] Often leaves of plants, gums and barks from trees, choice oils, dry rushes, and boughs of certain shrubs, were burnt in combination. Most of the seventeenth-century treatises on Witchcraft give rules and proportions for the composition of this incense.

often leaped off the tripod, went into convulsions, and then the wild sounds and pithy sentences uttered by her—often ambiguous enough,[1] but occasionally only too definite—embodied the actual revelation or communication of the genius of the Oracle—an example of clear-seeing or *clairvoyance.* The answer was commonly in the form of a verse, usually an hexameter; and these responses were held in the greatest veneration, not only in Greece, but in all the countries of the Mediterranean; for the people—shrewd enough, watchful, and taught by experience—had a sincere faith in its counsels, warnings, and directions.

Other oracles—those, for example, of departed leaders of men and warrior heroes, called "oracles of the dead,"[2] in which sacrifices were directly offered to the "gods" or demons of the lower world, and the spirits of

[1] Let it be noted that, *mutatis mutandis*, on a ruder platform, and by a coarser method, the incantation-scenes in Shakespeare's "Macbeth" perpetuate the tradition of the more refined pagan Oracles.

[2] These oracles were founded on the reasonable belief that dead heroes still took an interest in the welfare of their country, and could aid it—a conception quite true and reasonable in itself, and perfectly in harmony with Christian belief regarding the departed; and no doubt an imperfect and distorted conception of the traditional teaching of primitive religion—the worship of One God and the intercommunion of His servants.

the dead warriors and sages were consulted—had an existence, and were likewise held in great respect. One of the most ancient and renowned was situated near Lake Aornos, in the country of the Threspasians; another was at Heraclea on the Propontis, to both of which allusions are made in the writings of the Fathers.[1]

Sacrifices—the highest types of divine worship, let it be especially noted—were offered to the genius, demon, or devil of the place: incense for the tripod; oil, money, beasts for the altar-offering, specially a black ram or a he-goat; while corn and fruits were also sacrificially presented. Sometimes, after lavations, fastings, and abstention from lusts, the applicant for advice or information concerning the future was introduced to the inner place, and led to worship the demon's image, after which the oracle was consulted.

In some oracles—as at that of Creneste—the answers were made by the use of lots. Pieces of oak, with signs and writings cut on

[1] Early Christian writers did not at all dispute the *fact* of the powers exhibited—in truth, no reasonable being could have done so—but distinctly attributed them to the influence of evil spirits and the Prince of the Powers of the Air.

them, were first shaken up in a vessel, and then two or three were drawn out by a trained youth, on behalf of the person seeking counsel or advice. In other oracles responses were made by dreams, by watching the flights of birds, or by examining the intestines of the sacrificed animals; sometimes by gazing into a well or a polished mirror; occasionally by sounds coming from the temple or shrine, which were duly interpreted by its appointed officers and guardians.

The theories that these Oracles were plain impostures, and were "managed" by members of certain favoured and aristocratic families for their own interests, may be dismissed as absurd. A German writer, F. A. Wolf, has written a most laborious, learned, and curious treatise to show that the keepers and workers of these oracles were acquainted with "animal magnetism" or "mesmerism"; but without at all denying his assumption, there can be little doubt that witchcraft and necromancy were the actual principles by which such oracles were worked.

The rise of "Spiritualism," as it is now called, in America, is at length well known—

the subject having been systematically dealt with by many writers—and its spread to the European continent equally so. Thousands of persons in the former country, and numbers of enthusiastic supporters of the system in Germany, Russia, France, Belgium, Italy, and England, are its ardent votaries. It only differs from ancient forms of the Supernatural by being better adapted than they would be to the tastes and sentiments of the present age.

Let a few distinct and definite testimonies, as to facts and occurrences, be now considered. Here follows a certain categorical statement concerning a *séance* from the published 'Narrative' of Professor Crookes:—

"I was sitting next to the medium,[1] Miss Fox, the only other persons present being my wife and a lady relative, and I was holding the medium's two hands in one of mine, whilst her feet were resting on my feet. Paper was on the table before us, and my disengaged hand was holding a pencil. A luminous hand came down from the upper part of the room, and after hovering near me for a few seconds,

[1] The modern name for "witch."—F. G. L.

took the pencil from my hand, rapidly wrote on a sheet of paper, threw the pencil down, and then rose up over our heads, gradually fading into darkness."[1]

And here is another equally remarkable extract from a publication by a certain Dr Sexton :—

" Under the strictest test conditions, I have seen a solid self-luminous body, the size and nearly the shape of a turkey's egg, float noiselessly about the room, at one time higher than any one present could reach standing on tiptoe, and then gently descend to the floor. It was visible for more than ten minutes; and before it faded away it struck the table three times, with a sound like that of a hard, solid body. During this time the medium was lying back, apparently insensible, in an easy-chair. I have seen luminous points of light darting about and settling on the heads of different persons; I have had questions answered by the flashing of a bright light a desired number of times in front of my face. I have seen sparks of light rising from the table to the ceiling, and again falling upon the table,

[1] 'Narrative Concerning Spiritualism.' By Mr W. Crookes, F.R.S.

striking it with an audible sound. I have had an alphabetic communication given by luminous flashing occurring before me in the air, whilst my hand was moving about amongst them. I have seen a luminous cloud floating upwards to a picture. Under the strictest test conditions, I have more than once had a solid, self-luminous, crystalline body placed in my hand by a hand which did not belong to any person in the room. In the light, I have seen a luminous cloud hover over a heliotrope on a side table, break a sprig off, and carry the sprig to a lady; and on some occasions, I have seen a similar luminous cloud visibly condense to the form of a hand, and carry small objects about." [1]

The following is the authentic report of a spiritualistic meeting, held at Notting Hill on a Sunday evening in the month of February 1878 :—

" One speaks in a mesmeric trance, and in that condition discourses fluently, on a moment's notice, on every subject, abstruse or popular, that may be suggested. Improvised poetry also is the outcome of this somnam-

[1] 'Defence of Modern Spiritualism.' By George Sexton, p. 12.

bulic state, the subject of the verses being chosen by the audience. Spiritual prevision, second sight, clairvoyance, or the discerning of spirits, is likewise encouraged. . . . Another phase of these strange manifestations is the ecstatic state into which many who attend these services are thrown under the influence of some power *ab extra* of themselves, speaking with other voices than their own, and seeming to be for the time, while the afflatus is upon them, altogether different beings, and not themselves—certain in this condition speaking in Chinese, Hindustanee, and other foreign tongues, of which they in their waking state had no knowledge."

Here in what follows the same writer replies to those scientific persons who apparently advise their followers to boldly and thoroughly reject the evidence of their senses:—

"Viewing the manifestations as owing to a mechanical cause, they were inexplicable by any known law of physical science, unless viewed as the action of the human beings with whom they had been associated. Nothing is better established than that weight is necessary to move weight. Archimedes said, 'Give me where to stand, and I will move the world.' It was necessary to have a place to stand; and so in all my experience, whether as a chemist or as a natural philospher, I found it was necessary, in order that weight should be removed, that weight should react with it. An isolated body will not budge in obedience to any imponderable influence, whether of electricity or heat. If the imponderable cause of these affections be generated within a body, an explosion may result from the reaction among themselves of the constituent particles of the body; but according to the laws of *mundane* nature, *action* cannot exist without *reaction*. Pursuant to these views, I sanctioned the opinion of Faraday, that if there was a table moved when a human being was present, since the table was an inanimate body, incapable of self-motion, it was of necessity to be inferred that the human being moved the table, unconsciously, if not wilfully. I did not take this opinion from Faraday. I formed it independently, as every man must who endeavours to explain the *phenomena* in question by the physical laws universally admitted by men of science. Accordingly I published my opinions as coincident with those of Faraday. From my long acquaintance with the laws of motion, and with the chemical and electrical reaction, I was confident that the result could not arise from any of these causes; that there was no physical cause, under the name of electricity or odic force, or anything of the kind, which could account for these motions." [1]

With many of the following accounts most persons at all interested in the subject are more or less familiar. It will, however, be wise and well for those persons desiring to be accurately informed on the subject, to have the distinct statements of the advocates of spiritualism set forth in their own language and form. The following further extracts, therefore, are taken from Dr Sexton's publications:—

"It occurred, Serjeant Cox tells us, 'in the house of Dr Edmonds,' a sceptic, and in the presence of other sceptics; 'a dining-table of unusual weight and size' was moved most palpably, when no person touched it, all present kneeling on the chairs, the backs of which were turned to the table. 'In that position,' he says, 'of the entire party, a heavy dining-

[1] 'Defence of Modern Spiritualism.' By G. Sexton, p. 6.

table moved six times—once over a space of eight inches at a swing. Then all the party, holding hands, stood in a circle round the table at the distance from it, first two feet, and then three feet; so that contact by any person present was physically impossible. In this position the table lurched four times; once over a space of more than two feet, and with great force. The extent of these movements, without contact, will be understood when I state that in the course of them, this ponderous table turned completely round; that is to say, the end that was at the top of the room when the experiment began, was at the bottom of the room when it concluded. The most remarkable part of this experiment was the *finale*. The table had been turned to within about two feet of a complete reversal of its first position, and was standing out of the square with the room. Suddenly the table was swung violently over the two feet of distance between its then position and its proper place, and set exactly square with the room, literally knocking down a lady who was standing in the way in the act of putting on her shawl for departure. At that time nobody was touching the table, or even within reach of it, except the young lady who was knocked down by it."[1]

Here, again, is a remarkable case of noise and motion. As so many persons of intelligence have witnessed similar *phenomena*, it seems impossible to pooh-pooh such independent testimony :—

"Very loud sounds, as of violent blows, came from a large loo-table which stood alone in the centre of the room, nobody being near it. We turned to look at the table, and, untouched, it tilted up almost to an angle of forty-five degrees, and continued in that position for nearly a minute; then it fell back; then it repeated the movement on the other side. None of us were standing within five feet of it at that time. The room was well lighted with gas, there was no cloth upon the table, and all beneath it was distinctly visible. Only four persons were in the room, and no one touched it, nor was near enough to touch it had he tried."[2]

Again: the same writer asserts what is set down in that which follows :—

[1] 'Defence of Modern Spiritualism.' By G. Sexton, p. 8.
[2] Ibid., pp. 8, 9.

"The *phenomena* I am prepared to attest are so extraordinary, and so directly oppose the most firmly-rooted articles of scientific belief—amongst others, the ubiquity and invariable action of the law of gravitation—that, even now, on recalling the details of what I witnessed, there is an antagonism in my mind between *reason*, which pronounces it to be scientifically impossible, and the consciousness that my senses, both of touch and sight—and these corroborated, as they were, by the senses of all who were present—are not lying witnesses when they testify against my preconceptions. But the supposition that there is a sort of mania or delusion which suddenly attacks a whole roomful of intelligent persons who are quite sane elsewhere, and that they all concur to the minutest particulars in the details of the occurrences of which they suppose themselves to be witnesses, seems to my mind more incredible than even the facts they attest."[1]

Again to the same effect:—

"On one occasion I witnessed a chair, with a lady sitting on it, rise several inches from

[1] 'Defence of Modern Spiritualism.' By G. Sexton, p. 10.

the ground. On another occasion, to avoid the suspicion of this being in some way performed by herself, the lady knelt on the chair in such a manner that its four feet were visible to us. It then rose about three inches, remained suspended for about ten seconds, and then slowly descended. Another time two children, on separate occasions, rose from the floor with their chairs, in full daylight, under (to me) the most satisfactory conditions; for I was kneeling and keeping close watch upon the feet of the chair, and observing that no one might touch them."[1]

Once more. The same writer describes the appearance of what are known as "spirit-hands":—

"I will here give no instances in which the phenomenon has occurred in darkness, but will simply select a few of the luminous instances in which I have seen the hands in the light. A beautifully-formed small hand rose up from an opening in a dining-table, and gave me a flower; it appeared and then disappeared three times at intervals, affording me ample opportunity of satisfying myself that it was as

[1] 'Defence of Modern Spiritualism.' By G. Sexton, p. 11.

real in appearance as my own. This occurred in the light, in my own room, whilst I was holding the medium's hands and feet. On another occasion a small hand and arm, like a baby's, appeared playing about a lady who was sitting next to me. It then passed to me, and patted my arm, and pulled my coat several times."[1]

In certain of the following statements of Mr Thomas Grant, another lecturer and writer on this subject, some allowance must be made for his want of exact information as to the action of the Catholic authorities in America. It is utterly incredible that any Catholic clergy should have sanctioned the use of mediums; for the whole subject of Spiritualism having been long and carefully considered at Rome, the current practices have been distinctly condemned and directly forbidden.

But Mr Grant shall make his own statement, in his own words, which, however, must be taken *cum grano salis*:—

"In the course of twenty years, notwithstanding the most violent and unscrupulous opposition from the press, the Men of Science

[1] 'Defence of Modern Spiritualism.' By G. Sexton, p. 12.

and Religion, the regular intelligent communication with departed friends had become so thoroughly established as a family practice in America, that at a Convocation of the Roman Catholic Archbishops and Bishops, held early in 1867 at Baltimore, to consider how the matter should be met by the Church, it was found that the aggregate estimate by all the Bishops of the number of Spiritualists in their several dioceses amounted to between ten and eleven millions, with 50,000 *media*, whilst Romanists and Protestants together only numbered eight to nine millions, with 45,000 preachers. It must be remembered these were statements made by the enemies of Spiritualism, and the result was to cause Spiritualism to be acknowledged by the Roman Catholic authorities in America, who from that time have not only ceased opposition, but have established *media* in their own institutions, and are endeavouring to induce their flocks to confine themselves to the *media* under their control."[1]

Here is another quotation from the same writer, dealing with the appearance of lights,

[1] 'A Scientific View of Modern Spiritualism.' By T. Grant, p. 6.

and of other *phenomena* not unknown to students of Oriental mysteries:—

"Spirits, through outward *media*, can sometimes exercise perfect control over fire, to the extent of placing hot glowing coals from the grate in the hands of persons, or upon their heads, without burning or even singeing a hair. They can also produce lights of various magnitude and intensity, from a faint phosphoric appearance the size of a pea, to a brilliancy almost rivalling that of the sun, and as large as a man's head. Manifestations exhibited in a dark room are sometimes made visible by means of these spirit-lights."[1]

A careful consideration of these authoritative testimonies, extracted from the writings of the most devoted adherents of this system, will show how entirely in harmony the modern practices are with the ancient systems of magic, necromancy, and witchcraft, as followed of old and elsewhere.[2] The same evil

[1] 'A Scientific View of Modern Spiritualism.' By T. Grant, p. 11.

[2] "The very titles of the art and its professors have been altered: what was necromancy is now spiritualism; and the presiding high priest or priestess of the mysteries is no longer called 'witch' when of the feminine gender, and 'wizard' when of the masculine, but both are now styled in common by a less expressive appellation—

principles are still at work, adapted perhaps to modern needs; the same methods as in times past, *mutatis mutandis*, are still adopted by those who would seek the aid of disembodied spirits, powerful but lying demons, or inferior spiritual intelligences;[1] which the restless, the sad, the weary, and the tormented

that of 'medium.'"—"Apology for Spiritualism" in the 'Englishwomen's Domestic Magazine.'

Five American writers make similar admissions, thus:—

1. "The time is past when these new things (spiritual *phenomena*) would have been ignorantly termed demonism, necromancy, and witchcraft."—Andrew Jackson Davis.

2. "The history of Salem witchcraft is but an account of spiritual manifestations, and of man's incapacity to understand them."—Judge Edmonds.

3. "Simon Magus was, of all men, Prince among the workers of spiritualistic miracles."—Professor Brittain.

4. "All the magic, the mysteries, the witchcraft, and the necromancy of the ancient world, from the time of the Delphic Oracle, are explained by the modern manifestations."—Governor Tallmadge.

5. "Modern spiritualists can do all that the Egyptian soothsayer and sorcerers could accomplish—so there is nothing new under the sun."—Robert C. Reeves.

[1] "These pretended spirits often lie. Messages are received purporting to come from departed persons, and giving the particulars of their decease, who prove on inquiry to be still alive. I have known this in several instances. Of course this does not disprove a communicating intelligence. . . . If we admit the physical phenomena of Spiritualism, and concede that communications and revelations are really made by beings ordinarily invisible to mortals, we are still surrounded with difficulties. What assurance can we have in any case of the identity of a spirit? A bad or mischievous spirit may, for aught we know, personate our friends, penetrate our secrets, and deceive us with false communications. Where is the proof of identity?"—'Forty Years of American Life,' vol. ii. pp. 63, 64.

amongst so-called "civilised nations" take up, in order to fill the void in the hearts of the multitude made by the absence of True Religion and the one True Faith. As regards success in experiments, everything depends upon the persons operating and operated upon *giving up their wills*[1] to some unknown power, the chief of the fallen angels or his missionaries.

When the beauty and value of their literature are pointed out, what is actually found? A mere bundle of negations, hazy assertions, a batch of pietistic sentiments—which, when duly considered and carefully weighed, are seen to run directly counter to the fundamental doctrines of Christianity—are alone found in the writings of this important and increasing sect. "Another Christ" is looked for by some of their writers. Save, however, that the doctrines of a Supreme Being and of the

[1] "The Devil has always striven hard to get men to yield to him the dominion of their will; and our magnetisers and spiritualistic operators tell you they can do nothing unless you make your will over to them; but if you do that, then they can do almost anything. This is so fearful that I cannot but think it one of the worst parts of these revived mysteries."—"Ancient and Modern Spiritism," p. 95, in 'Essays on Religion and Literature.' Third series. London: 1874.

immortality of the soul[1] are invariably most urgently and passionately maintained by the Spiritualists, there is little that is distinct and definite taught:—

"Hitherto we have deemed it only as a science; but when we remember that its scientific facts are to lead us to a knowledge of our hereafter, and the best means of attaining to it—that they are exploring the secret depths of our character—that they are bringing before us the causes of life's many failures—that they are showing us the secret foundations upon which character is built up, and giving us the strongest motives for improving, amending, purifying, and strengthening all the good that is in us—can we come to any other conclusion than that this Pentecostal day is indeed *to lead us to the*

[1] "A universe without a God and a man without a soul present little to boast of in the shape of the consolation they can bring to suffering humanity."

"If Spiritualism were only the enjoyment of the hour, beautiful as it is, gladdening to the heart and cheerful to the mourner as it has proved, it were nothing but some personal attribute which we have no need to herald forth to the World. But Spiritualism teaches of that God Who is a Spirit, of that immortality which constitutes the very gist of human existence, of that life-practice for which religious systems have been established as a guide. What more do we require to constitute the elements of a Religion? If it be not a Religion it is nothing!"—'The Creed of the Spirits,' a Spiritualistic Tract.

coming of a second Messiah?[1] *He is not yet in our midst: we are only listening to the voices that are crying in the wilderness.*"[2]

The doctrine of the Blessed Trinity is here categorically denied, though the denial is clothed in novel and strange jargon and in redundant verbiage. Let the statements be duly weighed:—

"For ourselves we believe that all truth is of God, and Christ embodied in His form as much of Deity as the truth He expressed: that He was the Son of God, and that He represented the possible of man, inasmuch as He promised the same gifts to others that He himself possessed. But we certainly decline entering into any discussion upon the creed of the Trinitarian or Unitarian, or any form of theological controversy. *Christ's words, when He says 'I and my Father are one,' did*

[1] *Note by the Author.*—This notion had been previously set forth in a theologically-slipshod and inexact verse by Lord Tennyson in his powerful and touching poem, "In Memoriam," thus:—

"Ring in the valiant man and free,
The larger heart, the kindlier hand,
Ring out the darkness of the land,
Ring in the Christ that is to be."

—'In Memoriam,' sixth edition, p. 164. London: 1855.

[2] 'On the Spirit Circle,' p. 11. By Emma Hardinge. London: J. Burns.

not mean He was God. If He and His Father were one, it simply signified *they were one in spirit.*"[1]

The fact of the Incarnation—flowing from the doctrine thus denied—is here likewise deliberately and distinctly regarded as, and declared to be, a point of no consequence, an "open question":—

"Meanwhile there came a voice in the East, simple like that of a child. There dawned a star, there beamed a day; and the Wise Men saw that the Christ they had long expected had come. Now it does not matter, in our opinion, whether, as the Infidel believes, this Birth of Jesus is a tradition; or whether, as the Christian believes, it is a reality. The influence of that supposed Birth upon the World is precisely the same; and whether

[1] 'Spiritual Ethics.' By Mrs Cora L. V. Tappan, pp. 11, 12. The Lectures of this American lady were delivered in London in the year 1874 and 1875, and they were certainly full of fire, power, and beauty of imagery. They set forth very forcibly—though often in exceedingly ambiguous language—the special watchwords and obvious principles of Spiritualism. Certain of her doctrines were plausible enough; while the method adopted to win adherents was exactly of a character to attract Christians whose faith was vague and nebulous. I may here add that a spiritualistic treatise entitled 'A Forecast of the Religion of the Future,' may be profitably studied in order to note how directly anti-Christian the system and principles of Spiritualism are.

you take it from the standpoint of the Secularist or the standpoint of the Religionist, it does not matter."[1]

It is obvious, therefore, that as against blank infidelity, the principles of Spiritualism are of extremely little value, being distinctly and most dangerously anti-Christian. So much so indeed, that not only are they being formulated into a system, but that a new religion is being founded upon them, and a regular "School of Sorcery" is being established, and is even now being worked, in France.[2]

The following is what is still further maintained in regard to the doctrine of the Atonement and the need of a Mediator between God and man.

[1] 'Spiritual Ethics.' By Mrs Cora L. V. Tappan, p. 7. An oration delivered 28th September 1873.

[2] In the 'Standard' of September 13, 1878, was printed an account of a new religion, then recently founded in France by a M. Piérart, under the name of "Esseno-Druidism." This enthusiastic person endeavoured to establish at St Maur a regular "School of Sorcery." It was to be "a spiritualistic seminary, a field for pneumatological and thaumaturgical experiments, a college of prophets and *illuminati*, guided by the rules of a wise discernment. The magnetic experiments, performed by the Marquis de Puysegur, . . . will be reproduced. A spiritualistic doctor will be attached to the establishment." A somewhat similar institution—to inquire into the authenticity of facts which all save Atheists, Materialists, Agnostics, and Darwinites, acknowledge to be true—has been established in England, under the shadow of Westminster Abbey.

"Christ taught that between the human soul and the Father there is no intercessor but Love; and the divinest feature of His teaching was, that it left the individual in the hands of Deity, instead of in the hands of an outside God who might or might not listen to prayer. More than this, instead of offerings of bloodshed and burnt-offerings and sacrifices, He taught that the only offerings were those of the human spirit; that the only sacrifice was the sacrifice of the senses; and that to the spiritually-minded there is no need of an intercessor, for God is there and will listen."[1]

In that which follows, vague enough in its definite teaching, the Christian doctrine of rewards and punishments hereafter is likewise altogether rejected :—

"So far as Spiritualism is concerned, it distinctly, emphatically, and conclusively repudiates the whole scheme [of rewards and punishments] from beginning to end—thoroughly and completely repudiates any connection therewith, *thoroughly and utterly places out of conception the theological idea of Heaven and Hell.*"[2]

[1] 'Spiritual Ethics' &c., p. 8.

[2] 'Heaven and Hell, in their Relation to Spiritualism.' By J. J. Morse. P. 7. London: 1874.

Again to the same effect :—

"There is no room for either the theological Hell or the theological Heaven."

"The destiny of all souls in the world of spirits is progression; due punishment, and only due punishment, is administered—*and that self-inflicted*, by virtue of the fact that every law that you seek to violate brings down upon your own head the punishment due."[1]

"Ever onwards and upwards to God, though never reaching Him. Always going on, with eternity before us, ages and ages of eternity yet to be unfolded; and when these are past, there are ages and ages of eternity yet to come. On and on, for ever progressing! ever aspiring towards Beauty and Truth—to Heaven, if you will!"[2]

The so-called "creed" of the spiritualists, as far as the system can be said to own a creed, is thus summed up :—

"Thy first and last duty upon earth, and all through thy life, shall be to seek for the principles of Right, and to live them out to the

[1] 'Concerning the Spiritual World.' By J. J. Morse. Pp. 13 and 15.

[2] Ibid., p. 13.

utmost of thy power; and whatever creed, precept, or example conflicts with those principles, thou shalt spurn and neglect, ever remembering that the laws of Right are,—in morals, justice; in science, harmony; in religion, the fatherhood of God, the brotherhood of man, the immortality of the human soul; and compensation and retribution for the good or evil done on earth."

The Christian religion is thus contemptuously spoken of:—

"Though Christianity to-day declines and is losing power and vigour, yet in its day it has done great and glorious good in the work of human redemption. It was an advance upon the religions that preceded it, and was the dawning of a glorious day in the World's history. . . . The Christianity of to-day and that of its Founder are distinct in every particular."[1]

To sum up, therefore, and the summary is not unworthy of careful study:—

1. Spiritualism denies the facts of original sin, the fall of man, and consequently the disorganisation and corruption of his moral nature.

[1] 'What of the Dead?' By J. J. Morse. P. 5. London: 1873.

2. It wholly and systematically repudiates the doctrines of the Blessed Trinity, of the Incarnation, of the personality of the Holy Ghost,[1] of the divinity of our Lord, and of the Atonement.

3. It likewise scornfully and absolutely repudiates the doctrine of the resurrection of the body, and denies that there will be any day of judgment, either particular or general.

4. It furthermore absolutely rejects the existence of any place of punishment, and the eternity of that punishment; and finally,

5. It distinctly and categorically denies the existence of a personal Devil.[2]

To those guided by sentiment or fancy, or misled by pulpit claptrap about "eternal hope," who either secretly disbelieve in Christianity,

[1] "*The Holy Spirit is not any particular Spirit*, but is a name that represents the divine proceeding,—the totality of good, pure, and superior spirits, who are sent by God to comfort His children. God hears the prayer, however faint it may be; He answers it by sending *His souls of light* to bring comfort and further spiritual revelation to those who seek for it."—'Old Truths in a New Light,' by the Countess of Caithness.

[2] "Hence it will be seen that the personal Devil has no existence, except as a distorted, deformed, and monstrous representation of the good and true personified in each individual, as long as he continues in opposition to God, who is wisdom, goodness, and love in one."—'Old Truths in a New Light,' by the Countess of Caithness. See also 'Spiritualism a Satanic Agency,' by Thomas W. Greenwell, Member of the Victoria Institute, &c.

or own no very decided faith in our holy religion, there will of course be something singularly attractive[1] in holding communion, as some assert and maintain, with the disembodied spirits of dead friends. Few people know how widely this system is practised—sometimes openly, sometimes in secret—how numerous are its dupes, what a mischievous effect it often exercises both on mind and body,[2] how the practice frequently tends to make its votaries lunatics, and how the vain hopes and fantastic beliefs of its degraded dupes turn out to be only fond delusions or mischievous day-dreams, and to ensure for such both moral and physical decay and ruin.[3]

[1] This is the case with a minister of the Scottish Establishment, who has thus written :—

"The results of being present at *séances* are such as many rejoice in and are devoutly thankful for. The tears of many mourners have been dried, because they have come to believe that they were not parted far from those who have become for the time lost to sight—friends who perished by shipwreck, and never heard of, are objects of painful doubt no longer. It has, in a word, become impossible for mourners to grieve as they had grieved before, and the thought of leaving this world no longer produces the chill impression that it once produced. One says, I ought to have derived all this comfort direct from the Bible, but did not."—"A Case of Extacies," by a Scotch Minister, 'Spiritual Magazine,' p. 408. London : 1877.

[2] Mischievous physical results frequently follow—violent headaches, constant sickness, intense debility, and sometimes wasting away.

[3] I myself have been again and again asked by strangers, as well as persons of whom I have some knowledge, whether they might not

The following warning words, with which this chapter is closed, are well worthy of due consideration and attention :—

"For myself, I look with alarm and uneasiness at the growing taste for these scenes and experiences displayed by many otherwise worthy souls, and destined at length, I fear, to corrupt them. It is the 'willing worship of demons.' It is not impossible that it may end in real formal idolatry—an idolatry coming in, not perhaps under any of its old forms, and yet a real formal idolatry. Let us not be too sure. I do not mean the worship of Mammon, for instance, with which saying we are so familiar—I don't mean the covetousness which is the service of idols,—I mean rejecting God from our heart and from our belief, and yielding ourselves, our very wills, as a possession to another to be filled and guided by him,—perhaps a soothing, sensual, intellectual, and sense-flattering god—a demon. What has been may be. We are not the wisest and most cultivated of all men that ever were. Paris and London are not equal in culture and

consult and hold communion with the disembodied spirits of their departed friends,—in other words, whether necromancy is not a perfectly good and lawful practice.

refinement to Athens and Corinth. And although it would appear incredible that men could descend from their present standing and stoop to the absurdities of ancient idolatry, we may somewhat demur to granting this, seeing what we do see — grave and sensible men looking on eagerly and believingly, while invisible spirits are endowing with intelligence the dull and lifeless furniture of a room, making tables and heavy articles turn, and run, and skip, and make obeisances, and though not themselves intelligent, give, when asked, intelligent replies concerning things absent, unknown, and future, even concerning the mysteries of heaven; ponderous sofas and pianos raised by this spirit agency many feet above the ground, floating in the atmosphere, making the circuit of the room, and gently falling into their places again; human hands floating in the air, spirit-writing, spirit-drawing, spirit recitals at the piano,—whoever believes all this will believe anything, except the revelations which come to us in God's own way. If these things are true (and I cannot deny them as matters of fact deposed to by multitudes of shrewd and observant men), I can only say that a Catholic can have no doubt or difficulty in saying from whence they come. Therefore, I say, do not let us be too sure that men, sensible and clever in commerce, politics, and literature, or what you please, may not lapse into formal idolatry. When a man has driven the one true God from his soul, he will easily give place to a whole hierarchy of other gods, and 'all the gods of the Gentiles are devils.'" [1]

[1] 'Essays on Religion and Literature.' Pp. 107-109. Third Series. London: 1874.

ORIENTAL MAGIC AND JUGGLERY, ETC.

CHAPTER VII.

ORIENTAL MAGIC AND JUGGLERY, ETC.

THE fact of Oriental Magic—the reality of the strange performances which are to be seen in India and other Oriental countries—are not denied by that considerable number of curious and astonished persons who from time to time have seen them.[1] In some cases, however, the marvels witnessed were so evidently believed to be supernatural, that, rather than admit this fact, fearing adverse criticism, certain Europeans have declined to express any opinion at all as to what they have witnessed.

[1] "It is almost impossible to escape the conclusion that the marvels of the Old Testament were, on the part of magicians, an exercise of unlawful knowledge, handed down from primitive times; and in this I am fortified, as well by what I myself have seen with my own eyes, as by the assertions of the Oriental magicians themselves, who profess to be assisted by *genii* or Ginn."—Archbishop Steins.

"I was so utterly appalled, and altogether driven into a corner, by what I saw with my own eyes," wrote a spectator to myself (one whose account is given later on), "that, rather than subject myself to the charge of believing in the diabolical nature of Oriental magic, I would prefer to be silent and to say nothing. But my astonishment, I am free to confess, was in some cases without bounds."

"Of one point I feel confident," wrote another correspondent, "that the singular things I saw can only be accounted for by the use of a sort of supernatural agency on the part of those who did them. I was never more impressed by many accounts of the Old Testament, or convinced of the fact of witchcraft (call it what you will), than when I stood round, with a hundred others, and saw the weird doings and operations of Burah Khan."

The miracles recorded in the Old Testament, however, are quite conclusive as to the magical practices current of old amongst those nations of antiquity which came in contact with the Jews. Moreover, omens, warnings, dreams, the powers of evil spirits and the protection of good spirits, are recorded in many a narrative of ancient literature; and no doubt, in these particulars, do not contradict the Hebrew records, but tend most directly to maintain and support them. There is little now done in Eastern countries of which a parallel may not be found in the Sacred Books of the Old Testament, in which of course such practices as witchcraft and commerce with evil spirits are expressly condemned. Of course those persons who deny the existence of the Great Creator, and place men on a level with animals, as a consequence reasonably enough reject the truth of the existence of the Supernatural.

These men, as Daniel De Foe wrote, begin "with denying the God that evidently made them. If you pretend to argue from reason, from nature, from visible things to invisible, they reject it all and all for demonstration. They will have Heaven measured geographically, as it were, by scale and compass; . . . they will allow of nothing but what they can see with their eyes and feel with their hands, nor will they believe any such thing as an incomprehensible. They will have all heaven resolved into nature, all religion into reason, and all God into philosophy."[1]

One modern writer, but one of no great point nor depth, remarks that these "magicians and sorcerers *boasted* of a power in consequence of their occult science, and maintained that they were the depositaries of such power." Another, that "the dealer in the 'Black Art' *professed* to possess supernatural powers." A third writer, referring to the particular sorcerers mentioned in the New Testament — Barjesus and Simon Magus — asserts that these two persons "deceived the common people[2] by *asserting* that they possessed the power of working false miracles." Of course the true point at issue is not whether they either *boasted* of owning a power, or *asserted* that they owned it, but *whether this power was truly theirs*, and whether the direct and obvious consequences of their acts—ap-

[1] 'A System of Magic,' &c., p. 121. London: Printed and sold by Andrew Millar—1728.

[2] The Author need not stay to show that it was not the "common people" only who believed in the reality of the Old Testament miracles, in witchcraft and necromancy, but the men of learning amongst the Jews—the Scribes and Pharisees, the interpreters of the law of Moses,—all, in fact, save the Sadducees, who stood apart from their brethren by the rejection of the Supernatural.

prehended by reasonable people, in their right senses and in the light of day—proved that the sorcerers in question actually possessed it. Another remarks—"If these odd exhibitions of spiritualism be true, who cares? If there be spirits, angels and devils, who cares?"[1]

After a laborious inquiry and much careful examination of certain well-selected passages, both in sacred and profane authors—after setting forth a considerable amount of curious and interesting evidence as to the practice of magic, necromancy, and witchcraft,—a contemporary writer in Dr Smith's 'Dictionary of the Bible,' Mr Reginald Stuart Poole, draws

[1] "Who cares? . . . The atheist, in spite of himself, must care; because, even in the faint uncertain light thus furnished, his gloomy dreams must dissolve and perish. That worst enemy of the age, Materialism, will possibly care, because the ground on which its professors have built a temple to their own pride and glory will crumble from beneath them. It will discover that the *ultima Thule* of human knowledge has not yet been reached, and that there may be yet more vouchsafed to the humble investigator than is dreamed of in the proud philosophy of Unbelief; that the forces, which may be weighed, handled, and measured, are not the only forces that circulate through this life-brimming universe. If the excision from the human garden of this foul weed, Materialism—this, in the words of Sir Humphrey Davy, 'cold, heavy, dull, and insupportable doctrine, necessarily tending to Atheism'—be the ultimate result of this new philosophy, motley, chaotic, nay, repulsive as its elements may yet appear, how great a boon to humanity will be from thence evolved!"—'Sights and Sounds,' by Henry Spicer. P. 470. London: 1853.

the following notable conclusion. This is quoted as a fair and faithful sample of the singular method by which so many modern writers deal with the ordinary laws of evidence—when the result of an application of such laws tends directly and forcibly to overthrow their own preconceived and narrow opinions:—

"Our examination of the various notices of magic in the Bible gives us this general result. They do not, as far as we can understand, once state positively that any but illusive results were produced by magical rites. They therefore afford no evidence that man can gain supernatural powers to use at his will. This consequence goes some way towards showing that we may conclude that there is no such thing as real magic; for although it is dangerous to reason on negative evidence, yet in a case of this kind it is especially strong. . . . The general belief of mankind in magic, or things akin to it, is of no worth, since the holding such current superstition, in some of its branches, if we push it to its legitimate consequences, would lead to the rejection of faith in God's government of the world, and the adoption of a creed far below that of Plato."[1]

Anything more pointless, jejune, and poverty-stricken, than this lame conclusion of an elaborate but very partial inquiry, could scarcely be conceived.[2] The wise, the great, and the experienced, law-makers, jurists, judges, and common people, have during previous years, in thousands of cases, directly testified to facts which could not be explained away, and to conclusions which appeared inevitable. The grandiloquent climax of the extract relating to a "rejection of faith in God's government of the world" as a logical consequence of a belief in the reality of magic and the sin of witchcraft, it cannot be denied, closes the sentence most suitably.

Of course every example of the Supernatural, whatever form it may take, must stand on its own merits, and on the testimony forth-

[1] 'Dictionary of the Bible,' vol. ii. p. 205. Article by Reginald Stuart Poole. Ed. 1863.

[2] In a milder form, the Rev. H. N. Oxenham makes a somewhat similar criticism when dealing with the subject of "Christians and the Old Testament," 'National Review,' June 1884, thus: "The somewhat elaborate special pleading in Smith's 'Dictionary of the Bible' appears to me more ingenious than convincing, and it scarcely ever touches any part of the Scriptural evidence except the story of the Witch of Endor."

coming of its reality. But is any person justified in assuming and asserting that the almost universal belief and conviction of mankind as to that subject is a delusion? Is there any good and solid reason for holding that the too general scepticism and disbelief of the present age are alone accurate and reasonable? Were all the various ancient and independent writers who have expressed their conviction of the reality of the Supernatural — Greek, Roman, Hebrew, Christian—under a complete delusion, and the mere victims of phantasies and fancies? Were the laws of the kingdom of Israel against witchcraft and enchantments, so wise and needful, so precise and distinct, enacted only to take captive a cloud, to clip the wings of an idea, or to suppress a fantastic intellectual delusion? Yet this is what some credulous persons would have us accept. In their profound admiration for their own admirers, and in their admirers' mutual profound admiration for them, History, Facts, Experience, and Testimony are one and all swept aside as worthless, and are entirely, but somewhat short-sightedly, put out of all proper consideration.

The following account of a strange incident is taken from a well-known but vaguely written and mystical book,[1] devoted to a consideration of the Oriental wonder-worker:—

"About the end of September my wife went one afternoon with Madame Blavatsky to the top of a neighbouring hill. They were only accompanied by one other friend. I was not present myself on this occasion. While there, Madame Blavatsky asked my wife, in a joking way, what was her heart's desire. She said at random, and on the spur of the moment, 'to get a note from one of the Brothers.'[2] Madame Blavatsky took from her pocket a piece of blank pink paper that had been torn off a note received that day. Folding this up into a small compass, she took it to the edge of the hill, held it up for a moment or two between her hands, and returned saying that it was gone. She presently, after communicating mentally by her own occult methods with the distant Brother, said he asked where my wife

[1] The 'Occult World.' By A. P. Sinnett. Pp. 61-63. London: 1881.

[2] A band of persons who duly study the practice of magic, and who have introduced their so-called "system" into Paris, Vienna, Berlin, and London.

would have the letter. At first she said she should like it to come fluttering down into her lap, but some conversation ensued as to whether this would be the best way to get it, and ultimately it was decided that she should find it in a certain tree. Here, of course, a mistake was made, which opens the door to the suspicions of resolutely disbelieving persons. It will be supposed that Madame Blavatsky had some reasons of her own for wishing the tree chosen. For readers who favour that conjecture after all that has gone before, it is only necessary to repeat that the present story is being told not as a proof but as an incident.

"At first Madame Blavatsky seems to have made a mistake as to the description of the tree which the distant Brother was indicating as that in which he was going to put the note, and, with some trouble, my wife scrambled on to the lower branch of a bare and leafless trunk on which nothing could be found. Madame then again got into communication with the Brother, and ascertained her mistake. Into another tree at a little distance, which neither Madame nor the one other person present had approached, my wife now climbed a few feet and looked all round among the branches. At first she saw nothing; but then, turning back her head without moving from the position she had taken up, she saw on a twig immediately before her face—where a moment previously there had been nothing but leaves—a little pink note. This was stuck on to the stalk of a leaf that had been quite freshly torn off, for the stalk was still green and moist — not withered, as it would have been if the leaf had been torn off for any length of time. The note was found to contain these few words: 'I have been asked to leave a note here for you. What can I do for you?' It was signed by some Thibetan characters. The pink paper on which it was written appeared to be the same which Madame Blavatsky had taken blank from her pocket shortly before."

The basket-trick[1] of the Indian Magicians has been witnessed by hundreds,—by shrewd

[1] It appears that this basket-trick is sometimes performed in England, and that those who accomplish it have learned the secret of their art from certain Oriental magicians. In the 'Standard' of November 18, 1878, a woman who had advertised for four small children to appear at an entertainment, is reported to have stated that "the child was wanted for a trick, to be placed under a basket on a table, and when the basket was raised, the child was gone."

critics as well as several "great thinkers,"—and few persons, save those superficial and shallow ones who profess to believe that it is done by sleight of hand, pretend to explain it except by the conviction that it is wrought through supernatural agency. It is commonly performed on a traditional system by one method, and the circumstances and details do not materially vary in the several accounts received from spectators of such performances.[1]

The Magicians in question invariably aver that it needs no preparation. It can be effected in a room, in a paved courtyard, or on any spot selected at random. This is the accustomed method: A child of either sex, possibly trained for the purpose, is placed upon a spread rug or carpet six or eight feet square,

[1] The late Lord Mayo, Rev. C. J. Serpart, S.J., the late Sir Bartle Frere, Bart., G.C.B., Professor J. Wheeler, M.A., Colonel H. C. B. Barnett; my brother-in-law Colonel Ostrehan of the Bombay Staff Corps; the late Most Rev. Walter Steins, S.J., Archbishop of Bosra in Western Bengal, and the Rev. Father Gannon, sometime Chaplain of St Thomas' Mount, near Madras, have each furnished me with details of such occurrences. Mrs J. B. Speid, in her volume, 'Our Last Years in India,' pp. 107-111, deals with the subject of Oriental Magic, pertinently remarking that "the Mahometans admit the fact of supernatural power, and believe it to be of Satanic origin. They say the secret has been handed down from a remote antiquity, and preserved in certain families alone—an heirloom of unlawful knowledge, gathered in some old time from the Forbidden Tree."

laid upon the floor. Over the crouching child is put a tall conical basket of wickerwork, closely woven, which can be examined inside and out. This being done, the magic-worker, taking and unsheathing a long sharp sword, thrusts it through and through the basket. Sharp screams, as if from a suffering and wounded child, arise; but the performer still thrusts his weapon again and again through the basket, and when the sword is withdrawn it is seen to be covered with blood. Then, when the screams, growing fainter, have ceased, and the victim seems to have sunk exhausted, overcome, and death-stricken, the basket is all at once removed, to find nothing and nobody underneath it. The child has vanished during the process; there being no traces of it, and no signs of blood anywhere apparent within. In a few seconds, however, the child will be seen perfectly unhurt, some distance off, running into the presence of the astonished spectators.

Here follows the account, given almost exactly in the narrator's own words,[1] of another singular performance — so frequently done,

[1] Lieutenant-Colonel Gordon.

however, as to have been witnessed by thousands :—

On one occasion we saw a living shrub spring steadily from a pot filled with earth or mould. Here there was no possibility of deception, for the watchful and critical eyes of at least eighteen or twenty interested spectators were upon the performer. The empty pot, an ordinary common piece of Oriental crockery, was examined; the mould with which it was in our presence slowly filled was examined; the single seed which was deposited therein was handled and examined likewise. So that deception was simply out of the question.

Yet we saw the first sprout of the shrub; we beheld it at once grow upwards and shoot out. We marked the coming and unfolding of the leaves, and in less than a quarter of an hour had before us a perfect tree on a small scale. The performer, having planted the seed, simply waved his hands and stroked the air, as it were, when the various consequent results specified took place before our very eyes.

The following singular parallel to the above,

effected by a person named Coal, is related[1] as having occurred in England, *circa* 1795:—

"Himself being a collier, and leaving work one winter evening about ten o'clock (about twenty-five years since), he went to refresh himself at a little public-house he pointed out to us with his finger, not far from us. He sat down in company with said Coal and six or seven other persons, amongst whom was the landlord of the house, who had been joking and laughing at Coal about his pretended art of conjuration, telling him he believed nothing of it, and that it was all mere imposition. Upon this Coal told the landlord and company,

[1] The above and the following are preserved in a MS. album belonging to Canon F. K. Harford, M.A., of Dean's Yard, Westminster, and are marked: "From the papers of Mr Joseph Beck of Frenchay, my paternal great-uncle, C. J. Harford, M.A., F.S.A. (A.D. 1810).

"Original letter addressed to Edward, Bishop of Gloucester, dated Bristol, 2d August 1703.

"Therein the writer avers as follows:—

"'About thirteen years ago, whilst I was curate to Dr Reid, Rector of St Nicholas, in this city, I began to be acquainted with one Thomas Perks, about twenty years of age, who lived with his father at Mangotsfield, by trade a gunsmith.'

"NOTE.—William Llewellen had in his possession about twenty years ago the book [which] T. Perks made use of in raising spirits, for more than half a year to peruse; it was the fourth book of Cornelius Agrippa's 'Occult Philosophy.'

"That J. Perks died of a consumption at about twenty-one years of age, or rather wasting distemper, thought to be occasioned by the fright he induced from the spirits the last time he raised them, without anything remarkable attending his death."

if they were willing to see a specimen of his art and would sit still and quiet whilst he was performing it, he would soon convince them by causing a tree to grow up before their faces, and men, too, to come in and cut it down. That they promised to sit still; upon which Coal, retiring to a corner of the room, with his back towards the company, seemed to take something out of his pocket; but immediately afterwards he and the whole company very distinctly saw by the light of the candle in the room a small tree, an inch or two thick, gradually rise out of the stone floor of the room, to the height, as he thinks, of three feet, with branches and leaves, and in all respects like a natural tree; that when it was thus grown up, this informant and all the rest of the company saw two little men, each about one foot high, dressed in short jackets, with caps on their heads, their complexion sunburnt, and bearing their axes, begin to cut it down with great celerity, the chips flying about at every stroke; that the tree seemed to fall with great force, and as soon as this was done, the tree, chips, and little workmen went from their sight they knew not how, leaving all the company in a great consternation, except this informant himself, who says he beheld the whole from beginning to end (which he thinks was about half an hour) without any sensible degree of fear, though at the same time he confessed he wished he had been elsewhere. That he observed one of the little workmen, during the gathering up of the chips, to look about very angrily, and that Coal observing the same also, said he was sure some one of the company had taken away and concealed some chips of the tree, but whether it was so, this informant said he does not now well remember.

"The great simplicity and seriousness with which this man delivered his whole narrative was so very remarkable, that there was not the least room to suspect his having any design to impose upon us, or that he himself did not really believe he saw what he related. He assured us he was in no way disordered by liquor at the time it happened, nor does he remember any of the company were so; and said Coal had the character of being a sober serious man, much given to mathematical and other studies, that he died to all appearance of old age, and without anything extraordinary attending his death. STEPHEN PENNY."

But to return. Another well-known Oriental wonder-worker—one whose powers over inanimate matter had made his acts and deeds so remarkable and unaccountable for a long distance round his place of residence, that numbers of persons had arranged to come to witness a fresh exposition of them—was to exhibit those powers to a select gathering which had been formally invited by an Englishman of rank and position.[1] Seven or eight officers were there, some with their wives; a judge; two commissioners; two Catholic priests, one of them a member of the Society of Jesus;[2] several chaplains of the Society for the Propagation of the Gospel, and other Church of England clergymen; three barristers; a physician who is a materialist, disbelieving in the Supernatural altogether; and many other persons, with a few natives and several servants.

[1] A member of the staff of the late Sir Bartle Frere.

[2] The above account is compiled from three letters of eyewitnesses—the main facts of which were admitted to have been "most carefully stated and set forth" by a well-known Jesuit Missionary Apostolic, Archbishop Steins.

The performer or wizard, who dwelt amongst the tribes to the south of Chaibassa, owned a remarkable reputation. The natives who lived near him one and all acknowledged his supernatural powers. The miraculous effects he had often produced had long been spoken of with amazement by those who had witnessed them. He could charm away sickness; and, as some affirmed,[1] he could produce it in any case—though this seemed doubtful to others. In some cases it was distinctly asserted that he *had* undoubtedly produced it, and as undoubtedly removed it; while his power over animals was more than remarkable. He could arrest the footsteps of the most dangerous wild beasts, and compel them to remain stationary at a distance.[2] He could lull to sleep serpents, and so confuse and dazzle tigers (by his gaze, as some asserted, or by the passing

[1] "In 1875, the Chaibassan magician caused a child to have a most severe fever, which so enraged the relations of it that on the following day he took off the sickness, and within a quarter of an hour's incantation, and singing, and humming, the child, though weak, had perfectly recovered."—Letter to the Author from H. B. Williams, M.D.

[2] "I know several persons who have witnessed the effect of the strong will of an oriental magician in disarming wild beasts. One man was perfectly able to keep them at a distance from him by the power and effect of his glance. This has been verified by the personal testimonies of three officers, one of whom belonged to my regiment."—Colonel Le Geyt.

or motions of his hand) that they dropped their stare, turned tail, and fled. He used no instruments, but merely uttered certain *formulæ* or incantations, spreading out his hands and lifting them upwards, or kneeling down with his face to the earth, and, with groans and heavings of the body, seeming to hold conversations with spirits of the earth.

On the present occasion he produced a living tree or plant from an empty pot subsequently in the presence of the spectators, filled with common earth and a seed. The plant began to sprout before the spectators' eyes,[1] as he waved his hand in circles over the earth and pot; the green stem gradually increased, striking upwards; a leaf came out here, another there; until at length the plant seemed perfectly complete. It should be noticed that in the present instance the plant soon faded, withered, and died, and within three hours of its production had fallen to dust. A particular leaf, which one of the spectators had taken possession of as a curiosity and had placed in a used paper envelope,

[1] In two cases, of which I have written accounts, the pot of earth was covered over during the operation; in one instance by a cone of wickerwork, in the other by a silken shawl.

became a few mere particles of what seemed like grey ashes.

But the most remarkable action was that now to be recorded: He borrowed from the wife of one of the English officers a small embroidered empty silk bag, about an inch and a half square, drawn together at its mouth with a ribbon, which had been used to contain a reel of floss silk. It was of Indian make, and there were flowers embroidered on either of its purple sides in gold thread.

Having handed it round for the inspection of the people, who were standing or seated in groups in a kind of circle round about him, it was passed from hand to hand, and then returned to him. He then borrowed from various spectators seven gold coins, upon which he asked all those persons who had thus provided them to make some slight mark, by which they would all be able to identify their particular pieces of money. This was done.

While the pieces of gold were being notified, marked, or otherwise specially identified, he begged one of the spectators, an Indian judge, to elect some place to which the bag, into which the coins were then placed, should be despatched.

The judge mentioned a well-known station, fourteen miles off. This was at once agreed to be too far off for convenience' sake. It could not be easily reached, and no test of reality could be had in a reasonable period.

Another suggested a place some miles off; and a third—a Roman Catholic priest, who laughed at the whole proceedings, and showed his scorn both in words and manner—suggested the extreme topmost branch of a tall and slender tree about fifty yards away.

This the performer accepted, and all eyes were at once turned to the top of the tree in question. Nothing unusual, however, was to be seen there; and in the meantime the performer began his incantations. He sang and cried out, and, crossing his arms, beat one palm of his hand against another. Then he danced and sang again, holding the bag with the marked coins in it between his teeth. Then he knelt down upon the earth, laughed wildly, then cried, then howled with his face towards the ground, and appeared to be in convulsions.

Rising suddenly, however, in a state of calmness, he handed round the bag and coins, which were taken out again and examined by their respective owners, who identified each piece of money. These were placed into the bag once again by the Indian judge and handed to the performer, who took them between the flattened palms of his hands. Now the crisis was to be looked for.

The spectators at once crowded nearer, but were waved back again by the performer.

He continued to rub the bag and the coins with a circular motion of his two hands. Round and round he moved the right over the left hand, between which was supposed to be the bag. Round and round, with a singsong kind of chant, to which he kept moving his feet and swaying his body, he continued to move his hands; and then opening the same, and holding the left one in a kind of cup-shape, he exposed to the gaze of all the curious, watchful, and astonished spectators, seven small and poisonous snakelets—seven little snakes!

He tossed them from palm to palm; they curled together. He lifted up one by its tail and showed it in this direction; then he lifted up another and showed it in that. There could be no doubt that the bag and coins were gone, and that these small snakes were in their place.

Then, to the still more utter astonishment and disgust of the spectators, he took snakelet after snakelet by its tail, lifted it up, threw back his own head, opened his mouth wide, and—swallowed with a gulp and grimace each of the seven living creatures. The eyes of more than forty people had been and were upon him. He had no concealed apparatus. His legs and arms were bare. Saving a tunic and trousers of linen and a shawl, he wore nothing. No one could doubt that the bag and seven coins had gone, that the snakes had been found in their place, and that the performer had actually swallowed the seven small living snakes.

In a moment, as by common intuition all eyes were turned to the tree. Upon the topmost branch, something purple undoubtedly glittered. Most of the onlookers saw it. The performer, turning thither, intimated that thereon the identical bag and coins would be found.

At once one of the officers volunteered to secure it. He went towards the tree, in company with three other Europeans—one, the physician already referred to. Nearing it, and looking up, there without a doubt hung the bag. All saw it as with one glance. With some little difficulty it was reached with the aid of a long lance; and both bag and marked coins were each identified by their respective owners.

Such is my record of facts.

The following account, kindly communicated to me by another friend,[1] was witnessed at Attock in the year 1861, in the presence of five military officers, and of several persons of repute and position :—"After placing some cardboard figures on a cloth spread out on the bare floor of our mess-room, the conjuror, a well-known local magician, began playing upon a reed instrument. In a moment up jumped the cardboard figures, one after the other, and began dancing in time to the music. After this singular performance was over, the operator placed a rupee at one corner of the

[1] It appeared, in part, in one of the English newspapers, having been supplied by an eyewitness to the late Mr J. T. Delane of Serjeant's Inn.

mess-table, and one of the officer's signet rings at the other.[1] Then, upon the music being recommenced, the ring wobbled across the table, clawed the rupee, and carried the prize back to its own corner, as a spider would a fly."

On another occasion an Indian conjuror took a pack of cards, and presenting them *seriatim* to the colonel of the regiment stationed at Attock, bade him mentally select eight cards, which he did. The conjuror then, breathing on the pack, flung the whole on to the table with their faces downwards, and then commenced to play a tune upon a common reed-pipe. In due course one of the cards, the king of hearts, rose and began to dance or posturise at the sound of the strain: then another, the queen of hearts, joined its companion; then two more, one after the other, the king and queen of clubs; and fin-

[1] A somewhat similar incident has been sent to me by the Rev. Canon P. A. Wood, M.A., Rector of Newent, Co. Gloucester, in the following terms: "A man named Hyett of Newent told me that he was in a public-house many years ago, when a stranger came in. This stranger offered, in return for some refreshment given him, to show the party assembled, three or four people, the following exhibition. He put a sixpence down in the centre of the apartment. The coin untouched moved along the floor to the wall, ascended it, and then traversed the ceiling until it arrived over the spot it started from, and then dropped down upon it. Hyett remarked that he was much relieved when the stranger departed."

ally the whole eight court cards in pairs as selected by the colonel. When the music was slow, the motion of the cards was slow; when the music quickened in time, the cards, still keeping time, danced furiously. When the music ceased, the cards at once correspondingly fell flat and motionless.

A Professor of Magic, a Frenchman, was utterly astonished at what was effected, having carefully seen that no apparatus nor contrivance of any sort or kind was used, and acknowledged himself wholly unable to account for what he had seen. He repeatedly offered the oriental magician large sums of money for these avowed secrets: but the tempting bribes were invariably and firmly refused.[1]

Here is another curious feature in this and similar cases. Why should these men, who are apparently the poorest of the poor, prove superior to the power of money? Yet such is invariably the case. Their occult secrets are valued, and are certainly not necessarily disposed of.

[1] "A friend of mine offered the man a large sum of money to impart the secret to him; but though the magician was poor, he promptly and somewhat scornfully rejected the offer—scarcely giving it a moment's consideration."—Note from Mr J. Wheeler.

Here is another example :—

"A man is now in Calcutta, hailing from Delhi, of the name of Burah Khan,[1] who has attained a simply wonderful excellence in the magical art. We ourselves had the pleasure of witnessing some astonishing feats achieved by him a few days ago at the hospitable residence of the Dutt family, of Wellington Square.

"I record only one out of several feats performed by Burah Khan and his company, which consists of three females. One of these, a young woman, was tied with cords most securely. Her hands, feet, and body were so fastened that she could only stir and no more. She was, in fact, deprived entirely of the power to turn her limbs to any use. She was then placed under a conical-shaped cover. People sat close round the skirts of the cloth, which had been thrown over the cover. No means of escape whatsoever was left to the young

[1] The above account was sent to me, in consequence of my communications with Father C. J. Serpart, S.J. of Chaibassa, Bengal, in regard to Oriental magic. I am informed that this well-known necromancer, Burah Khan, whose performances are inexplicable, has received very valuable testimonials of his efficiency in magical experiments and occult powers from the Prince of Wales, Earl de Grey, General Gordon, Sir R. Phayre, the Editor of the 'Pioneer,' Mr Gough, and many others.

woman. But yet, after the lapse of five or ten minutes, the cover was removed, and the woman was found to have disappeared altogether.

"When her name, however, was called out by Burah Khan, her voice was heard from the verandah above.

"This performance took place in the compound of the family residence of our friends the Dutts, and the verandah is in the lofty second storey, forming part of the female apartments. She was there found responding to the call of Burah Khan, to the surprise of everybody present. The woman did not and could not know the topography of the house. But how she extricated herself and made her way high above to the verandah from within the cover, surprises us to such a degree that we cannot account for the feat on any natural grounds. Even if she was furnished with wings, it is inexplicable how she got out of the cover, unseen and unperceived, except on the supposition that some supernatural agency had been employed."

The following account deals with another detail of the wide subject of Oriental magic, and bears a striking resemblance to certain traditionary stories of the Western world :—

TREASURE-RAISING BY MAGIC.[1]

On the evening appointed, the Moroccan and three others, besides myself, left the city as the gates were closed, and reached the appointed place when only two hours were wanting to midnight. After a short rest our guide took us to a fragment of ruin on the southern slope of a hill, where he desired us to remain perfectly silent, and instructed us not to be intimidated by anything we might see or hear. He could not tell precisely what would happen ; but "whatever may transpire (he said) give no utterance to your feelings, whether of fear or of joy, for if you do our labour will not only be in vain, but the treasure itself will have to continue in the bowels of the earth for another century."

He then lit a small lamp and began his incantations. He stood in the centre, and we at the four cardinal points of the compass, only about four or five arm's-lengths from him.

[1] From a narrative by Dr G. A. Herklots.

Then he blew into a small flame the coals he had brought in an earthen cruse, and threw a variety of incense into it. No sooner did the smoke commence to ascend than he made a last imploring sign to us neither to move nor to utter a sound, and then flung himself flat on the ground.

In a few seconds we felt the ground beneath us heave like the waves of the sea, so that we had the greatest difficulty to stand erect; tremendous noises, like the sound of thunder, at the time assailed our ears. By the dim moon we could discern hosts of cavalry in the plain below, galloping up to us with their guns and lances aimed at us. They rushed upon us in the most furious and threatening attitudes, but no sound—not even that of hoofs—could we hear; and horses and riders seemed to vanish when only within a few yards of us. But this strange army thickened; the fierceness of their countenances and their threatening position increased, while, at the same time, we distinctly heard the clangour of chains and other extraordinary noises underground.

Although trembling from fright, we stuck

to our posts, and obeyed to the very letter the Moroccan's instructions.

But one huge mass of rock above us began to stagger, and, as if hurled by some supernatural and invisible force, commenced rolling down with the utmost velocity in the direction of the spot where we stood, threatening us with instantaneous destruction.

The fear of death overcame our love for treasure. We fled with the speed of lightning, and called for mercy at the top of our voice, never stopping nor looking back till we found ourselves in safety.

The Moroccan joined us soon afterwards, giving utterance to the greatest rage and fury, as soon as he could make himself audible; and, had we not been four to one, he would, I believe, have there and then committed murder that night.

The work, he said, was on the eve of being completed, and the stones opened the gap for us to possess ourselves of vast treasures.

"Your cowardice has frustrated all. You might have been wealthy by this time; but beggars you were when you came here, and, through your own incredible folly, beggars you return."

And the following account of a certain magician of the Lebanon is reproduced from the pen of Colonel Churchill, because it helps to complete a series of examples of the magical art as practised in the East:—

THE MAGICIAN OF THE LEBANON.[1]

At times Bashir Talkúk will place a jug between the hands of the persons sitting opposite to each other; then, after the recital of certain passages, taken indiscriminately from the Koran and the Psalms of David, it will move spontaneously round. A stick, at his bidding, will proceed unaided from one end of the room to the other. A New Testament, suspended by a piece of string to a key, will, in the same way, turn violently round of itself. On two earthenware jars being placed in opposite corners of a room, one being empty, the other filled with water, the empty jar will, on the recital of certain passages, move across the

[1] The above is substantially from the pen of Colonel Churchill, whose interesting researches in the Lebanon, and whose curious book on the subject, are so well known.

room; the jar full of water will rise of itself on the approach of its companion and empty its contents into it, the latter returning to its place in the same manner that it came. An egg boiling in the saucepan will be seen to spring suddenly out of the water and be carried to a considerable distance. A double-locked door will unlock itself. There cannot be a doubt that an unseen influence of some kind is called into operation, but of what nature, those may conjecture who like to speculate upon such matters.

But it is in more serious cases of disease or lunacy that the supernaturally-derived powers are called into play. Previous to undertaking a cure he shuts himself up in a darkened room, and devotes his time to prayer and fasting. Fifteen and sometimes thirty days are passed in this state of abstinence and self-denial. At last one of the genii (*Jinn*), described by him to be much of the same appearance as human beings, will suddenly appear before him and demand his bidding. He then states his position, and requires assistance in the case he is about to undertake. The genius replies at once that his request is granted, and encourages him to proceed. The wife of Shaykh Ahmed Talkúd had been for more than two years afflicted with a swelling, which had been mistaken for pregnancy. Shaykh Bushir, after the usual preparatory discipline, passed his hand over her person, and in five minutes she arose perfectly cured. Shaykh Yúsuf Talkúk was brought before him a confirmed lunatic; in two days he returned to his home, perfectly restored to health and reason. You see how shrewd was the apostle of Allah, when he disclaimed the gift of miracle-mongering. That the Shaykh stoutly maintained his intercourse with spiritual agents to be real and effective was unquestionable; and indeed the belief in magic, and in the interposition of an order of unseen creatures in worldly affairs, at the bidding of those who chose to devote themselves earnestly to such intercourse, is universal throughout the entire population of every religion and sect. . . . Instances could be multiplied in which the most extraordinary and unaccountable results have been brought about, by the introduction of individuals who make this communion the subject of their study and contemplation.

But, as the ears of Europeans would only be shocked by assertions and statements which they would not fail of holding to be utterly fabulous and ridiculous, the subject is merely alluded to in these pages, to indicate the existence of a very prominent and prevalent belief in the Lebanon.

But now, to sum up by a narrative with which I have been favoured, with a more remarkable instance of oriental magical powers than any yet given :—

"After witnessing a variety of marvels, so astonishing in themselves that a series of states of wonderment in all our minds followed each succeeding marvel, the conjuring man received his *honorarium*, a very small sum, and prepared to bring the proceedings to an end and depart. But his performances were not quite exhausted. He ended with one which quite overwhelmed us with astonishment.

"Taking out of his pocket a long, thin, silk rope, curled up, however, into several folds, and made into a circle, the ends of which were bound round and round this circle, he threw it on to the ground, where it lay. Alternately humming a wild air, whistling, and singing a monotonous chorus, knocking two sticks together all the time, and dancing to the noise or sound, the tied cord on the ground began to move about, to twist hither and thither, to gyrate in circles, to leap up a couple of feet in the air, and then gradually to unfold itself, till at length it appeared to be only a tangled mass of rope. In a few minutes, however—the performer all the time playing louder, singing more vigorously, knocking his sticks together violently, and leaping about almost in a fury—the tangled mass became unravelled, and the rope was at once seized by him.

"Taking it in his right hand, yet holding one end in his left, and with a vigorous shout and great bodily exertion, he threw it perpendicularly into the air. It fell. He threw it again. Each time it went higher, though it fell several times. All the while he kept muttering, gesticulating, whining, imploring, expostulating, crying. At length—warning the spectators, who were crowding upon him, to keep the circle around as wide and broad as at the outset—he gathered the rope once more into circular coils in his right hand, and with a supreme effort and a wild shriek, threw it up a great height toward the sky. He then all of a sudden pulled it with the greatest violence two or three times. It fell not, however, but on the contrary seemed tightly fastened. With a yell of triumph, half laughing and then shrieking, he at once climbed up the rope, first with one hand then with the other, his legs equally agitated and acting, he rose higher and higher, and then—actually vanished out of sight in the air."

Another correspondent in India writes to me thus:—

"As to the reality of the performance of the oriental jugglers, I can only speak of what I have seen, and testify to the truth of what I have witnessed.[1] The tricks are wholly unlike those done by common conjurors; and conjurors themselves—I know two professional Frenchmen in the conjuring line—admit most frankly that they themselves are quite unable to act

[1] "The childish comments of one of the English newspapers here," writes the above correspondent, "could only have been made by a person deplorably ignorant of obvious facts, and who had never had the opportunity of witnessing what *we* saw. If Mr Jones distinctly *saw* a certain act done, it is no proof that the act was never performed because Brown and Robinson *did not see* it."

the Orientals. And why? Because our Western folks do their tricks by sleight of hand and clever apparatus; whereas the Orientals perform them by the aid of supernatural powers, the *Jinns* or genii of oriental belief.

"I saw a man at Calcutta, in the year 1869, change a staff into a serpent, like the old magicians of Egypt, and then change the serpent back again into a stick. He had no apparatus, no means of concealing anything on his person; for he wore little else than a pair of drawers and a short tunic. With nothing in his hands, for he had handed his staff round to the spectators to examine, he began to mutter and cry out and pray. Then, taking the staff in his left hand, with his right hand he stroked it down several times. In a few minutes it appeared to wave and bend; and then, lo! the staff was gone and behold a snake. There would be no possible doubt about this change, made before the eyes of fifty or sixty acute and carefully-watching people. But what could we say,—what could we think, when the same man changed the same snake into a stick again? I ought to have said that the snake was handled by one of the spectators,

Professor Dowson, a celebrated doctor who was entirely at his wits' end to account for what he then saw."

Several variations of the remarkable narratives and records now set forth have been furnished to me by friends in India, who, one and all, acknowledge the reality of the deeds done.

It is not my intention either to reconcile the accounts one with the other, to add to them, to systematise them, to explain them, or to explain them away. Here I have dealt with facts; and in closing this chapter cannot do better than reproduce that which is set forth just as it was originally written, regarding

THE KOH-I-NOOR DIAMOND.

The following remarkable letter, in which ancient oriental traditions are intertwined with recent history, was published about ten years ago by Mrs Burton, the wife of the celebrated traveller and consul at Trieste, Captain Richard Burton :—

I brought out a book this season called 'The Inner Life of Syria.' That book has met with a success which cannot fail to gratify the most ambitious author, but especially a beginner like me. The reviewers have accorded me terms of praise far beyond my deserts. But they have had a duty to perform to their public, and though they have done it conscientiously, they have also, to their great honour, doubtless on account of my sex, handled my foibles (?) most tenderly and courteously. For this I thank them. The gem of my book, to which the rest is but a framework (to my thinking), is a dream which fills the whole of Chapter xxvii.—some fifty pages. This is the raw which the press has been obliged, however delicately, to touch up. Some say I write like two persons, or with a double nature. Some say one thing, and some another; but all, thank God! gave me credit for honesty, and they are right. It would surprise them to know how many persons who have read my book have come to me and said (privately, of course), "I am so thankful to find that some one else has dreams besides me: I often have them, but I should not dare to own it for fear of being thought foolish." Now I knew that it would be thought foolish, but I could not resist giving the public a specimen of those things to which I, amongst many, am subject. There is some excitement in not being believed when one is speaking the truth, and I am forced to cry with Galileo, "E pur si muove." I have read my dream over carefully, and I have now picked out what I conceive to be the silliest-sounding thing in it—the passage about the Koh-i-noor. I will reduce that to practical common-sense, and I think that I could perform the same office, in course of time, for every line of my dream. I must remark that when I dreamt and wrote in 1871, I was not aware that the Koh-i-noor had any history or antecedents, but as I dreamt so I wrote. Since my dream has been set before the public, one friend sent me 'Rambles and Recollections of an Indian Official,' by Lieutenant-Colonel Sleeman (1835); and another friend, who held a high post in Hyderabad, has given me a quantity of interesting information from various old Indian sources relative to this wonderful ill-fated stone, now in the possession of our Queen.

Do you not see, sir, what a vein of Dreamland runs through our two inspired books, canonical and uncanonical — the Bible and Shakespeare. In the Bible everybody "dreams a dream," and these have become visions and revelations. Shakespeare meant the same thing when he said—

> "And therefore as a stranger give it welcome.
> There are more things in heaven and earth, Horatio,
> Than are dreamt of in your philosophy."

Do you believe that any one man, in one life, could have known so much of human passion, if he had not been inspired by dreams? And do you believe that, because we have become a practical £ s. d. kind of people, that there are no more dreams going about, amongst the highly wrought, nervous, sensitive exceptions who live a higher kind of life? I do believe it—nay, I knew it.

I will now give you the true history of the Koh-i-noor as I believe my dream was given me to do. I know how the English nation glory in the possession of the thing, simply because it is worth a million—how reluctantly they would part with it. I know they like a veil to be drawn over their hidden sores, and abhor the knife and cautery, therefore, if I would contribute my mite to saving our country a disaster, I must do so at the risk of my own popularity. But if, after reading it, Englishmen agree with me, let me tell them that there are two ways of getting rid of it. To break it up, sell it, and give the proceeds to the poor would be the Eastern way of dispelling the ill-luck. My way would be to sell it to Russia for less than its worth (£800,000), pass our ill-luck on to our bugbear, and use the money to send our future king out to India as an emperor should go. But it is not for me to suggest, but only to give its history.

The Koh-i-noor, or "Mountain of Light," is the largest and most celebrated diamond in the world, and is famous throughout the East as the "Accursed Stone" that brings misfortune and eventual destruction upon the dynasty of every successive royal possessor of it. In the East there is a belief as to good or evil fortune attending particular precious stones. It was the same in England in the reign of Elizabeth and the first James, and Shakespeare alludes to this belief in one of his minor poems; but the modern £ s. d. Englishman rejects the absurdity, despite the fact that evil fortune has actually always followed the possessor of this particular gem, showing how curiously actual fact co-operates with superstitious theory. The Koh-i-noor was first discovered in the mines of Golconda about the year 1650, so that it has cursed the world for 225 years. The famous Mir Jumla was the farmer of the diamond mines, and the king's chief minister, a Persian who had been brought young to India and rose by rapid gradations of power, and was famous for the sagacity of his plans and the ruthless cruelty with which he carried them out. The poor people under compulsory labour had to give their services for a bare subsistence to the public farmer of the mines, and under Mir Jumla their condition was desperate, and this tempted them occasionally to elude the vigilance of their taskmaster and secrete a stone if they could. The cruelties inflicted on them on the smallest suspicion of such a fault rendered the mines a perpetual scene of horror, especially under Mir Jumla; and it is supposed that some frightful act of fiendish brutality occurred at the finding of the Koh-i-noor which was cursed by the innocent victim,—a curse which ever since, according to the natives of India, has remained attached to it and its possessors. Certain it is that before the King of Golconda had long been in possession of it he quarrelled with Mir Jumla, who in return treacherously invited the Mogul Emperor of Delhi, Aurungzebe, to invade his master's territory, promising to join him with the whole of the forces under his command. This he did, and the King of Golconda had to sue for peace, which was only granted by Aurungzebe on his giving him one of his daughters in marriage, making over to him a large portion of his treasures, including the Koh-i-noor, as well as a considerable slice of his territories, and consenting to hold the rest as a fief of the Great Mogul Empire. Some time after the King of Golconda thought he saw a favourable opportunity to recover his territories, rose against his oppressor, and lost all the rest of his kingdom—nay, all that he possessed. Mir Jumla died a miserable death of disease in exile. Aurungzebe, the second royal possessor of the Koh-i-noor, was at the time of getting it in the zenith of his power, but immediately trouble after trouble rained upon him, and accumulated till he died in 1707. After his death a war began amongst his progeny. The first who succeeded him, the third royal possessor of the Koh-i-noor, was Shah Alum, who died in 1712, five years after his succession. The next king of Delhi, the fourth possessor of the Koh-i-noor, met the same fate in 1719, in the course of which year two other occupants of the throne (sixth and seventh possessors of the Koh-i-noor) passed in the same way thence to the grave.

So in twelve years from the death of Aurungzebe, five princes of his line who had ascended the throne and possessed the Koh-i-noor, and six others who had been competitors for it, had come to grief. Moreover, the degraded state of the royal authority during his period had introduced an incurable anarchy, and a disposition in all the governors of provinces to shake off their dependency on the head of the empire. The next king of Delhi, the eighth possessor of the Koh-i-noor, was the Emperor Mahmoud Shah, under whose reign the once great empire of Aurungzebe speedily fell to pieces. He succeeded in 1719, twelve years after the death of Aurungzebe, being the son of Akter, youngest son of Shah Alum, the son and immediate successor of Aurungzebe; and it was in 1739 that the final blow was given to his authority, and his ill-fortune culminated in the capture of Delhi by the celebrated Nadir Shah, who in that year invaded India, and after defeating the army of Shah Mahmoud at Kurnaul, entered as a conqueror into the capital. Then, in consequence of hostile acts of some of the people, he delivered over the whole city to massacre and pillage, and from the dawn of light till the day was far advanced, without regard for age or sex, all were put to the sword by his ferocious soldiery. Fifty-eight days afterwards, Nadir Shah commenced his march homewards, carrying with him treasure amounting to twenty millions sterling, jewels of enormous value, and the Koh-i-noor, which was considered by the Persian conqueror to be his greatest prize. Nadir Shah, ninth possessor of the Koh-i-noor, was no more fortunate with it than the previous owners had been; for after his return to Persia, in the height of his glory, everything went wrong with him, and he was shortly afterwards assassinated, leaving no heir to his kingdom; while Ahmed Abdallee, chief assassin and once his trusted officer, went off, carrying with him most of Nadir Shah's treasure, and amongst it the Koh-i-noor. He meant to found a kingdom for himself out of the territories forming what is known as Affghanistan. The dynasty which Abdallee, the tenth possessor of the Koh-i-noor, founded, having been crowned at Kandahar in the year 1747, met with the same fate that attended the dynasties of all the possessors of this celebrated stone. His son Timour, after a short and inglorious reign, left his throne to his eldest son Humayoon, twelfth possessor of the Koh-i-noor, who fell into the hands of his next brother Zemaun Shah, the thirteenth possessor of the Koh-i-noor, who in turn fell into the hands of another brother, Mahmoud, who also put out his eyes and succeeded him, but who was in his turn soon conquered by another brother, Shah Shooja, afterwards our Affghan ally. This last did not long maintain his position, and after various vicissitudes, fled to the Punjaub with his brother Zemaun Shah, the thirteenth possessor of the Koh-i-noor, of which Shah Shooja was fifteenth and last Mohammedan possessor. His fate is known to all who have heard or read the story of our fatal expedition to Cabul and its consequences, including Shah Shooja's end. Shah Shooja being now dependent on Runjeet Sing, the then sovereign of the Punjaub, for his very existence, soon found himself compelled to yield to the requirements of this powerful and most unscrupulous potentate, who insisted upon the Koh-i-noor being given up to him. The captive prince had no alternative, and yielded, when the great Sikh potentate became the sixteenth possessor of the Koh-i-noor. At that time no native sovereign of India was so great as Runjeet, and no kingdom seemed more likely to last than the great Sikh monarchy he had founded; but by a curious coincidence, the same ill-fate that had always followed the possessor of the Koh-i-noor pursued it into this great family. Runjeet himself died in his prime, and was succeeded in 1839 by his son Kurruck Sing, who died by poison the following year. Before the funeral ceremonies were completed, his son was purposely killed by a falling beam. A competition for the throne (now vacant) ensued between the widow of Kurruck Sing and a reputed son of Runjeet Sing, named Shere Sing, who, though born in wedlock, had been stigmatised by his father as illegitimate. Shere Sing, however, succeeded; but his triumph was of short duration. Near the close of 1843 he was assassinated, and this led to widespreading anarchy, culminating in the two successive wars with the British, that of 1846 and 1848-49—ending in the final annexation of the Punjaub by the British, and the acquisition by them of the celebrated diamond of the Koh-i-noor. The natives, with their belief as to the peculiar properties of the stone, prophesied what would happen. The East India Company broke up almost directly after the "accursed" had entered their hands. When Lord Dalhousie, the Viceroy of India, presented it to her Majesty, 3d July 1850, it was considered the most sinister circumstance that could have befallen our Royal family by all loyal natives. Lord Dalhousie did not live very long, and died a miserable death just as he might have expected to be raised to the highest honours of the State. The Duke of Wellington, who gave the first turn to the cutting, died three months after. We then lost Prince Albert, and I do not believe we any of us knew what we were losing until he was gone. When my friend, the then Collector of Hyderabad, was sitting with the Nawab Mahmoud Khan—the former minister of the State, and one of the Queen's most loyal subjects after the conquest of the province—he informed the Nawab of the stone's destination. The latter spat upon the ground, and with an expression of horror uttered the usual Mohammedan exclamation under the circumstances: "Toba Nosbilla! Repentance in the Name of God! Are they going to send that accursed thing to our Queen? May she refuse it!" All natives spit with an exclamation of horror whenever they hear it mentioned. It is impossible for me to go into the cause, nor perhaps ought I to say how, according to Eastern theory, the curse might be averted. Nevertheless I have done so. May I ask if, barring £ s. d., our position or prestige has progressed or declined since we became the possessor of the accursed stone? I ask all non-£ s. d. Englishmen whether they consider the Koh-i-noor a comfortable ornament for the English crown, or a pleasant legacy for our most deservedly popular and well-beloved Prince of Wales.

Will the press absolve me from utter imbecility in my dream? Here is the most ridiculous item. Our ancestors were not so sceptical, and many a noble foundation or splendid action has had its origin in beliefs, or if you like it better, in superstitions, of a not very dissimilar kind.

ISABEL BURTON.

14 Montagu Place, Montagu Square,
September 25, 1857.

MIRACULOUS INCIDENTS AND MARVELLOUS CURES

CHAPTER VIII.

MIRACULOUS INCIDENTS AND MARVELLOUS CURES.

A BELIEF in the Supernatural in general, and in miracles in particular—even those recorded in Holy Scripture—is now regarded by many as an act of mental weakness;[1] while a general belief in the Supernatural, as it was current amongst all the nations of antiquity, is held to be an obvious but deplorable superstition. On the new theories, which some maintain to be so enlightened and truly philosophical, little is explained, while everything is explained away.

[1] Many writers—as some recent literature on the subject proves—are now ashamed to acknowledge that they believe in the truth of miracles, and often humbly and most laboriously apologise for appearing to do so. If they make a statement, which on the surface seems to admit the reality of miraculous occurrences, they take good care in the succeeding sentence to contradict it, or weaken it by some antagonistic admission or assertion.

There are, in fact, three kinds of objectors to the reality of miracles: the popular, who take their opinions, without much examination, from the newspapers and current serials; the scientific, from persons well enough satisfied with themselves, who lay down scientific dogmas, excluding everything supernatural, often with remarkable dogmatism, considerable arrogance, and no little nescience; and the experimental—those who have never seen a miracle, or any example of the Supernatural, and who apparently would only be convinced by an examination of a spirit under a microscope, or by the vivisection of an apparition by a dissecting-knife.

Some so-called "scientific" people—whom their friends often describe as "great thinkers"—stand forward either to deny the existence and power of the Maker of heaven and earth, or else to criticise the laws of creation, and to prescribe limits to His liberty of action. They assume the complete and absolute omnipotence of Science. The language of Nature, as they understand it at the moment,—for this language varies, and is often misconceived and misunderstood,—is made to silence the voice of

God.[1] Some people, moreover, are constantly speaking about "the facts which Science in the future may bring to light;" but we are certainly no nearer to the discovery of any law by which the raising of a dead man, like Lazarus, to life again, could take place without miraculous intervention, than the world was two thousand years ago. Science, with all the boasting and mutual admiration of its votaries, has not discovered, and is not at all likely to discover, any law by which any man can make a dead man to live again.

But what does the Almighty's divine reve-

[1] As an ancient writer well remarks,—"The Devil's business, and all his aim, is not to destroy, but to damn mankind; not to cut him off, and put his Maker to the trouble of a new creation, but to make him a rebel, like himself: and even this he is fain to bring to pass by subtlety and art, making use of man against man, arming flesh against spirit, and setting nature in defiance of the God of nature; and this by secretly corresponding with some of the worst and vilest abandoned wretches that he can find; instructing them, and teaching them his own methods, and so making them traitors to their own kind; drawing them in to engage with him in ruining the souls and bodies of others, and concerting measures with these corrupted instruments, whose principles he has first debauched, that they may act and do for him, and in his name, all the mischief which he finds it is not for his purpose to do himself.

"While he thus lies behind the curtain himself, and is not seen, or at least not publicly, he corresponds most punctually with these agents, empowering and directing them, by a great variety of hellish arts and contrivances, to work wonders, amuse and impose upon mankind, and carry on all his affairs for him. And this is what we call the black art."

lation teach—a revelation imperfect of old, but definite, clear, and complete under the Christian dispensation?

It teaches, firstly, that in the natural order man consists of body, soul, and spirit, created after, and made in, the image of God; that man is destined to live here for a while, but for ever hereafter. It further, and secondly, teaches that God Almighty hath made man lord of the whole earth: "The earth hath He given to the children of men."

In the supernatural order, man, on his part, acts towards God by prayer, adoration, homage, sacrifice, faith, hope, love, and obedience. God Almighty, on His part, acts towards man by grace, revelation, the voice of conscience, the ministry of the Church, and by appointed sacramental operations.

Both the Natural and Supernatural are directly from God, Who reminds man, through things around him which are seen, of the Supernatural and of that which is not seen.

Now what is a miracle?

According to Thomas Aquinas, "A miracle is an act performed by God out of the ordinary course of nature."

All miracles may be divided into two classes :—

1st, Raising a dead person to life belongs to the first class, because in the ordinary order of nature the event never occurs.

2d, Restoring a person to health all of a sudden, by a word spoken, by a deed done, by a command given, or by delegated authority duly exercised, belongs to the second class; because, though not at all unnatural that sick persons should recover from their sicknesses, it *is* unnatural that they should recover all at once, suddenly, and without any apparent cause.

Popular objections against miracles, founded either on prejudice or want of information, may be passed by.

As to scientific objections, it may be reasonably and properly enough asked, "Is not the Author of the natural order its obvious Superior and Lord?" For surely the maker of a law can unmake it, or suspend its operations, as and when he wills: though the suspension of a law does not alter that law.

Moreover, the conclusions of Science are at best but probable and conditional. Many such conclusions in the past having turned out to be unfounded and erroneous, are rejected even by the scientific: many in the present—made most dogmatically by equally confident people —will no doubt prove to be equally untrustworthy.

Furthermore, when it is maintained that change implies contradiction in Almighty God, it may be very properly and reverently answered that, as experience too truly teaches us all, change is ever in the creature and in things created, not in the Eternal and Uncreated. And when it is still further objected that we cannot rightly tell what a miracle is unless we know all the laws of nature, our reply, simple and reasonable enough, is, that we know quite enough to be perfectly convinced that raising a dead man to life, or changing water into wine, or feeding a great multitude with a few loaves and fishes, or cleansing an incurable leper, are each and all miracles. The Catholic Church, the Greek Church, theologians of the Established Church, and many most eminent philosophers and authors,[1] are witnesses of their reality.

[1] "With the accumulative evidence of these Churches [*i.e.*, the Catholic and Greek], with the collective mass of intellect which adorns

But, independent of the long line of remarkable miraculous interventions recorded in Church history,—examples of which have been noted in every age since the Day of Pentecost,[1]—the present existence of the Jews, an independent nation scattered amongst other nations, itself partakes of the supernatural and miraculous. So, too, does the existence of Christianity.

On this point here is the forcible and profound utterance of St Augustine of Hippo :—

"Christianity was either founded by miracles or it was not. If it was, then miracles exist. If it was not, this is the greatest of miracles, that a religion opposed to human prejudice and so much resisted should, without the help of miracles, have made and held

them, with some names upon whose reputation the sun never sets, and with such names as the following as independent witnesses—Lord Bacon, Hooker, Laud, Grotius, Bull, Pearson, Locke, Butler, Campbell, Paley, Leibnitz, Burton, Whately, Babbage, and many others—if you pretend to yield to authority and to submit to intellect, to bend to great names, then you must believe in miracles."—'Five Discourses on Miracles,' &c., by Very Rev. D. Gilbert, p. 44. London: 1866.

[1] For example, the miracles wrought by the apostles and recorded in the New Testament, the appearance of the Cross of Constantine, the events which occurred when Julian the Apostate boastingly endeavoured to rebuild the Temple at Jerusalem,—recorded by Cyril of Jerusalem, Gregory of Nazianzum, and Ambrose of Milan,—are all supernatural events in question.

its progress in the world. If a man will only admit personal evidence he is unreasonable, asking for himself that which he denies to others."

As to the power of working miracles remaining in the Christian Church, evidences of which have been known in every past age since the Day of Pentecost, in the lives and actions of the saints as well as by the instrumentality of sacraments and sacramentals, the following is certainly a reasonable and careful statement of the case :—

A power to work miracles is as formally granted to the Church in the Gospel as any other of her powers. That power has never been revoked, although from time to time sin may have suspended the exercise of it. The arbitrary conditions under which modern writers in general would have miracles to be, are, to my idea, extremely profane. For instance, we are told that the purpose of a miracle must be obvious, otherwise the manifestation is useless; again, that it must not be puerile; again, that the end must be a good one. Such canons are as stupid as profaneness usually is. How can we know sufficiently of God's purposes that they should be obvious? It is not the general character of God's purposes to be obvious. They are mostly obscure, to be sought out of them that love and fear Him. Besides, a miracle is not necessarily a manifestation. The miracles of the Conception and Resurrection were both secret; *and a miracle, as well as all other proofs of Divine sanction or interference, is not meant to convince where there is no moral preparation of the heart.* Then, to say a miracle must not be puerile is unmeaning, for who is to judge of the puerility? And if the fact of superhuman agency be ascertained, what is to be done then? The agency may have been exerted in what a man chooses to call a puerile way; but such an agency being proved on credible testimony, the puerility of the manner, or of the occasion, will not subvert the fact. Let a man reverently consider whether the circumstances of some of our Blessed Lord's gracious miracles would not be found to militate against his arbitrary canons, if natural good feeling and a happy inconsistency did not lead him to shrink from applying his principles to the Gospel narrative, to which those principles, if sound, should be equally applicable. Men talk at random, and lay down canons without at all seeing where they lead them. But men say that the legend-loving times were times of greedy and facile credulity, and that this accounts for the miracles. *Of course, faith in miracles will multiply miracles, for it is faith which works them.* To him that hath shall be given; that is the Gospel rule in all things. *Times of strong faith, therefore, will naturally be times of many miracles.* It is one of the ways in which such faith is rewarded. People say we should be convinced more if a miracle were worked in these unbelieving days. The Christian answer is simple, and, of course, admits of being sneeringly put. The Church cannot work miracles because of your unbelief. You first tie her hands, and then ask her to work. The Divine influence withdraws in hard-hearted times, and will not manifest itself. It withdraws itself, partly out of chastisement to you and partly out of mercy, lest, by slighting it, you should incur a still more grievous chastisement. *The demanding of a sign is an infallible proof of a temper unfit to receive a sign. The Jews were bid to look at the past. So are you.* Then men will say, "But what is the good of a miracle if it cannot be worked when it is wanted, in order to our conviction?" I answer, that *it does not appear that the end of miracles is to convince.* Our Saviour's miracles do not appear to have convinced. The Christian evidences do not convince without a moral temper going beforehand. Just as the Devil was permitted to work miracles then, so as to cloud our Lord's miracles, put an excuse into the mouths of the unbelieving, and be a trial to faith, so might he be permitted in these later times to set abroad false legends and lying rumours, the discovery of whose falsehood would cast a slur upon the truth. There are two kingdoms in the world ever at work to enlarge their borders; and what is done in the kingdom of light is forthwith imitated, in a fearful way, in the kingdom of darkness.

As to the general question, there is nothing more illogical and unhistoric than for a Christian writer to endeavour to define the period when miracles ceased. All such attempts are idle, profane, and arrogant, arising out of a sceptical spirit, and, as a consequence thereof, are much to be deprecated. For they are well enough calculated to delude and mislead the shallow. The miracles of our Lord, Who had expressly declared that His followers should work even *greater* works than His, were succeeded by the miracles of the apostles. These, in their turn, by those wrought during the earliest ages of the Christian Church. History abounds with such. It is impossible to take up any volume by a faithful Christian historian in which these tokens of the power of God are not either described or alluded to; while the lives of the saints,—from those of apostolic times, through every succeeding age down to the present day, from the raising to life again of Dorcas by St Peter to the marvellous and manifold cures wrought at Lourdes only yesterday,—abound with tokens of the presence of the Comforter in the Church, and of unmistakable evidences of the continuous fulfilment of the gracious and consoling pledge which our Blessed Saviour made to His followers.

Or, to take another detail of the Supernatural, what can be more striking than evidence both of history and tradition[1] to the punishment for Sacrilege?

In England, as elsewhere, as the observant inquirer may readily enough discover for himself, the punishment for Sacrilege still goes on. The solemn curse pronounced of old against all who should seize upon lands and properties given to the Almighty, and formally consecrated to His service, still works—even new families getting possession of abbey lands feeling its force. Let those who doubt this fact, or slur over the deeply interesting records of history, or the telling and forcible traditions of any particular locality, study them once anew, so that no mistake be made. Let the fate of those noble families in the past, which, co-operating with the Tudor monarchs,[2]

[1] Sacrilege has been defined both as "an invading, stealing or purloining from God, any sacred thing, either belonging to the majesty of His Person, or appropriate to the celebration of Divine service;" as also, "a violating, misusing, or a putting away, of things consecrated or appropriated to Divine service or the worship of God; and hath many branches—viz., of time, of place, of persons, and of functions."—From the definition of St Thomas Aquinas.

[2] "As the nobility spoiled God of His honour by parting those things from Him, and communicating them to lazy and vulgar persons, so God to requite them hath taken the ancient honours of nobility, and communicated them to the meanest of the people—to shopkeepers, taverners, tailors, tradesmen, burghers, brewers, and graziers."—MS. Letter of Sir Henry Spelman, *circa* 1630.

have participated in sacrilege, be specially searched out and carefully noted. Let the sad history of individuals be traced out and fully faced. Here may surely enough be read "sermons in stones."

Who has not heard, for instance, of the Curse of Cowdray? Who has forgotten the striking incidents which occurred to Sir Anthony Browne? He had been specially favoured by the Tudors, and his coffers were enriched to overflowing with Church plunder. In the abbot's hall of a once grand and stately religious house—from which the monks had been cruelly and illegally cast out—a feast was being held, as is recorded, the first great feast or house-warming given by this popular knight on taking possession of the consecrated building. A crowd had gathered, and the guests from far and near were numerous. When the feast was going on, an outcast monk, uninvited and unexpected, is reported to have made his way through the assembled gathering, and boldly walking up to the chair where sat Sir Anthony, cursed him to his face with all the force and solemnity of the ancient and accustomed malediction.

He ended his forcible sentences thus: "By fire and by water your race shall come to an end, and it shall utterly perish out of the land." Two hundred and fifty years passed, and then that curse was exactly fulfilled. Cowdray House was completely destroyed by fire; and soon afterwards the eighth Lord Montagu and his two nephews, his heirs, were drowned.

No matter to what part of England or to what county the reader may belong, if a careful historical and genealogical investigation be made, it will be almost invariably found that the possession of monastic lands has brought no blessing with them. Swineshead Abbey in Lincolnshire, Glastonbury, Fountains, the Cistercian Abbey of Thame Park, St Edmundsbury, Melrose, and St Alban's—one and all tell the same tale. He who runs may read.

For example. The Curse of Tinterne is believed to have been experienced on the battle-field of Moodkee. Newstead Abbey—I purposely avoid details—can scarcely be said to have brought other than sorrow and misery upon its various owners. Again: in two centuries and a half no less than twenty-one different possessors have owned Leeds, in Kent; and eleven families as owners have there come and gone. Repton Abbey, in Derbyshire—where one Thacker, to whom it had been granted, pulled down the church on a Sunday in the early part of Queen Mary's reign, saying, "If the unclean nest is thoroughly destroyed, the birds can scarcely build again,"—brought no blessing nor peace to its possessors. Unrest followed temporal loss; the deaths of heirs succeeded to the ravages of fire; while lunacy or unusual loathsome diseases filled up the cup of bitterness. The history of the owners of these places sets forth only too forcibly the punishment for sacrilege.[1]

[1] "For the most part, so unhappy have been the purchasers of Church lands, that the World is not now to seek for an argument from long experience to convince it that though in such purchases men have usually the cheapest pennyworth, yet they have not always the best bargains. For the holy thing has stuck fast to their sides like a fatal shaft, and the stone has cried out of the consecrated walls they have lived within for a judgment on the head of the sacrilegious intruder, and Heaven has heard the cry and made good the curse. So that when the heir of a blasted family has risen up and promised fair, and perhaps flourished for some time upon the stock of excellent parts and great favour, yet at length a cross-event has certainly met and stopped him in the career of his fortunes, so that he has ever after withered and declined, and in the end come to nothing, or to that which is worse. So certainly does that which some call 'blind superstition' take aim when it shoots a curse at the sacrilegious person." —'Sermons by Robert South "At the consecration of a Church."' London: 1692.

In two inland English counties with which I myself am well acquainted, the reasonable theory that punishment follows sacrilege (which Sir Henry Spelman[1] set forth with such power—illustrating the theory by undoubted facts and a record of occurrences,) has obtained many distinct examples of support during the last two centuries, while many who are thoughtful and observant have duly noted them; facts known to every person in the locality in question, and generally acknowledged to be such, cannot be overlooked nor ignored.

To give names and places; to set forth dates of misfortunes, and to describe the kinds of death undergone; to point the moral and proclaim the obvious and patent consequences of distinct sacrilege, would be, of course, to give pain[2] to many still living,—friends and

[1] 'The History and Fate of Sacrilege.' By Sir Henry Spelman, Knt. London: 1698.

[2] "I hesitate to give you names and places where punishments for Sacrilege, coming down to the present day, are still experienced; because obviously *the families still suffering often feel their position most acutely*. But I undertake to show, from the history of the last three centuries, that in this county the owners of monastic lands—a curse upon the alienators of which was solemnly pronounced—find that the consequences of the curse still track them; and that, while children suffer for the sins of their forefathers, Sacrilege has seldom gone unpunished."—Letter from a Norfolk Rector to the Author.

connections of those upon whom the shadows of loss and suffering have from time to time fallen, and who are reasonably enough very sensitive on the point, however much they may profess to deny the Supernatural, and to maintain that sacrilege goes unpunished.

A certain ecclesiastical foundation, with chapel, hall, and buildings, had remained untenanted for nearly two centuries. The buildings, used only by tillers of the soil, and not for many years as a residence, had become dilapidated and were fallen into ruin. The chapel, an architectural gem of First Pointed work, had been miserably desecrated.

About forty years ago, however, the property was purchased by a retired merchant, and after a considerable outlay, turned into a comfortable and convenient dwelling-house. But the new owner did not live to inhabit it for more than two years. It was then sold and conveyed to another. He in turn soon passed away, and his son and heir died prematurely. Two tenants in succession then inhabited the place, and both were soon carried to their fathers,—one by a sudden and shocking death, the other at an early age, and by a painful and wasting disease.

In another case, that of an old religious house of abbatical rank, and its adjacent lands, these never once descended from father to son, through two long centuries and a half. All kinds of misfortunes and sorrows met various members of the noble family which had obtained the lands in question soon after the Tudor changes. Fire, and early death, and heavy losses overtook them during the Civil Wars. Though they had largely benefited in things temporal by the changes which overthrew the altars under Edward VI., they suffered still more sorely by those further changes effected by the usurpation of Cromwell when the throne was overturned and the monarch martyred. In later times, loathsome diseases, the failure of heirs-male, sudden deaths, and pecuniary losses have afflicted them, as also the more modern race to whom it had been transferred and now belongs. Its members, as one of them stated to myself, "have rather vegetated than prospered."

In a third case, that of another religious house for nuns, every generation of two distinct races who have owned it, has known unusual losses and remarkable sorrow. Sudden deaths, bankruptcy and financial ruin, wasting sickness, impotence of mind and imbecility, and long courses of extreme bodily suffering, have followed in sad and solemn succession, as their history, duly investigated, only too truly sets forth. The only son of a more recent owner, who was my friend and contemporary at Oxford—the direct heir to two now extinct baronetcies—having himself done the greatest credit to his intellectual and moral training, and after taking high honours at the University, died of brain fever, brought on by over mental work. At his home the old chapel of the nuns had long been the modern dining-room—a sufficiently leading and typical change of such changes in general.

Out of forty-two adventurers enriched with the spoils of the so-called "Reformation"—and to whom abbey lands were so liberally granted as a bribe for their aid and support by Henry the Eighth and his son—eight only at the present time have representatives in the male line. Upon these eight families, however, various terrible and direct judgments have fallen; while in some notable cases a dark shadow still lies upon their paths. Thirty-six of the families of the sacrilegious peers referred to have become utterly extinct. Their place knows them no more. They have one and all died out.

The history of the Veres, Earls of Oxford, to cite another example, is well known. In Tudor times they obtained monastic lands. In them was vested the office of Great Chamberlain of England, which had been theirs from the days of Henry I., but which soon afterwards passed, through the Lady Mary, sister of Edward Vere, to the family of Willoughby de Eresby, and in due course the Veres in the male line became extinct. The Ratcliffes, Earls of Sussex, the family of Hastings, Earls of Huntingdon, the Dacres' family of Gillesland, the Scroopes of Yorkshire, the Ferrers, the St Johns of Battersea, the Berkeleys of Gloucestershire, with many others, suffered because of sacrilege. This fact is almost indelibly imprinted upon various pages of English history.

"Even now," as a faithful and outspoken

writer[1] remarked, "after centuries of legalised sacrilege, a belief that it never thrives is strong amongst our peasantry. Abbey sites are 'unlucky'; abbey buildings are 'haunted'; it is 'unfortunate' to have anything to do with them—they will not 'stick by' any family. On the supposition that the hypothesis which we are supporting is ungrounded and superstitious, how impossible is it, and must it remain, to account for this general belief! Allow it to be the voice of God, and it ceases to be inexplicable. Therefore we conclude with St Ambrose that what is above nature proceeds from the Author of nature."

The following account of a royal apparition comes to me from Russia. Its details have never as yet been published:—

In the winter of 1881 the spirit of the late Czar is said to have been seen thrice in the Kazan Cathedral.[2] Except the dim lights from the silver lamps, the sacred building in question was almost in darkness; and on the

[1] The late Rev. John Mason Neale, D.D.

[2] I am indebted to a Russian ecclesiastic for the above. His account has been considerably shortened. I have since learned that "this apparition created a deep sensation amongst all classes," and that "the details of the affair, though inquired into, were carefully hushed up."

first occasion, only the custodian of the same was within it, pacing its solemn aisles in perfect silence. Suddenly, at midnight, as he was reciting his accustomed office, he asserted that he distinctly saw the royal figure, pale and sorrowful, glide out of the vestry, take a long taper, kindle it from one of the lamps, and then proceed to light the candles at the Holy Table within the screen. Then, standing near the sacred doors of the sanctuary and turning towards the nave, its voice was heard—"My son, come to me. Yours shall be the same fate as your father's," and then it suddenly vanished. The candles were left alight. On the following night, the external doors having been specially examined beforehand and the building carefully searched, the same apparition appeared to two persons—to the custodian already referred to, and another ecclesiastic who had remained with him. On the next night, in addition to a military watch outside the cathedral, a special sentinel was enjoined to keep guard inside its chief portal. At midnight the apparition a third time appeared, lit the tapers as before, uttered the same warning words, and then likewise vanished. The sentinel is said to have been "afterwards found half dead with fright."[1]

I now turn to certain recent events, obviously miraculous, which, however remarkable in themselves, are perfectly well authenticated, and which certainly deserve more respectful consideration[2] than they have yet received in the present sceptical age. It is, of course, easier to scoff and to sneer than to disprove obvious miraculous facts.

"You have heard," wrote Bishop Ryan of Buffalo, in America,[3] "of Bois d'Haine and Louise Lateau. Well, with the good Rector of the college, the Rev. Father Pulsers, we started on Thursday evening, and about dusk we reached that out-of-the-way place, now, however, world-renowned, and visited by strangers of every tongue and nation.

"I can only say that I carried the most Holy Sacrament to her on Friday morning, accompanied by a crowd of pious pilgrims, more than enough to fill twice over her little

[1] 'Guardian' newspaper, January 1882.

[2] For further details see 'Louise Lateau, the Ecstatica of Bois d'Haine,' by Dr Le Febre: London—Richardson, 1872; and 'Our Blessed Lady of Lourdes,' by F. C. Husenbeth, D.D., Provost of Northampton: London—Washbourne, 1870.

[3] From an original letter of the Bishop.

room. After administering to her the Blessed Sacrament, whilst she in ecstasy communed with her God, I uncovered the bleeding wounds of her hands to the gaze of all present, and looked myself in wonder and a species of awe, now at her ecstatic countenance, now at the blood flowing from the open wounds on the back of her hands.

"At ten o'clock I returned again, this time with the parish priest alone, and had this time the opportunity of seeing her and speaking with her, and examining the *stigmata*, not now bleeding, but fresh and open as if a nail had actually pierced her hands.

"Again at three o'clock P.M., a crowd had assembled, but this time men, for women are now excluded at this hour, much, indeed, to the disgust of several ladies who had come from a long distance. But there were there besides ourselves physicians and distinguished gentlemen, lay and clerical, from different parts of Belgium, France, and Germany: and there she lay in ecstatic rapture insensible to all around her, the blood flowing profusely from her hands. We recited prayers and psalms of the Divine Office: she seemed to unite with us at times, and even raised herself up with a wonderful expression of countenance at certain parts of the same. Physicians present wiped the blood from her hands and examined the same, others dipped handkerchiefs and other articles in the flowing blood. Relics of the Holy Cross and other blessed things were presented, and she smiled and bowed in recognition.

"I quietly took from my neck my episcopal cross and placed it over her, when she arose immediately to a sitting posture, stretched out her bleeding hands, and seized it with a holy joy. I left it for some time in her hands, and then gently withdrawing it, she fell back again upon the bed. I sat thus by her bedside and watched the varied expressions that were depicted on her countenance, which I must not now describe; and when all others but the parish priest were excluded, I saw her return from this wonderful ecstasy, and again spoke to her, while modestly and naturally she tried to hide her bleeding hands.

"I only relate the facts myself have seen; let others attempt to account for or explain the extraordinary *phenomenon*, remembering that for upwards of ten years, every Friday similar scenes have taken place, witnessed of thousands, and tested rigorously and scientifically by distinguished professors, physicians, and theologians."

The following interesting and authentic account of her death may be here suitably added :—

The little village of Bois d'Haine was in a state of much excitement on Saturday, the feast of good King Louis. Louise Lateau was dying. On the previous morning the administration bell had been rung, and, according to custom, every one hastened to the door and knelt as the Blessed Sacrament passed along to comfort and strengthen a departing soul. A presentiment seemed to come over all who heard the tinkling of the little bell. They knew the end was near, and therefore they left their work and followed Father Duclos, a Marist, to the humble cottage of Louise. That her death was close at hand, was evident to all; painful sighs and coughing testified to the acuteness of her sufferings. At the head of her bed stood her sister Adeline, weeping bitterly, and wiping away the cold drops of perspiration that fell from the pale brow.

After receiving the Holy Communion, Louise rallied a little; she seemed to suffer less, and listened with marked piety and consolation to the prayers and exhortations of the *Curé*. Towards three o'clock her agony began, and extreme unction was administered. The doctor, M. Lecrinier of Fay, found the pulse at 100, respiration difficult, the left hand greatly swollen, as also the right foot. All Friday night the agony lasted, not a word of complaint passing the lips of the dying woman. Towards six o'clock on Saturday morning, when the village church bells were ringing for mass, Rosine, the eldest sister, asked leave to go and assist, but was motioned to stay. Then, for the first time for three weeks, Louise spoke to her sisters, calmly giving directions for her funeral—it was to be as simple, simple as her mother's. Delirium shortly afterwards set in, during which she was heard to say, "St Louis, what a beautiful bouquet!" Then the sweet Name of Jesus was uttered, followed by one last, lingering sigh; and God's favoured child was dead. Since death, the face of Louise has preserved the quiet, peaceful, resigned expression so often witnessed during her illness. Her hands and fingers are white and strangely flexible. Around her bed are grouped her favourite objects of piety, and the Papal benediction accorded her by his late Holiness Pius IX. The grief of the villagers is great and genuine, crowds gathering round the house, awaiting in silence and respect their turn for admittance, and reciting in the open air their prayers for the dead.

On that last solemn Friday of Louise Lateau's life the *stigmata* did not appear, for the first time for some twelve years. Writing two months ago of her ecstasies and bleedings, M. Bridet, *Curé* at Lyons (Guillotière), said: "Being present at the Eucharistic Congress of Liège, I profited of the occasion to pay a visit to Louise Lateau, this living wonder of the Blessed Sacrament. One Friday I saw her three times—once when she communicated in the morning, again during her ecstasy between two and three in the afternoon, and again later. All that I saw appeared to me to be in perfect harmony with what we know of the life of Our Lord Jesus Christ, of His religion, and of His saints. I was struck with the simplicity and uprightness of her character. I was edified and touched with this perfect Christian, this voluntary victim, who seemed to suffer for the salvation of men and the glory of God, and who unites the most angelic humility with heroic obedience. I was witness to the flow of blood from the wounds in her hands. I saw the ecstasy—her eyes, widely opened, seeming to follow the scenes and passages of our Lord's Passion. In a word, this simple and poor peasant was to me an invincible demonstration of the Supernatural." I need not add to this latest account of a visit to Louise, any history of her career, which has been already made familiar to the pious reading world by Dr Le Febre of Louvain.

In July 1862, a certain Frenchman, M. Henri Lassare, had lost his eyesight from some affection which the two celebrated Paris eye-doctors, M. Desmares and M. Giraud-Teulon, attributed to what is termed "hypertrophy of the optic nerve." In truth he could not read even three or four lines of the largest print without experiencing a great fatigue in the upper front of the eyes, rendering it quite impossible for him to continue reading. The doctors in question advised him to use douches of cold water upon the eyeballs, cupping on the back of the neck, and in turn various other ordinary and special treatments. But these were all of no avail. As regards reading, it was impossible, and to all intents and purposes he had lost the sight of his eyes.

Three months after the period in question—*i.e.*, in September 1882—M. Lassare received the following suggestive and practical reply to a letter of his own, which he himself had dictated, but was quite unable to pen, from M. de Freycinet, subsequently Prime Minister of France, and said to be also a man of considerable scientific acquirements :—

My dear Friend,—Your few lines have given me pleasure, but, as I have already said to you, I long for a sight of your handwriting. This last few days, on returning from Cauterets, I passed Lourdes (near Tarbes). I visited there the celebrated Grotto, and I heard of such marvellous things in the way of cures produced by its waters, principally in cases of diseases of the sight, that I press upon you very seriously to try them. If I were a Catholic and a believer like you, and if I were ill, I should not hesitate to try this chance. If it be true that some sick persons have been suddenly cured, you may fairly hope to increase their number; and if that is not true, what do you risk in making trial of the waters? I add that I have a little personal interest in the experiment. If it were to succeed, what an important fact it would be for me to record! I should be in presence of a miracle, or at least an event of which the principal witness would be beyond all suspicion. Adieu, my dear friend; give me news of yourself, and arrange for me to see you soon.—Your old friend, C. DE FREYCINET.

It appears that at the outset M. Lassare was by no means willing to make such an experiment. In a subsequent conversation with M. de Freycinet, he explained himself fully by admitting it was rather that he dreaded success than that he was afraid of a failure.

"A miracle of that kind, of which I myself were the object," wrote M. Lassare, "would impose on me the obligation to give up everything, and to become a saint. It would be a terrible responsibility, and I am so much of a coward that it makes me tremble. With a physician I should be quits for a little money; but if God cures me, what is it He will want of me? That is horrid of me, is it not? But such, unfortunately, is the pusillanimity of my heart. You suppose my faith faltering? You imagine that I fear to see the miracle not succeeding? Undeceive yourselves, I am really afraid of its taking place."

To which M. de Freycinet replied as follows: "You are not less obliged to be virtuous now than you would be as a consequence of the miracle. And besides, even if your cure were brought about by the agency of a physician, that would be just as much God's gift; and your scruples would have just as much right to raise their voice against your weaknesses or your passions."

As a consequence, M. de Freycinet himself wrote to the *Curé* of Lourdes, the letter in question being signed by M. Lassare, asking for some of the Lourdes water, which was charitably and duly forwarded.

And with this issue: the cure was quite sudden and perfectly complete. Since then, during the last twenty years, M. Lassare's eyesight has never failed him—surely a standing and unquestionable case of a remarkable recent miracle.

Of the following remarkable incident, which took place in London, I can vouch for the perfect truth :—

In the autumn of the year 1870, a clergyman, working in one of the poorest parts of London, became utterly prostrate through a most severe attack of rheumatic fever. His constitution, however, was naturally good, and, by the favour of God and the assistance and advice of competent physicians, he was attended and watched carefully through the severe illness in question, which lasted several months. But the pains he suffered were exceedingly excruciating, and more than usually keen and prolonged. Utterly helpless, and unable to move a single joint or finger (at one time lifted off his bed to a couch to die), his limbs were racked with agony; one of the attendant doctors remarking that the physical pains he endured for several weeks were almost as great as it was possible for any person to bear.

The sufferer being possessed of a relic of

one of his own patron saints, St Thomas of Canterbury—a relic which had been brought to him from Rome twenty years previously—expressed a devout wish, in his extreme suffering, that it might be placed on one of his most pain-stricken limbs, in the hope that, if it pleased God, and by the favour and intercession of the Blessed Virgin Mary and the holy martyr St Thomas, its application might somewhat assuage his pain.

After having duly recited certain appropriate devotions, and commended himself specially to God, the silver reliquary containing the relic was placed on the limb in question, when almost at once—certainly in less than five minutes—a marked and manifest cessation of pain ensued. This occurred on the Feast of the Immaculate Conception (A.D. 1870), from which holy day the pains of the sufferer not only marvellously diminished, but the patient began slowly to mend, and eventually entirely recovered his health, and became quite well in the latter part of the spring of 1871.

The following relates to Lourdes :—

The number of the 'Annales de Notre Dame de Lourdes' for October 1878, like almost every other part of that interesting serial, contains accounts of the twenty-one great pilgrimages made to the Grotto during the month of September. These pilgrimages were signalised by several most remarkable cures, two of which are so striking, that I briefly extract their chief features.

The first case is that of Joachine Dehan, of Hainault, in Belgium, aged 29. In the year 1866, in consequence of an attack of cholera, she had a large abscess in her right leg, extending from the hip to the knee. She was also afflicted with luxation of the right hip-joint, depriving her of the use of that leg, and contraction of the muscles of the same leg, causing club-foot. All the remedies that surgical skill could employ had been used, without the slightest benefit. Joachine was sent to Lourdes by a benevolent lady, the Countess Limminghe, and felt so much confidence in the certainty of her cure that she took with her shoes and stockings, which she had not been able to wear for twelve years previously. On the 13th and 14th of September she bathed eight times without obtaining a cure; but she persevered, and at the ninth bathing a cracking sound was heard in the sinews of her right leg, and the pain became so intense that she fainted. On recovering from her swoon, she said, "I am cured," and walked without the aid of her crutches. The club-foot had been restored to its natural shape, the contracted muscles had regained their normal action, and the immense ulcer had healed up in a moment, leaving only a redness of the skin to show the place where it had been. Joachine returned home to Belgium perfectly cured.

The other case was that of Sister Mary of the Angels, a poor Clare of the Colletine Convent in the Rue Sala, at Lyons, who was afflicted with a cancerous ulceration of the liver, and was reduced thereby to a state of utter prostration, after eleven years of extreme suffering. These facts are attested by a certificate signed by Dr Keisser, a physician of Lyons, and dated 8th October 1878. Sister Mary was sent to Lyons under obedience, by order of her religous Superior, and was carried to and from the railway stations at each end of her painful journey, looking more like a small wax-figure than a living being. She was laid down in the Chapel of the Grotto, her head being supported by the altar-step. The Bishop of Agen came in to give his blessing to the pilgrims from his diocese, who were then assembled and praying in the Grotto. He also specially blessed the poor nun who was lying at his feet, upon which she was instantaneously cured, without bathing, and walked without assistance to the convent of her order at Lourdes, about half a kilometre distant, where she now performs all the duties of the community.

The cure at the same place of Francis Macary, a carpenter of Lavaur,—a town about forty miles distant from Tolouse—is likewise most wonderful. No mere stimulus given to the nervous powers by Faith and Hope can possibly account for it. Macary himself, as he avers, was a perfect unbeliever in Christianity, and had suffered long and patiently (in truth, for thirty years) from varicose veins. Having, however, heard of several cases of miraculous cures effected at Lourdes, he was led, as he asserts, to procure a bottle of the Lourdes water, for which he made a respectful request, and which duly reached him. He at once put aside his special stockings and bandages, and applied the water in question to his legs, soon afterwards falling into a deep sleep. Waking up, he cried out to his wife that he believed himself to be quite cured. But overpowered by sleep almost immediately, he did did not again awake until the next morning, when he discovered to his great joy that all the varicose veins and knots in his leg, and the consequent pains, were entirely gone. He rose early to work, as he had not done for several years, and was there found by his astonished son. He lived for four years afterwards, and died suddenly a few years ago.

The following are translations of the three original testimonials as to the above-recited cure :—

No. I.—*From* Dr SEGUR.

I, the undersigned, declare, that for about thirty years, Mr Francis Macary, carpenter, had been suffering from varicose veins in the legs. These varicose veins, which were of the thickness of a finger, and complicated with "de cordons noueux et flexueux très-développés," compelled him to wear up to the present time a regular compression ("une compression méthodique"), exerted partly by twisted bandages, partly by means of dog-skin stockings. In spite of these precautions, ulcers frequently showed themselves on both legs, and whenever they did, compelled complete repose and a long course of treatment. I have visited him to-day, and although his under limbs were stripped of all clothing, I have only been able to discover a few traces of these enormous varicose veins. This case of spontaneous cure appears to me all the more surprising, because the annals of science record not a single fact of this nature.

SEGUR,
Doctor of Medicine, Member of the Mutual Aid Society of St Louis.

LAVAUR, *August* 16, 1871.

No. II.—*From* Dr ROSSIGNOL.

I, the undersigned, certify, that for about thirty years, Mr Macary, carpenter, of Lavaur, has been attacked by varicose veins with enormous nodosities in the legs, frequently complicated by large ulcers, in spite of the compression exerted by appropriate stockings or bandages; that these symptoms have disappeared suddenly, and that to-day there only remains a nodosity, sensibly diminished, in the inner and upper part of the right leg.

ROSSIGNOL,
Doctor of Medicine.

LAVAUR, *August* 25, 1871.

No. III.—*From* Dr BERNET.

François Macary, sixty years old, carpenter, of Lavaur, member of the Society of Saint Louis, consulted us about twenty years ago for varicose veins, which filled up the left popliteal hollow and inside of the knee and of the leg. We then observed towards the lower third part of this limb a varicose ulcer, with thickened edges, with considerable and painful engorgement of the tissues. There was besides, both in and outside the upper part of the calf, two large old scars, which had nothing to do with the affection for which we were consulted, and which were the result of a gunshot received by the patient twenty years previously. There were so many enlarged veins, and they were enlarged to so great an extent, that, so far as we were concerned, the surgical means with which one treats this disease were formally contra-indicated. Macary appeared to us to be the victim of an infirmity which would last him his life, and we advised only palliatives, which several of our brethren had already advised. Eighteen years later,—that is, two years ago,—Macary presented himself to consult us again. The state of his leg had grown much worse. We confirmed our former prognostic, and told him it was of urgent necessity for him, to get the ulcer to cicatrise, to submit himself, as the only means, to absolute and prolonged rest in bed, and to the application of regular dressings. To-day, August 15, 1871, Macary appears for the third time. The ulcer is perfectly cicatrised. There is nothing compressing the leg, and nevertheless there does not exist the shadow of engorgement. What surprises us, above all, is, that the varicose knots (*paquets*) have entirely disappeared; and that where they were before, one can feel some small strings, hard, empty of blood, and yielding under the pressure of the fingers. The interior saphene vein has its normal direction and volume. The most attentive examination affords no trace of a surgical operation. According to the account of Macary, this radical cure was produced in the course of a single night, and under the influence of nothing but the application of some compressers wetted by water drawn from the Grotto of Lourdes. We conclude that, apart from Macary's story, Science is impotent to explain this fact; for [medical] authors give us no experience of anything at all similar. They are all unanimous on this point, that varicose veins, left to themselves, are incurable; that they are not cured by palliatives, and still less spontaneously; that they go on getting worse steadily; and that one can only hope for any radical cure by the application of surgical means, which involve grave dangers to the patients. And though the fact asserted by Macary would not be proved by evidence taken from any one else, still it would not the less remain for us a fact of the most extraordinary kind, and—let us say it out plainly—a supernatural fact. In which faith we sign the contents of the present report.

BERNET,
M.D. of the Faculty of Paris.

August 15, 1871.

The following remarkable record of a miraculous cure of paralysis relates to the same holy[1] and God-favoured spot :—

The Abbé de Musy, priest of the diocese of Autun, had been ill with paralysis and other complaints for twenty years—*i. e.*, since the year 1853. During the last eleven years of that period he had only said mass twice, and was utterly unable to walk, and at times could neither read nor write. On Friday the 8th of August 1873 he was taken to Lourdes, but being so ill, and moved with danger, he was attended by two friends and two men-servants. The venerable *Curé* of Lourdes, M. Peyramale, called upon him on his arrival; and the Baroness de la Rue, who, having suffered from paralysis for twelve years, had just been suddenly cured in the Grotto of Lourdes, came likewise to recount and testify to the miracle by which the Almighty had so mercifully relieved her. The Abbé de Musy was

[1] I myself possess nearly fifty records, given by and gathered from various Catholic and Church of England friends, who are personally acquainted with the subjects upon whom remarkable miracles have been wrought at Lourdes, detailing facts which cannot but rejoice all true Christians; and proving conclusively that amid the atheism and indifference with which civilised society in Europe is so greatly afflicted, the recent miracles at Lourdes and elsewhere still fulfil the pledge and promise of our Divine Redeemer to be with His Church unto the end of the world.

earnest in his devotions, and implored the favour of God and Our Lady at the services of the sanctuary day by day. Others devoutly joined their prayers with his.

On the morning of the Feast of the Assumption the Abbé was carried down to the crypt, where another priest, the Abbé Sive, was to say a third mass in the hope of securing the poor sick priest's recovery. The Abbé de Musy had already heard one mass, and had received Holy Communion, and during the second mass which he had attended, had made a prolonged and deeply earnest thanksgiving. Just before the elevation in the Abbé Sive's mass, he rose with some difficulty from his chair of repose, in which he had previously been reclining, and to the astonishment of his friends knelt down upon an ordinary *prie-dieu*. In a few moments it became apparent to his attendants and to other suffering persons near that his prayer had been there and then answered, and that a miracle had been wrought. This, thank God, was so. He rose without assistance, to the awe and astonishment of the bystanders, and he walked as he had not walked for twenty years. All tokens of paralysis and sickness had passed away. Only physical weakness remained. Tapers were lit, thanksgivings were offered up, and the now perfectly cured Abbé gave his blessing to the many who had crowded round. All this was done in the face of the Church. A lapsed Catholic, who was believed to have become an atheist, was reconverted to the faith on the spot; and the increased devotion of those who had witnessed the miracle was marked and manifest. All this and more is on record. It was publicly proclaimed at vespers by the Abbé Peyramale to hundreds, and more than forty persons testified in writing to the certain reality and completeness of the miracle.

The following cure of blindness at Hal has been penned from a statement by the subject of the cure :—

I became ill at Thowrout on 11th January 1867. Having a severe rheumatic affection, I went to Brussels for medical advice, as on the subsequent 6th of May all the members of my body were paralysed, and I became still further perfectly blind.

On the 24th of June of the same year I consulted M. Vallez of Rue St Lazare, a distinguished oculist, who gave me little hope of any recovery of my sight, and I returned home.

In March 1868 I again was taken to Brussels, with the intention of getting relief at the Ophthalmic Hospital there. Dr Libbrecht, the eminent oculist of Ghent, whom I also consulted, declared that it would be very difficult to restore my sight, and exceedingly unlikely that it ever would be restored.

At Brussels, in April of the same year, a consultation on my malady and case was held between Drs Warlemont, Van Roosbroeck, and Lebrun, who unanimously agreed that, owing to my general weak state of health, nothing could be attempted except an issue at the back of my neck; and that even that remedy was asserted to be dangerous.

M. Moren, a distinguished oculist from Dusseldorf, also saw me, but gave no further hopes than the other doctors. They one and all agreed that my case was hopeless, and told my wife so. She was urged not to make this known to me, lest it might have a too great depressing influence. But I demanded of her the full and frank truth, and after a while obtained, " Your case, as the doctors one and all declare, is without hope."

I then began to turn my thoughts to Almighty God, and often specially prayed for relief and a cure. Those saints whom I venerated I asked specially to lift up their holy hands to God on my behalf.

On the 19th of July I went a pilgrimage to the shrine of the B. V. of Hal, and again did the same on the Festival of Lady-Day in harvest—that is, upon August 16th.

Penetrated with feelings of faith, hope, and confidence, and desiring to be in charity with all men, my wife and my little daughter accompanied me to Hal on this second visit.

We arrived on the 14th, and, early on the morning of the feast, attended the Pilgrims' Mass. At the beginning of the most solemn time of it—when the Sanctus-bell was being rung, and just before the Elevation—I enjoined upon my wife to redouble her devotions, and I myself prayed most fervently. I was perfectly collected, and, placing my hands before my face and resting my head thereupon, bent down in lowliest adoration.

Judge of my joy when, on raising my head, I found that I distinctly saw the celebrant at the altar. I went up alone, without guide or assistance, to receive my spiritual food, and found that, by the mercy of God and the intercession of Blessed Mary ever virgin and St Ignatius, though I had been blind for two years and two months, I could then see.

As a consequence, — overpowered myself with joy, gratitude, and happiness, — I proclaimed God's goodness. One of the clergy, who had seen me go blind to the church, demanded complete particulars of my loss of sight and sufferings, and of my cure. These were frankly and faithfully given. Of the physicians whom I had consulted, there was not one who did not look upon my recovery as distinctly miraculous.

All this is the truth, and only the truth. For the greater glory of God, I am ready to affirm as much on my oath. And this I do.

VICTOR FLEMING.

3 PLACE DU GRAND SABLON, BRUSSELS.

The following account of an appearance of the Blessed Mother of God may be here very suitably produced :—

The village of Dietrichswald, in the district of Allenstein, East Prussia, has lately (A.D. 1877) been, and still continues to be, the scene of some interesting occurrences. Crowds of persons come to the place, it being reported that our Blessed Lady has several times appeared there.

In a garden attached to the parish priest's house, and close to the churchyard, there is a splendid maple-tree, which forks at a height of about twenty feet from the ground. A little below this a long dry branch runs out from the trunk, and about six feet lower, but still eleven or twelve feet from the ground, there is the stump of another dry branch, upon which are now hung wreaths of flowers. It is between these two dry branches that the apparitions are said to take place. Two girls, Augusta Szafrmski, about fourteen years old, and Barbara Samulowski, about twelve years old, first saw a white figure of brilliant appearance on the spot mentioned. They were much frightened, and went and reported the matter to the parish priest, who told them to be silent about it. But they continued to see the appearance daily at the same hour, and they seem to have been moved in some way to recite the Rosary. On July 23, 1877, the appearance was seen three times during the day. Subsequently several other persons declared they witnessed it. It is worth noting that all those persons, including the children, perceived during the space of five days similar appearances in other places, but they seem to have had an instinctive apprehension that these were not genuine. In one case the apparition recommended a young woman to go to Communion more frequently than her confessor wished, which incitement to disobedience was at once judged to be a sign of the source whence the pseudo-apparitions came. Usually the apparition lasts eight minutes, and comes while the Rosary is being recited, usually during the second part, and then disappearing during the third part. When the two young girls are present they are not permitted to be near each other. But invariably at the same instant both sink on their knees to the ground, and remain perfectly motionless, with their eyes raised towards the tree, and an expression of extreme devotion on their countenances. During this period they remain quite insensible to all external impressions. After about four or five minutes the children bless themselves, probably at the moment when, as they say, the apparition blesses all present. They then remain for three or four minutes without movement, and prostrating themselves on the earth, they gradually come back to consciousness. They are invariably taken to the parish priest, who interrogates them separately as to what passed, and the statements of both thoroughly correspond. To complete the report, the appearance, at first, represented the Divine Mother seated on a throne with the Infant Jesus, surrounded with angels; but subsequently the apparition took the form usually known under the title of the Immaculate Conception. Crowds go to pray in the churchyard and around the maple. The greatest order is observed, and hitherto the police have not interfered; already several strange cures of afflicted persons who have been to the place are reported.

In the year 1880 remarkable sacred apparitions were likewise seen in Ireland at the Catholic Church of Knock, about five miles from Claremorris, the parish priest of which is Archdeacon Bartholomew Cavanagh.[1] The church itself is cruciform in construction, the sacristy being placed behind that eastern part containing the high altar. In the gable of the sacristy is a window about five feet high by two feet broad, its lowest part being about twelve feet from the ground.

On Thursday evening, about half-past seven o'clock, on August 21, 1880, as some persons were going along the road leading to this church, in a drizzling rain, they perceived the external wall of the sacristy to be marvellously illuminated by a strange white light, in which stars, as it were, twinkled and flickered. On approaching it—for as many as twenty persons witnessed it—there appeared an altar, upon which stood a lamb, with a cross behind, on which was a figure of our crucified Redeemer.

[1] I am indebted for the above facts and accounts to various friends in Ireland, who sent me written details of them; and to others—some acquaintances, some strangers—who have personally obtained records from Archdeacon Cavanagh, Canon Bourke, and others; as also to the local serials, the 'Tuam Herald,' the 'Nation,' and certain newspapers published at Cork.

On the gospel side of the altar were figures of the Blessed Virgin, St Joseph of Nazareth, and St John the Evangelist. The eyes of Our Lady were raised heavenwards, the palms of her outstretched hands being turned towards the onlookers. St John, who had a mitre on his head, held a Book of the gospels open in his left hand, and raised his right in the act of giving a blessing. St Joseph was in a posture of adoration, bending towards the Virgin Mary.

These figures, round which moving angels were seen gliding about, remained visible until ten o'clock in the evening, and the light on and over the gable-end of the church was seen by many.

The Blessed Virgin appeared again on New-Year's Day, just after divine service at noon, and subsequently upon the eve of the Epiphany, January 5th, 1881. The extraordinary light was visible from eleven o'clock on that evening until two o'clock the following morning, when it is said to have slowly faded away. Two members of the Irish Constabulary witnessed it for some time.

One of these, introduced to a special correspondent of the 'Daily Telegraph' by the parish priest of Claremorris, the Very Rev. Ulick J. Bourke, sometime President of St Jarlath's College, and Canon of Tuam, declared as follows:—

"On a certain night, about twelve o'clock, I and a comrade set out on patrol, our road taking us past the chapel. When opposite the building we saw people and heard the sound of praying; so we went in to look round and ascertain that all was right. Down to that time, though others had professed to have witnessed the apparitions, we had not. On going round to the east gable, some one cried, 'There's the light!' and then both I and my comrade saw the end of the church covered with a sort of rosy brightness, through which what seemed to be stars appeared. I saw no figures, nor did my comrade; but some women who were praying there declared that they beheld the Blessed Virgin, and one went nearly frantic in consequence. We stood and watched the light for some time before starting again on our rounds.

"'How do you explain the light?' he was asked.

"'I can't explain it.'

"'Did you look around to see where it came from?'

"'I did; but everything was dark. There was no light anywhere except on the gable.'"

The Archdeacon's housekeeper was one of those who saw the apparitions.

He himself gave an account of two miraculous cures in the following words:—

1. Some little while ago I received a sick call late at night to a man who was said to be vomiting blood, and in extreme danger. Hastening to the house, attended by a boy with a lantern, I met the father of the patient coming to hurry me, in distress lest I should be too late.

On reaching the cottage I found the young man covered (so to speak) with blood, and apparently very near death, but conscious. After ministering to him I called for a glass of water, sprinkled on it a few particles of the mortar from the gable wall of the chapel, and bade him drink. He did so, at once began to recover, and is now well.

2. I can speak of a man from Cork, afflicted with a polypus which extended into his wind-

pipe, and, so said the surgeons, required a dangerous operation. He was here performing his devotions for several days, and then, to his astonishment and joy, expelled the abnormal growth (I saw it) and returned cured.

The same dignitary has recorded a long list of miraculous cures—some wrought almost suddenly, and known to be cures by those who first saw the sufferers, and then the direct consequences of their prayers and pilgrimage.

3. Bridget Nearney of Strokestown, blind for seventeen years, was made to see.

4. Maria Conolly, a cripple for thirteen years, after being carried into the chapel, was miraculously made to walk, which she is now able to do.

5. John O'Brien, of William Street, Cork, born blind, has now the perfect use of his eyes, and can see.

6. Belinda Mash, of Bellina, who was dumb for six years, can now speak.

7. Patrick Boyle, of Glasgow, so afflicted with heart disease that he was warned by a doctor there not to attempt the journey to Knock, came, prayed, received the Blessed Sacrament there, and left the place cured.

8. Michael Marin, of Lisakullen, subject to epileptic fits, and at times troubled with evil spirits, visited Knock, and, by God's favour, returned quite well.

9. John Roache, of Roosky, County Roscommon, who had been stone blind for seventeen years, came to Knock and left it able to see.

10. John O'Connor, of Ardagh, came to Knock with a bent leg, supported by an iron band and crutch, returned home, leaving the crutch, and able to walk.

Of these and suchlike examples of God's favour and power, so exactly suited to a race which, above all others, has clung so close and devotedly to the faith of their forefathers, it need only be remarked once again, that "he who runs may read," while it may be reverently noted how the past is linked with the present by the power of the Supernatural.

The miracles of Egypt, in truth, most real as regards those worked by magicians (though not from God); the wonders wrought in the desert; the opening of the dry rock for water; and the gift of manna; the dividing of the Red

Sea and the waters of Jordan; the many and varied miraculous exhibitions of the Eternal's might and mercy from time to time to the children of Israel, with all the marvellous wonders of the New Testament, and of ecclesiastical history,—leave no doubt that the Natural and Supernatural, each from God, are wonderfully blended, and that our own Glimpses in the Twilight here are a faint but most true earnest of the breaking of the everlasting day. To the devout believer in God's perfect revelation by His Son, miracles and miraculous interventions are, in fact, so strikingly interwoven with the history of the Catholic Church, that no age can be said to have been without them. St Augustine of Canterbury as well as St Augustine of Hippo testify to this fact;[1] while, from the days of the Apostles down to the Beatification or Canonisation of the last addition to the Church's Kalendar, the same truth is universally acknowledged by the faithful and thus authoritatively proclaimed. The miracles wrought at the tombs of St Martin, St Germanus, and St Hilary of old, or by St

[1] See 'De Utilit. Credendi,' cap. iv. 'Sti. Aug. Opera.,' and as regards St Augustine of Canterbury, Bede's 'Ecclesiastical History,' book ii. chap. 3.

Gregory, the wonder-worker of Neo-Cæsarea, find their counterparts in the various tokens of God's presence, care, and power, evidenced in the lives of St Dominic, St Francis Xavier, and others of quite recent days—even of our own. For the arm of God is evidently not shortened, and His mercy is still over all His works. The powers of the Church did not come to an end in apostolic days, as some vain babblers would have us believe: nor has the gracious promise, "Lo, I am with you all days, even to the end of the world," failed and been brought to naught.

On the contrary, Christianity, as both Past and Present declare, has overcome mighty obstacles, while the Supernatural both survives and is potent. Neither the impatience, nor the scoffs, nor the anger of modern sceptics, mars that innate belief in a World Unseen—in the battalions of the living God, and in the domination and activity of malignant spirits—which is widespread, energetic, and powerful still. The fall of Jerusalem under Titus scattered a favoured nation; but its sacred teaching and traditions with regard to Almighty God, the holy angels, Satan the enemy of souls, and his legions, still live.[1] Gentile thought, the speculations of Stoic and Epicurean, have had their day. Heresies bred amongst Christians could not destroy that fundamental teaching which related to the conception of a better Eve, to the incarnation of the Eternal Son of God, to His death and resurrection, His ascension and divine kingdom, to His own miracles, and to those of His Apostles and their true successors. This same Christianity, moreover, has survived the Ten Great Persecutions, the fall of ancient Rome, with all its disturbing and disorganising consequences. It has seen the rise and collapse of Mohammedanism, and it will no doubt witness its final decay. The disastrous schism between East and West, and the distressing and demoniacal divisions of the sixteenth century, have partly paralysed the Church's power, and certainly circumscribed her corporate influence. "He could there do no mighty work . . . because of their unbelief," is still true of several nominally Christian countries. Still Christmas by Christmas the miracle of

[1] The liturgical books of the Jews, as still in use, and their devotional traditions, are rife with details and sentiments involving a distinct belief in the Supernatural.

the Incarnation is celebrated with song and thanksgiving, and the message of the angels is handed down the quickly passing ages for the comfort and consolation of mankind. Sunday by Sunday the central marvel of God's merciful scheme of redemption—the resurrection of the dead in Christ—is commemorated north and south, east and west; while the Passion and Cross of Good Friday, and the empty tomb of the first Easter morning—with all that these imply, with all that they involve—are thus by stately rite and ancient orison stamped indelibly on the minds of many who in faith and patience watch and wait. Omen and warning of God's presence; punishment following sin; the grace of sacraments; the power of exorcism; the dire influence of evil spirits; the active ministrations of glorious angels; spiritual armour for the last conflict here, and the potency of prayer,—have one and all sunk deeply into the minds of the baptised. At the same time, human thought, whether sober or fantastic, has had its varied revolutions, its changes, its crazes; but amid all such, the mysteries of the World Unseen, on which the Lamp of Divine Truth has always shed its beneficent rays, remain mysteries, though Glimpses of that World are sometimes mercifully afforded, and foretastes of its promised peace and perfect harmony are dreamt of still. Let those who are strangers and pilgrims below never close either eye or ear to any mysterious sign or mystical token which tells of a Better World; so that, as they watch link after link of the social chain which binds them together here on earth mercifully removed,—for the circle of friends of all of us is found to be year by year steadily decreasing,—they may both piously believe and properly hope that the spiritual circle is being duly enlarged up above, where, for all who have been true and faithful to their Divine Lord and Master, no links shall be broken, and no loss nor separation shall ever come.

INDEX.

THE END.

PRINTED BY WILLIAM BLACKWOOD AND SONS

www.ingramcontent.com/pod-product-compliance
Ingram Content Group UK Ltd.
Pitfield, Milton Keynes, MK11 3LW, UK
UKHW021546100325
4931UKWH00035B/291

* 9 7 8 1 0 1 7 0 5 7 2 7 0 *